The Theatre of Drottningholm – Then and Now
Performance between the 18th and 21st centuries

The Theatre of Drottningholm – Then and Now
Performance between the 18th and 21st centuries

Willmar Sauter & David Wiles

The Friends of the Drottningholm Theatre (DTV), established in 1935, have generously supported the production of this book.

Design: Kerri Sandell
Cover: Eva Spångberg
Cover photos: Max Plunger, Mats Bäcker

© Willmar Sauter & David Wiles
and Acta Universitatis Stockholmiensis, 2014
ISBN 978-91-87235-91-7 (PDF)
ISBN 978-91-87235-92-4 (printed book)
ISSN 1400-2132
Printed in Sweden by Taberg Media Group

Distribution:
Stiftelsen för utgivning av teatervetenskapliga skrifter (Stuts)
c/o Theatre and Dance Studies, Stockholm University, 106 91 Stockholm
www.stuts.nu

Thomas Postlewait

PREFACE

Written by two renowned scholars of European theatre, this book offers a fascinating history of the Drottningholm Theatre. Professors Willmar Sauter and David Wiles describe the history of this court theatre from its eighteenth-century origins in the era of King Gustav III (1746-92) to its revival in modern times as a distinct performance space for opera. They recount how Drottningholm was the center of court activities during the reign of Sweden's famous 'Theatre King', who wrote plays and librettos, patronized the arts, and founded the Swedish Academy (1786). But after 1792, when King Gustav was assassinated (the topic of Giuseppe Verdi's famous opera *Un ballo in maschera*; *The Masked Ball*), Drottningholm, rarely used as a theatre, was closed down. The doors were shut, performances were discontinued. Indeed, for over a century the building served mostly as a governmental storeroom—dusty, densely packed, and disorganized. But then in the 1920s the theatre, newly discovered, was carefully restored to its past glory. Today Drottningholm, which the United Nations has identified as a World Heritage Site, is an international tourist attraction and the home of an annual summer festival for classical opera.

Because Drottningholm exists before us today as a fully reconstituted theatre from the eighteenth century, the building provides a special resource for performers, spectators, and theatre historians. The past is made present. In this sense the building and the stage space provide a kind of historical laboratory for examining the performance qualities, methods, and aims of earlier plays and operas. Of course, even if Drottningholm had disappeared—as has sadly happened to most theatre buildings from earlier eras—theatre historians could still delve into the documentary records in order to discover some of the traits of the building and its performance space. We would then conjure with pieces of evidence and hypothetical ideas about a lost theatre. Luckily, however, Drottningholm exists in all of its charming tangibility. We have the good fortune of experiencing the actual building and its artefacts. It thus allows us to learn many things that we cannot recover from the remaining written documents. It offers a special opportunity for all of us because of the building's history, its architecture, its auditorium, its acoustics, and its stage platform and scenic equipment.

Drottningholm is both unique and typical. It is unique because the history of Drottningholm separates it from the history of any other European theatre building. There is no other surviving building just like it. Part of the challenge we face is to understand and appreciate the details and nature of that history, beginning with the definitive contributions of Gustav III and his court. We also must take into consideration its double identity today as both a national museum and an active performance venue for opera each summer. To what extent does this double or split personality contribute to its aims and functions?

Yet despites its exclusive traits, Drottningholm is also emblematic of theatrical building and practices from the baroque and classical eras. It thus offers theatre practitioners, spectators, and historians opportunities to revisit and recover at least some of the vital aspects of performance procedures that were typical or conventional in the previous era. In harmony with the Early Music Movement, which in recent decades has transformed the performance methods for pre-classical music, Drottningholm Theatre could serve as the catalyst and setting for the recovery of the performance methods of early operas. It has the potential to place us aesthetically in the setting and conditions of a lost era.

We are thus confronted by some key questions. How and why was this theatre, which was almost completely forgotten for several generations, recovered from its years of neglect? When and how was it discovered? Who was responsible? How were the original stage space and machinery restored to the operating conditions of the eighteenth century? What is the heritage and mission of Drottningholm today? Should it attempt to preserve the past as a 'living history'? We know that when Ingmar Bergman made his film version of Mozart's *The Magic Flute* in 1975, he was inspired by Drottningholm. In preparation for shooting the film he recreated a replica of the Drottningholm stage in the studios of the Swedish Film Institute. Should a similar kind of dedication to the integrity of this theatre and its definitive features determine and control its heritage? Should the operas of Händel, Gluck, and Mozart be restaged and experienced as they were performed in the eighteenth century? Is this mission appropriate; is it possible?

Responding to these and related questions, Professors Sauter and Wiles describe in substantial detail the history of the Drottningholm Theatre, including the artistic, social, and political practices that defined the cultural activities during the reign of Gustav III. They describe both the discovery and the revival of the theatre, which still has the moveable scenic flats and stage equipment that were used in the court theatre. Sauter and Wiles also recreate the aura and ambience of Drottningholm that visitors experience when they come to the island, observe the architectural features of the buildings, and attend performances in the 400-seat auditorium. And because performers, spectators, and historians continue to disagree over the feasibility—and even the value—of recreating 'authentic' historical performances in this 'original' space, Sauter and Wiles investigate the challenges, problems, and arguments for historical authenticity.

Willmar Sauter is Swedish; David Wiles is British. Sauter, who has taught at Stockholm University since 1974, has been a Professor of Theatre Studies since 1992. He is a former Dean of Humanities at the university, and also a former President of the International Federation for Theatre Research, the primary organization for theatre scholars throughout the world. He has written and edited several books on theatre history and performance methods, including *The Theatrical Event* (2000), which focuses on 'the sensory, artistic, and symbolic levels of communication' that occur in the complex relationship between 'theatrical presentations and perceptions.' This book is used as a classroom text in many countries. As part of his investigations into the 'aspects of theatre communication, Sauter has conducted and published a series of surveys since 1980 on Drottningholm audience members. And his studies of the traits and history of performance events have been featured in Swedish, Norwegian, Finnish, German, British, Israeli, Japanese, and American publications. Because of his professional standing, he has served on the board of the Drottningholm Theatre Foundation. Also, over the years he has guided many visitors and students on tours of the auditorium and the stage space. Sauter thus understands not only the administration of the Drottningholm Theatre but also the ways spectators have responded, in positive and negative terms, to its stage productions.

David Wiles, who holds a Chair of Drama at the University of Exeter in the United Kingdom, has taught in England, Wales, France, and the United States. His scholarship spans the history of Western theatre. Since the 1980s, he has published a half-dozen books on classical and Shakespearean theatre, including *Greek Theatre Performance* (2000) and *Shakespeare's Clowns* (1987). In his scholarship Wiles is especially concerned with the changing history of performances in Europe. In *A Short History of Western Performance Space* (2003), he traces how and why theatrical activities have taken place in diverse settings, from explicitly designed buildings to churches, streets, gardens, and temporary or empty sites. He also shows that these theatrical performances, whatever their locations and characteristics, occur within particular socio-political structures and conditions. For Wiles 'the context for a history of performance space is a history of *space*.' Part of our challenge, he contends, is to comprehend the ways the performance space is conditioned by an idea of space, be it sacred or secular, monumental or insignificant, absolute or abstract. Quite appropriately, this topic of various theatrical locations and their performance sites or spaces is central to the book that Wiles conceived and co-edited in 2013: *The Cambridge Companion to Theatre History*.

Given their collective accomplishments as theatre historians, Sauter and Wiles welcomed the opportunity to work together on a study of Drottningholm Theatre. Sauter's concerns with the elements of 'the theatrical event' and Wiles's concerns with the locations and social settings of 'performance space' overlap quite effectively. Yet each of them also brings his distinct perspective and set of ideas to the project. Sauter is an insider at Drottningholm; he has attended performances at the theatre for five decades and has been intimately involved in its operations. Wiles is an outsider; he made his first visit in 2008. Initially this vital difference in their personal experiences and knowledge of Drottningholm Theatre raised some concerns about a joint venture. But these differences, like certain differences in their published scholarship, have turned out to be a great benefit in the writing of this book. In order to take full advantage of their individual cultural experiences and judgments, they decided to divide up the specific topics for the book, thereby delivering two distinct historical viewpoints and voices on Drottningholm. Sauter wrote chapters one, two, four, and six; Wiles took on chapters three, five, and seven. Then in the last chapter they have provided a dialogue on the significance of the theatre. Sauter and Wiles make no attempt to conceal their different voices, but they successfully make a virtue out of these differences. And they reach some shared conclusions about the heritage of Drottningholm, its operations today, and its future. In the process, they have written a major study of the historical and performance features of Drottningholm Theatre.

This fine book thus meets the needs of several types of readers. It serves those summer visitors who want a well-written and accessible survey of Drottningholm that provides a reliable and detailed record of their immediate experiences; it serves theatre practitioners of theatre and opera who want to understand the challenges of crafting successful performances for this specific site and its special audiences; it serves teachers of theatre and opera who want a solid historical record of this theatre, including its architectural features and staging practices; and it serves theatre scholars who require an accurate and fully engaged study of one of the few remaining theatres from the Enlightenment era. To their credit, Sauter and Wiles address each of these potential readers. They invite us, chapter by chapter, to experience the historical context and artistic qualities of Drottningholm Theatre.

Thomas Postlewait
University of Washington
Seattle, Washington

x

ACKNOWLEDGEMENTS

We should like first of all to thank the scholars who participated in the initial phase of this project: Maria Berlova, Rikard Hoogland, Inga Lewenhaupt, Mikael Strömberg, Eske Tsugami and Motomi Tsugami. Their enthusiasm and critical approach to performance practices were a source of inspiration to us. Mikael Strömberg also contributed the basic bibliography for the book.

We received generous support for our research from the Drottningholm Theatre Foundation, in particular from the artistic director, Professor Mark Tatlow (2007-13), the director Sofi Lerström and the public relations manager Eva Lundgren, in addition to the guides and other theatre personnel. Kjerstin Dellert, director of the Confidensen at Ulriksdal, and Fredrik Forslund were equally helpful with their open attitude and practical assistance.

Several people came in at the completion stage, contributing invaluable hands-on assistance. Hélène Ohlsson traced many of the photographs and drawings; Stephe Harrop helped render the English language into a consistent and idiomatic form; Samuel Edwards, assisted by Jennie Nell, translated Swedish texts from the eighteenth and twentieth centuries. We are very grateful for the generous help they provided.

Various photographers and artists gernerously contributed their work to this volume. We thank all of them, especially Mats Bäcker, Beata Bergström, Ragnvi Gylder, Bo Ljungblom, Max Plunger, Enar Merkel Rydberg, Linn Sandholm, Bengt Wanselius, Rikard Westman, Michal Tuma, Cecilia Uhrstedt, as well as the photographers of early performances at Drottningholm. Ann-Christin Jernberg kindly supplied us with photographs from the palace and park at Drottningholm. We should also mention Marianne Seid and Magnus Blomqvist at the Library of Music and Theatre (Musikverket, MTB), who searched and scanned numerous illustrations from the early as well as later periods at Drottningholm. We also wish to thank the personnel of the National Museum and the Stockholm City Museum.

The board of the Friends of the Drottningholm Theatre and their chairman Christer Villard have encouraged this project from the beginning and contributed substantially to the production costs of this book. Financial support for publication was also provided The Swedish Foundation of the Humanities and Social Sciences (RJ), and the Department of Computer and System Science at Stockholm University. We are very grateful to these institutions for their understanding of our needs and wishes. Emi-Simone Zawall, Christina Lenz and Eva Språngberg, who represent Stockholm University's publishing agency, were helpful in all the various aspects of the publishing process. Kerri Sandell assembled the text and the illustrations into the handsome form that we envisioned for this book. We offer them our heartfelt thanks for their efforts and patience.

Finally, we want to express our deep gratitude to Tom Postlewait, who supported this project from the moment he heard about it. He discussed the structure of this book with us, negotiated options for publication, then provided detailed comments on several of our drafts. Asking him to write a preface to the completed book seemed a logical step and we are delighted that he was willing.

CONTENTS

PREFACE *(Thomas Postlewait)* V

ACKNOWLEDGEMENTS XI

1. THE REDISCOVERY OF THE
DROTTNINGHOLM COURT THEATRE *(Willmar Sauter)* 1

2. A GUIDED TOUR OF THE THEATRE *(Willmar Sauter)* 13

3. A VISIT TO THE OPERA AT DROTTNINGHOLM:
FIRST IMPRESSIONS *(David Wiles)* 47

4. EIGHTEENTH CENTURY COURT LIFE *(Willmar Sauter)* 59

5. A TYPICAL 'BAROQUE' THEATRE? *(David Wiles)* 103

6. DROTTNINGHOLM IN THE
TWENTIETH CENTURY AND BEYOND *(Willmar Sauter)* 141

7. EIGHTEENTH-CENTURY ACTING:
THE SEARCH FOR AUTHENTICITY *(David Wiles)* 185

8. TOWARDS THE FUTURE *(Willmar Sauter & David Wiles)* 215

APPENDICES	229
Supplement to the regulations of the Royal Theatre (1779)	229
Dutchess Hedvig Elisabeth Charlotta's letter to Princess Sofia Albertina (1783)	230
C.F. Adelcrantz' Memorandum (1794)	231
'Summerfestival at Drottningholm' (R. Engländer, 1948)	232
'Wonderful vibrant Così fan tutte' (Leif Aare, 1962)	233
'Mozart: Earthy and Brilliant' (Carl-Gunnar Åhlén, 1979)	234
NOTES	237
BIBLIOGRAPHY	255
LIST OF ILLUSTRATIONS	262
LIST OF REPERTOIRE DURING GUSTAVIAN PERIOD	270
LIST OF REPERTOIRE SINCE 1922	273
INDEX	289

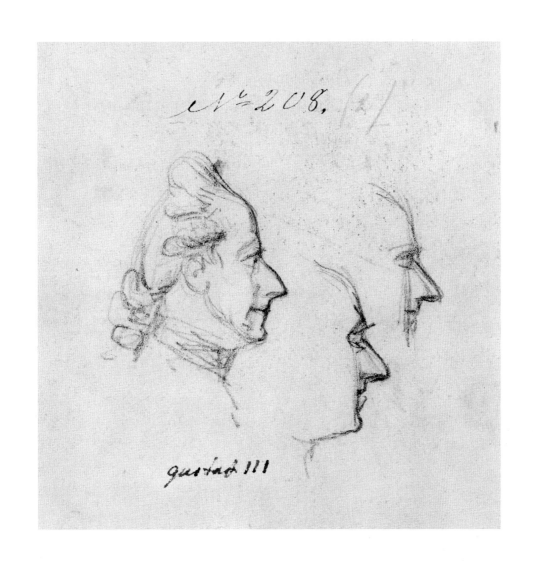

Willmar Sauter

1. THE REDISCOVERY OF THE DROTTNINGHOLM COURT THEATRE

The story has often been retold...

In the early spring of the year 1921, an assistant at the Swedish National Library was assigned the task of finding a painting by the late eighteenth-century artist Elias Martin. The painting had apparently been buried in storage for decades, but no records of its location existed. The young assistant searched in the backrooms and basement of the museum, but he failed to discover the painting. In frustration, he was preparing to abandon the search when one of his colleagues suggested that he might rummage through the old theatre barn at the Royal Palace of Drottningholm, situated on an island a few miles west of Stockholm. For over a century, the building had been used as a storeroom for the royal household.

The next day, after gathering the keys and bundling up against the cold, the assistant took the hour-long boat trip to the island. Ice was still gripping the edges of the waterway. After docking, the assistant walked up to the palace, passing what had formerly been the stables of the guard, crossed the gravelled yard facing the theatre building, and finally found the correct door to open. Because there were no lights in the building, the young man had to open some of the shutters. In this sparse light, he began his search for the missing painting by Martin. The building was filled with furniture, carpets, broken chandeliers, boxes of tableware, sacks of bed feathers, riding boots, a child's hobby horse, kitchen utensils, and, finally, numerous paintings. Everything was covered with a thick layer of dust, which had piled up over the decades.

As he worked his way through the piles of royal possessions and the ever-present dust, the assistant noticed that part of the space was filled with strange wooden objects, many of which were leaning against the walls of

1. View of Drottningholm from the English Park.

the stage. Trying to move them aside, the assistant suddenly realized that these large rectangular frames were flat wings—the original scenery for the old Drottningholm Theatre. During the second half of the eighteenth century, the building had been the royal theatre of Gustav III. Fascinated by his discovery, the assistant began to examine the stage space, including the area underneath the stage floor. There he discovered nothing less than its complete baroque stage machinery, including a capstan to move the scenery flats on and off the stage. Although the function of all these ropes and wooden structures was confusing to him, he understood that this machinery, and the scenic flats with various scenes painted on them, were the stage equipment of an original baroque theatre. This kind of stage equipment was not supposed to exist any longer, anywhere in Europe. But before his eyes the assistant observed the lost heritage of the baroque theatre.

The young man was enthusiastic. He went to the then Swedish king, Gustav V, and asked for permission to clear the debris in order to investigate the stage, the auditorium and the adjoining rooms. The king also informed him that he had allowed his 'boys' to take some of the ropes from the theatre to use for their sailing boats. For the young man, whose name was Agne Beijer, an intensive period of work lay ahead, during which he would work to reawaken the theatre that had lain forgotten since the day when Gustav III was shot dead during a masquerade at the Royal Opera in March 1792.

This saga of the discovery of the Drottningholm Court Theatre—an appealing Sleeping Beauty narrative—is today told repeatedly to tourists and theatre students who visit the theatre. This anecdote, though not entirely invented, is incorrect in many details. It is true that Beijer was searching for a painting by Martin, which he found. But he was not alone in this search. Two employees from the National Museum had accompanied him to the cold and uninviting theatre building. Together they opened all the windows to let the light in and the dust out. And the dust had not, in fact, piled up since the days of Gustav III, because the theatre had been used for various purposes since 1792. First of all, it was not closed immediately after the death of Gustav III, but had functioned as a theatre for another twenty years. Then, the Drottningholm Court Theatre had been used for performances on several occasions during the nineteenth century. Royal guards were sometimes housed in

2. The interior of the theatre in 1921.

the dressing rooms of the theatre. During the same period, some of its rooms had accommodated the household of the tutor of the royal children. And since 1898, parts of the theatre had been cleared to facilitate prayer meetings and concerts. In other words, the court theatre was not quite as deserted and forgotten as the legend would have us believe. It is true, however, that the auditorium and the stage were in great disorder and full of rubbish. What Agne Beijer and his colleagues discovered was not the theatre as such, but its historical, theatrical entrails: the numerous stage decorations, and the complete machinery with which the scenery could be displayed.

A century had passed, but practically everything was in place. These were not the ruins of a former theatre like Roman theatre buildings, or the empty shell of the renaissance Teatro Farnese in Parma in Italy. The Drottningholm Theatre contained everything that was necessary for theatrical performances. Although it had been misused as a storeroom, nothing of the original equipment had been destroyed. Actually, the various uses of the building since 1792, such as the delivery and removal of royal possessions, and occasional visits to the dressing rooms, had helped to preserve the building and its holdings. Fresh air kept damp and mould away and prevented the building from deteriorating. At the same time it was obvious that the theatre had not remained untouched – non-theatrical activities there had affected the place to some extent, even though no essential elements of the theatre itself had been taken away or replaced. The flat wings leaning against the walls had probably been placed there a hundred years earlier, but their condition was rather good in the sense that the paint and the wooden frames were well preserved. Most of the ropes belonging to the machinery under and above the stage were still there, although they ultimately had to be replaced because the hempen material had dried out over time.

To what extent, then, can we claim that the Drottningholm Theatre was still an authentic baroque theatre space? This vital question has been asked repeatedly, ever since Beijer and his colleagues rediscovered the theatrical space and its effects, and again with each and every step of the preservation and maintenance of the stage and the overall building. Have the processes of cleaning, restoration, and preservation since 1921 successfully returned the Drottningholm Theatre to its eighteenth-century glory? Or have these processes altered the state of an authentic theatrical environment? To what extent, from the perspective of authenticity, has the original baroque theatre been preserved or restored?

Much of the immediate work in the theatre, including the installation of electricity and the removal of nineteenth-century wallpapers, was directed by Agne Beijer, who himself became part of the myth of Drottningholm. He was at this time employed by the Royal Library. He was 33 years of age and had just completed his doctorate in Uppsala. Making a living as the theatre critic of a Gothenburg newspaper, he worked intensely towards the establishment of the Drottningholm Court Theatre as a museum. He succeeded with his plan within a few years, and from 1925 Beijer was the director of the Drottningholm Theatre Museum.

The past and the future

Agne Beijer was immediately faced with two tasks. One concerned the past: how had this theatre been used during the Gustavian period, or, more exactly, between 1766, when it was built, and the death of Gustav III in 1792? The other task concerned the future: how could this marvellous place be restored as a fully functional theatre? Would it be possible to bring this stage to life again so that contemporary audiences could experience the aesthetics of a long-gone era? Could the authenticity of the building be maintained despite the technical preservation measures that would necessarily have to be carried out in the twentieth century? Would it be possible, for example, to preserve the original building and operating conditions of the theatre while also complying with modern codes on fire prevention in public spaces?

The study of the conventions and practices of eighteenth-century theatres and, more generally, the baroque era, became Agne Beijer's priority. Of course, Beijer was not the first scholar to become interested in the Gustavian era. 'An aura spread over the days of King Gustav,' as one Swedish poet wrote in the early nineteenth century, celebrating the 50th anniversary of the Swedish Academy.[1] The theatrical activities of the period were also well described in several books.[2] It was well known that the present Drottningholm Court Theatre had replaced an earlier one that burnt down in 1762 during a performance. The Swedish Queen at the time, Lovisa Ulrika, sister of Friedrich the Great of Prussia and mother of King Gustav III, wanted to have the theatre rebuilt immediately to house her French theatre troupe. The court could not afford a luxurious building, so the architect Carl Fredrik Adelcrantz was urged to keep to the simple technique of using semi-timbered walls. Still, the theatre looks like a solid stone building because the wooden construction is well hidden beneath the plaster and paint. A closer look at the details of the theatre reveals the many ways in which the illusion of an impressive and expensive building for royalty was created.

The Drottningholm Palace mainly served as a summer residence for the royal family, and its theatre constituted an important and popular gathering place for court life. A French troupe performed the classical and contemporary repertoire of their country, and Italian operas were also performed, with a preference for the works of F.A. Uttini. Even before construction work on the new building was finished, while Donato Stopani was still

3. *Zemire and Azor*, performed in 1778 with a vision of Zemire's family seen through a mirror.

installing the stage machinery, the theatre reopened with the tragedy *Rhadamiste et Zénobie* by Crébillon, soon to be followed by J.-B. Lully and F.A. Uttini's tragi-comédie-ballet *Psyché*.

After the death of King Adolf Fredrik in 1771, Queen Lovisa Ulrika still remained in charge of the theatre, but could not afford to engage in theatrical activities. In 1778 she finally handed over the theatre to her son, King Gustav III, who immediately opened a new summer season at Drottningholm. A. E. M. Grétry's *Zemire and Azore*, an opera-comique performed in Swedish, was the first in a long series of theatrical court entertainments, in which both courtiers and professional singers and actors took to the stage. These theatrical activities came to a peak in the year 1786, when no fewer than 82 plays, operas and ballets were performed on the Drottningholm stage between March and December. In addition, performances and divertissements were presented in the French Garden and 'Carousels', which were theatricalised revivals of medieval tournaments, took place on the riding course between the theatre building and the palace. The king engaged Swedish poets and dramatists, German composers and a French stage designer to provide a never-ending series of spectacles. Gustav also participated personally in rehearsals and in the planning and design of the court entertainments. Throughout his life he wrote numerous libretti and plays, and in his younger years he also performed on stage. Although some historians and biographers have claimed that his interest and involvement in theatrical activities of all kinds overshadowed his political duties, others have insisted that Gustav III used the theatre cleverly in the service of his political ambitions. He turned theatrical events into political actions.

Gustav's passion for theatre was not limited to the Drottningholm Court Theatre. In 1773, the second year of his reign, he established a national opera company, which from 1782 performed in the newly erected Royal Opera House in the centre of Stockholm. In 1788 he founded the Royal Dramatic Theatre, and both of these national institutions continue to operate to the present day. Moreover, two other castles in the vicinity of Stockholm were equipped with theatres around the middle of the eighteenth century. The Confidencen Theatre at Ulriksdal was converted from a riding hall into a theatre in 1753 by the king's mother. And the theatre at Gripsholm Castle, originally furnished in 1773 by Gustav's wife, Queen Sofia Magdalena, was enlarged by the king's architect, Erik Palmstedt, in 1781. Later, after Gustav's year-long journey to Italy in 1783-84, it was adapted to reflect the Italian style of the theatre in Sabionetta. The theatre at Gripsholm, which is just as well preserved today as the Drottningholm Theatre, was quite popular with the court during the 1780s for performances during the Christmas season.

The theatrical tastes of Gustav III were rather complex. He was very fond of the French classics from Molière and Lully to Voltaire's plays, but he also liked Marivaux and appreciated Beaumarchais. Christoph Willibald Gluck was one of his favourite opera composers, but Wolfgang Amadeus Mozart's operas were never performed on the Gustavian stages. Gustav's own libretti, which were versified and brushed up by his Swedish literary collaborators, dealt primarily with the subject of Swedish history. His namesakes, the founder of the Swedish empire, Gustav Vasa, and the warrior king Gustav II Adolf, proved to be his preferred characters. These operas contained rather romantic plots, spiced with nationalistic, political ambitions.

Agne Beijer's major task immediately after the re-discovery of Drottningholm was to understand the workings of the baroque stage machinery, and its capacity to display the many flat wings and backdrops that were packed onto the stage at Drottningholm. He would also, as it turned out, discover equally well-preserved set of stage equipment in the theatre at Gripsholm. In his attempt to restore the Drottningholm stage, Beijer faced several problems arising from all these moving, rotating and sliding parts under and above the stage. For example, there were hundreds of ropes connecting the various carriages of the flat wings, and bringing them together at the central capstan. The trap doors had a special mechanism for opening and closing, synchronised with an elevator-like podium on which persons and things were lifted up to the stage level. The delicate mechanics of the light poles for the illumination of the stage, and their counter weights below the stage floor, constituted a living puzzle. The so-called chars for gods and goddesses to descend from heaven, amidst numerous clouds that could cover the entire stage with celestial revelations, were so narrow as to prompt questions about how any singer could dare to sit on them.

How did all these mechanics function, and how were they used on the baroque stage? To solve the problem of the mechanics, Beijer engaged some old sailors, who still had a working knowledge of similar constructions on commercial sailing boats. The hempen ropes were replaced, and the machinery came under the control of stage-hands who learned how to handle the capstans and wheels and levers. More problematic was the inventory of the flat wings and the backdrops. Which ones belonged with which stage design? In which order were they to be placed to form the illusionistic perspectives that were at the heart of baroque stage design? Most of the wings had names and numbers painted on their backs to identify the original production and their order on the carriages. He may have struggled with these practical details, but for Beijer, the understanding of baroque aesthetics was more pertinent at that time than developing a full inventory. His primary goal was to actually show how the sets could be changed in full view of the audience. This method of presentation, called changement à vue, was the practice on many European stages during the eighteenth century, and was the essential purpose of the whole scenic arrangement.

He succeeded quite quickly, at least as far as practical demonstrations were concerned. On August 19, 1922, the first divertissement was arranged. The date was chosen with care: it was the 150th anniversary of the coup d'etat that Gustav III had carried out in 1772, a bloodless seizure of political power from the then dominant Estates. In front of an invited crowd of theatre practitioners, journalists, historians and nobles, Beijer and his helpers rolled up the curtain and displayed four changes of scene. The ahhs and ohhs from the auditorium were eagerly reported in the next day's newspapers: "A festive performance, which despite of its quasi-improvised character provided an artistic experience far beyond what even a daring fantasy might have imagined," as one critic exclaimed.[3] This demonstration of the stage equipment was followed by five performances. Students of the Royal Ballet School danced one minuet to the music of Mozart's *Nozze di Figaro* and another to music by Carl Michael Bellman, a Swedish poet and composer at the court of Gustav III. Three arias by Gluck, Bellman and Händel, sung by Lillemor Montelius, concluded the presentation. The dances and songs were accompanied on a piano, played by Alice Tegnér, who later became famous for her children's songs that every Swedish child knows by heart. A first attempt to bring the Drottningholm stage to life in modern times had been accomplished: the stage machinery was, indeed, functioning and the acoustics were astounding.

Beijer's theoretical approach to the aesthetic and technical conditions of the baroque stage turned out to be a long-term project. Not until 1937, fifteen years after the first divertissement, was he able to publish his weighty book on *The Court Theatres at Drottningholm and Gripsholm* in a limited edition of 550 numbered copies.[4] The first part of the book traces the historical development of perspective stage design, from the late Middle Ages to the Italian masters of baroque scenery in the seventeenth century. It also presents sketches made by Louis Jean Desprez for the Swedish court theatres of the late eighteenth century. The second part of the book contains drawings, blue-prints of ground plans and cross sections of the Drottningholm and Gripsholm Theatres, as well as detailed drafts of all their machinery and constructions. Finally, there are photographs of their stage designs. In the year of its publication, the book was approved as an academic doctoral dissertation, and in 1940 Agne Beijer began teaching thea-

4. *The Magic Flute* in a performance from 1989. On the backdrop the palace of Drottningholm seen from the lake side.

tre history at Stockholm University. In 1946, he was awarded the title of professor, and in the same year he established the first department of theatre history in Scandinavia.

Since the reopening of the Drottningholm Theatre in 1922, many more divertissements and other events have been presented on its stage. In the 1940s, the first attempts were made to perform entire dramas and operas at Drottningholm. However, the theatre was still a museum first and foremost, and performances were meant to generate income for the museum and to provide a space for experimentation. When operas and ballets began to be produced on a more regular basis from the 1950s onwards, a new question arose: how did these modern productions relate to the basic aesthetic features of the baroque stage? How did various additions such as electric light, toilets and (more recently) a sprinkler system affect perceptions of the authenticity of this unique historical space?

The authors will first invite the reader to take a guided tour through the Drottningholm Theatre. We will report on what tourists are often told about this marvellous place, but we will also provide much more historical information and interpretive judgments. Drawing upon our professional experiences as theatre historians, we will expand upon what any standard tour can offer. We will also supplement the tour with information and viewpoints that are not included in public showings of the building. In Chapter Three, David Wiles will contrast the public tour with his own first impressions of Drottningholm as a theatrical space and as a place of performance. Chapter Four offers a panorama of theatre and society during the Gustavian period. We will investigate how Drottningholm and its theatre were originally used in the eighteenth century, and then consider how we can understand the aesthetics of that era. Then, in Chapter Five, we extend our analysis of the baroque theatre and its context. By offering a European perspective on baroque theatre and society, we will consider the challenges and problems of reviving that kind of theatre in modern times at Drottningholm. How has this court theatre been restored or transformed since the presentation of the first divertissement in 1922? Aesthetic approaches to this historical place have been manifold, and major trends during the twentieth century will be discussed in Chapter Six. Questions of authenticity will be extended to include the various attempts to cope with the historicity of the theatre's own aesthetics. Chapter Seven discusses performance style, and in particular modern acting and its relation to the aesthetic frames of Drottningholm. Finally, the issue of Drottningholm as a World Heritage site will be scrutinised in relation to the cultural policies and responsibilities of the Swedish state.

 The ambition of the authors is to give a concrete picture of the Drottningholm Court Theatre as a building, and as a place of historical and contemporary activities. At the same time, this unique theatrical space raises numerous aesthetic and scholarly questions that relate to many other historical theatres which – in various states of preservation – are still operating in Europe. Drottningholm offers a unique laboratory for performance, and it is a tool for the actor and musician, and as a site of social performance, that we shall analyse it. To reconstruct faithfully is impossible, but to perform in sympathy with the space means to understand the past, or more precisely, to imagine the past.

Willmar Sauter

2. A GUIDED TOUR OF THE THEATRE

Drottningholm was declared a World Heritage Site in 1992. This area includes the Royal Palace, built in the seventeenth century and refurbished several times before the reign of Gustav III, the theatre building of 1766, the French Garden, the Chinese Pavilion at the other end of the premises, various buildings for the military guards as well as the English Park that was added in the late eighteenth century at the end of the Gustavian period. All in all, the domain covers a large expanse of land on the island of Lovön, about twenty kilometres from Stockholm. Since 1974, it has been the home of the present royal family. From the city of Stockholm it can be reached by boat, by car or via public transport.

If visitors arrive in the middle of the day, they can observe the daily changing of the guard. This spectacle takes place outside the theatre building, in a fenced off area that is marked by posts and red and white striped ropes. Each day at noon, the military squad on duty lines up in a ceremonial manner. These soldiers wear elaborate parade uniforms, similar in their fanciful details to the military outfits that Swedish officers wore in the nineteenth century. One of the soldiers carries the folded Swedish flag, which he then delivers to the replacement squad upon its arrival. This second group of soldiers, also wearing elaborate uniforms, lines up opposite the first group. The two squads exchange military greetings. After performing several ceremonial drills, choreographed in accordance with traditional military commands, the flag is exchanged. The first squad then marches off, and the members of the new squad take up their positions at the guard posts, located before the Palace.

The ceremony of the changing of the guards at Drottningholm is not nearly as spectacular as the grand ritual outside the Royal Palace in the city, where solders on horseback and a large corps of musicians are involved in a magnificent military display. Nevertheless, even this minor event outside

5. Entrance of the Drottningholm Court Theatre

the Drottningholm Theatre emphasises a particular relationship between the past and the present. The soldiers of the squad are actually guarding the Royal Palace of Drottningholm, carrying rifles with bayonets. In a state of emergency, they have to protect the king's family in residence. At the same time, the formality of the ceremony, the historically informed uniforms, and the coded commands (nobody can actually hear what the officers are shouting) indicate a tradition that refers to past practices. The whole event maintains continuity between age-old traditions and the enactment of modern-day security procedures. The changing of the guards at Drottningholm lends a historical dimension to contemporary practices.

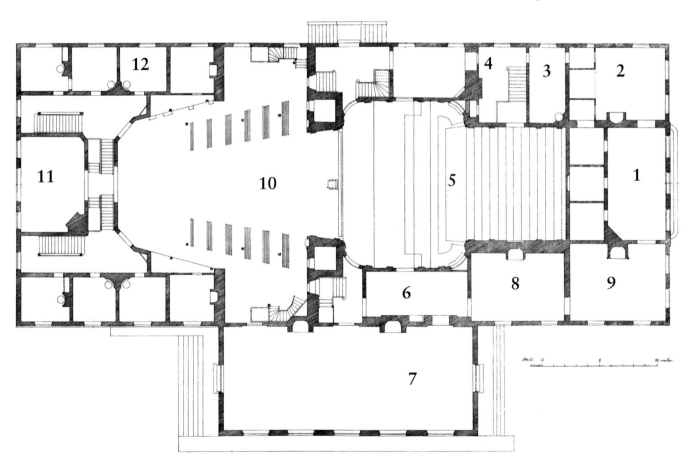

6. Groundplan of the Drottningholm Court Theatre. The numbers indicate the order of the rooms visited during the guided tours.

The open square upon on which the ceremony takes place offers a good view of the theatre. The façade of the east side of the theatre, with its main entrance, consists of three arched doors in the middle section and two high windows on either side. Seven smaller windows on the upper floor mark the extension of the building. The roof is flat and the gable is formed of a classical triangle with an oval window in its centre. The proportions, the sparse decorations, the small panes of glass in the windows, the double door – all of these details are recognisable features of a grand country house of the eighteenth century. There is no obvious sign that distinguishes this building as a theatre, but its historical style and origin places it firmly in the architectural milieu of the Drottningholm domain. A group of visitors waiting in front of the building, rather than any other visible sign, indicates that this is the entrance to the theatre.

Once the visitors are allowed into the entrance hall of the theatre, they are asked to leave their bags, coats and cameras in the tiny cloakrooms in order not to scrape the delicate wallpapers they soon will see (room 1). Various language groups are formed, since guided tours are conducted in Swedish, English, French, and German. In the future tours in Russian, Japanese, Chinese and Italian will probably become available. Entering the first room to the right of the entrance hall, the visitor's attention is caught by a large bed in the alcove of this beautiful chamber (room 2). The windows are covered with white transparent curtains to keep the sunlight out, and the guide introduces the group to the construction history of the Drottningholm Theatre, which will eventually explain the striking presence of a bed in this room.

A Bedroom

It all started with Lovisa Ulrika, a princess who was brought up at the Prussian court in Berlin together with her brother Frederick, later to be called the Great. Their upbringing was strongly influenced by classical French culture, theatre and music. In 1744, the 24 year old princess was married to the heir to the Swedish throne, Adolf Fredrik. Soon after her marriage, Lovisa Ulrika became involved in political intrigues over the monarch's constitutional lack of power. Then in 1751, when Adolf Frederik became king, the queen fought against the two leading parties in parliament, the 'Hats' and the 'Caps', over the power of the king concerning foreign policies, taxes and the election of members of national council.

Lovisa Ulrika considered Swedish culture to be in a deplorable state of backwardness in comparison to the French culture which she admired. In order to develop the court's cultural status, she transformed the riding hall at the Ulriksdal Castle into a fine rococo theatre, invited a French theatre troupe to come to Stockholm to perform at court and in the public Bollhuset Theatre, and she saw to it that all birthdays were celebrated with theatrical entertainments. Her sons, Gustav (1746 - 1792), who became Gustav III in 1771, and Karl (1748 - 1818), who became Karl XIII in 1809, were brought up in the French cultural tradition and learned Voltaire's plays by heart, naturally in French. There was already a theatre building at Drottningholm which Lovisa Ulrika had refurbished in 1755, but it went up in flames in dramatic circumstances in 1762.[1] Queen Lovisa Ulrika immediately wanted a new building to rise like a phoenix out of the ashes, but there was a problem: she did not have the money for it. As a result of all these circumstances, the tour guide finally explains why there is a bed in this room.

The queen approached the architect in charge of the royal buildings, Carl Fredrik Adelcrantz, to design a new theatre and, moreover, to invest his own money in the costs of the construction. The queen's promise to repay his expenses was never fully realised and, as compensation, the architect was offered this room as a bedroom, although it was originally designed as the king's own room in the theatre. The queen's lack of funds was also the reason why the construction, decoration and equipment of the building had to be kept to the lowest possible expense. Although plaster and yellow paint make the walls look like solid stone, they are semi-timbered rather than built with bricks. The structure of the building consists of timber joists, and the space in between was filled in with stones, a practice similar to that used to construct the Globe theatre in London.

In the architect's bedroom, the open fireplace seems to be framed with dark marble, but some defective edges reveal that it was actually built of brick and merely painted in an imitation of marble. These fake-marble details, as well as other illusionistic features, will appear in other parts of the theatre throughout the tour.

7. Queen Lovisa Ulrika (1720-1782).

The guide might not necessarily point out the almost invisible jib door, leading to the ladies restroom and installed in modern times, but will take the group to a small adjoining room, which is said to have been reserved for the architect's servant (room 3). Depending on the size of the group, the tour might linger for a moment in this room to have a look at the simple and efficient tiled stove which kept the place warm. Leaning towards the stove one finds a huge brush and next to it a bucket, the utensils that were used to quickly extinguish any glowing pieces of firewood that might have fallen onto the floor. This room also contains a bed, indicating that both the architect's servant and his master actually lived in the theatre. During certain periods, up to 150 people lived in the rooms that surround the auditorium, on the upper floor, and in the dressing rooms behind the stage. We have to imagine the place full of people – not just audiences, but actors and singers with their families and children, members of the court and their servants and even guests of the royal family. Few stayed there permanently, but summer seasons in the eighteenth century could last from early spring to late autumn.

8. View of the auditorium and stage upon entering the inner sphere of the theatre.

The Auditorium

The group continues through a corridor, climbing up some narrow stairs and finally entering the auditorium (room 4). The guide warns the visitors to watch their step, because the auditorium seems almost to lie in darkness (room 5). It takes a while to accustom one's eyes to the candle-lit hall and to find a seat on the benches. The candles are of course not wax candles, but electric ones with distinctive flickering flames that were invented especially for this theatre. While today's visitors might experience the auditorium as quite dark, the audiences of the eighteenth century, not spoiled by an overflow of electric light, found this illumination magnificent, grand and spectacular. But even during the Gustavian period, the theatre was mainly used during the bright summer months, when the sun sets close to midnight. The contrast between the sunny outdoor light and the gloomy candles in the auditorium helped to hide the fake details – then as well as today. What looks like marble, stone masonry and stucco reliefs is actually painted wood and papier-mâché. Adelcrantz had found cheap solutions for creating rich illusions.

The eyes of the visitors are drawn to the open stage rather than to the details of the auditorium. Behind the proscenium arch, six pairs of flat, painted wings and a backdrop form a perspective view which makes an amazing impression. Depending on the performances that are being prepared, the visiting group might see a park alley with trees, bushes and statues, a town street with houses or an indoor room with sunlight coming in through the windows. Of course, the 'natural' light is all painted on, and is always coming from the spectators' left side. All these views create a perfect illusion, although we are very well aware that what we see are painted wings. This is the first and most important perception of this baroque stage: the skillfully painted wings create an illusionistic perspective in a fully visible manner. We know, and we can see the technique, while our fantasy completes the imaginary harmony of the picture.

The ideal point in the auditorium from which to experience the seamless lines of this perspective view are the chairs of the king and queen in the front row. Spectators today are not allowed to sit in these two chairs. Nor are tickets available for the twelve chairs behind the regal chairs. These exclusive seats, which were once reserved for the highest ranking courtiers, are nowadays occupied by members of the board and distinguished guests during performance. (Plus ça change, plus c'est la meme chose.) But all spectators have a good view of the stage because the Drottningholm Court Theatre has a relatively egalitarian seating arrangement. The straight benches are all arranged parallel to the footlights, and the auditorium floor is raked enough to provide a fair sight line even for those sitting in the back row. The central space of the auditorium, where the king sat, is slightly wider than the rest of the hall, which is the same size as, and symmetrical with, the stage. Even in this respect, the harmony of proportions and the mirror effect between stage and auditorium are the dominating features of this theatre.

Here the guide will point out a peculiarity that is unique to Drottningholm: between the main part of the auditorium and the last eleven rows of benches, a curtain can be lowered. In Gustavian times, during intermissions and after the end of performances, this curtain shut off those who were placed on these benches – lower nobility and bourgeois citizens from town, as well as servants of the castle. Thus, they were prevented from mingling with members of the court. Today, the same curtain is occasionally used to diminish the size of the auditorium in the (rare) case of a performance not selling out.

There are no balconies in the Drottningholm Theatre. Instead there are six boxes in the central part of the auditorium, three on each side. The ones next to the proscenium arch do not allow a view of the stage, but are used as 'trumpet boxes' for musicians who will not fit into the orchestra pit, such as trumpet and kettle-drum players. The central boxes were reserved for the queen – to the audience's right – and the king, but were only used on rare official occasions. The remaining two boxes in the corners of the central audience space are called 'incognito boxes' with laced wooden shutters: from these one could see the stage without being seen. Are they still in use, you might ask. Well, one cannot see whether anybody is there or not!

At this point, our tour guide briefly leaves the auditorium through the door next to the stage, and very soon the visitors will hear a howling wind, which increases to a storm and then a rolling thunder which will batter the building. This is just a short demonstration of what parts of the stage

9. The auditorium photographed in the 1930s. The Royal chairs were, as in the Gustavian period, not yet surrounded by the benches; the shutters of the rear windows were pained in green. Clearly visible is also the false proscenium for the curtain to cut off the lower class visitors in the back rows.

machinery can still accomplish. The wind is produced by a big wheel with transverse staffs that scrape against a hempen cloth, and the thunder comes from a long wooden box, filled with stones that are rolled from one side to the other and back again –just by pulling a rope. If the group were to be lucky and some stage hands were around, they might move the 'sea' mounted upstage. This equipment consists of five horizontal beams stretching over the entire width of the rear of the stage. Each beam is covered with blue cloth in the form of a corkscrew. When the stagehands turn these beams, each provided with a handle, the illusion of rolling waves is created. The waves can represent a gentle sea – when the beams are turned slowly – but they can also appear as a stormy sea, supported by howling wind and repeated thunder claps. Even without any visible persons, the Drottningholm stage can produce the illusion of a stormy sea shore. Furthermore, a boat – painted on cut-out cardboard – can arrive on the shore. In the Gustavian period, a child would jump onto the shore, i.e. the boards of the stage, to give the full illusion of a distant place. The child would disappear through the flat wings upstage and reappear as an adult singer downstage, naturally in a costume corresponding precisely to the child's dress.

This little scene illustrates an essential aspect of the aesthetics of the baroque stage: illusion. Of course, illusion in this sense does not mean that anyone in the auditorium is fooled or even made believe in a real storm, as would be the case in a Hollywood movie. On the contrary, the visibility of the theatrical effects is part of the pleasure of the baroque stage. There is a playfulness involved in the creation of baroque illusion. To see and to understand how the illusionistic effects are accomplished, and to be aware of their artificiality, lies at the heart of theatrical productions on stages such as the one in Drottningholm. As the chapter on the Gustavian epoch will demonstrate further, the symbolic meaning of stage illusion had its equivalent expressions in the acting and singing style of the period, including costumes, make-up, and movements as well as the composition and execution of dance and music.

A Neo-Classical Extention

Meanwhile, the tour guide asks the group to leave the auditorium and brings them to the so-called Déjeuner-Salon (room 7). After the low light in the auditorium, the grand windows of this room let the sunshine flood in, blinding the visitors for a moment. The Déjeuner-Salon was built in the style of an Italian portico, designed by the stage designer Louis Jean Desprez and added to the theatre in 1791, just a year before Gustav III was shot dead. The high, French windows open upon a spectacular view out into the English Park revealing oak trees, meadows and a lake with various bridges to small islands. The ceiling of the hall is vaulted and contains a narrow gallery, and above this gallery a lovely summer sky is painted, giving the illusion of an outdoor space. The tour guide might tell the group that invisible musicians could be placed in the gallery to play heavenly sounds for royal personages dining in the hall. Although this can easily be imagined, it probably never happened. The Déjeuner-Salon was actually used for 'déjeuner', breakfast, and not for the king's family, but rather for the royal household, including servants and even peasants from the surrounding farms. Breakfast at the time meant a meal in the middle of the day, and Gustav III was eager to feed the court and all its employees every day. Earlier, these meals had been served in the Orangery, but now the food was brought to the Déjeuner-Salon, where the king and his family could – incognito – watch the crowd from the gallery. After the closure of the theatre in 1809, this room, with its

10. Painting of the carousel *The Conquest of Galtare Rock* by Pehr Hilleström from 1779.

direct entrance from the yard, was one of the building's most used spaces over the course of the nineteenth century. Artisans had their workshops there and for a while, farmers were allowed to store their potatoes with the result that its floorboards were completely destroyed. Therefore this is the only part of the theatre with a new floor, and that is also why only here is it permitted to serve drinks and food during the intermissions of performances, or on other special occasions. The lasting impression – with or without drinks – is that of a bright open space, decorated in the neo-classical style and contrasting with the darker rococo of the rest of the building.

Back in the theatre, the next room on the tour is called the Carousel Room due to its paintings depicting the Carousels or garden festivals of the Gustavian era (room 8). These events usually took place over several days, during which armed contests were interspersed with spectacular plots enacted in temporary locations specifically built in the park. In one large painting, a tournament in the medieval style is depicted: knights on horseback, in front of a large audience on specially erected scaffolds, are trying to pierce their lances through a ring at the centre of the arena. In another painting, a dragon is defending a medieval castle – built out of cardboard in the park – and the king himself is just about to kill the beast. This re-staging of scenes from the past for the entertainment of the court will be discussed in more in detail in the chapter on the Gustavian era. The guide of the tour might take this opportunity to point to the well-preserved wallpapers in this room. A closer look reveals that the wallpaper was not pasted to the wall, but that lengths of wallpaper were sewn together and then nailed at top and bottom to the boards of the wall. This technique allowed the wallpaper to be removed and set up in some other place whenever this was desirable. The last room to be commented upon by the guide is the corner room, symmetrical to the architect's bedroom, where the tour started (room 9). There is a well preserved fireplace with a hearth brush leaning towards it, but no bed. Instead the focus is on a painting of the actor Jacques-Marie Boutet de Monvel, who is said to be the father of the art of acting in Sweden. The guides usually exaggerate the significance of his teachings – Swedish actors of the time were not as poorly educated as we are led to believe – because Monvel's life lends itself to dramatic stories. He arrived in Stockholm in 1781 with a French troupe which performed at the royal palaces and also,

11. The actor Jaques-Marie Boutet de Monvel.

later, in a public playhouse. Monvel did not like Stockholm and was eager to return to Paris, so Gustav III posted guards in front of Monvel's living quarters to prevent the actor from escaping. He received an extravagant salary, but after five years he was granted permission to travel to France and he never returned to Stockholm again. Through this tale, together with some accounts of his amorous adventures with noble ladies, Monvel provides an arresting example of Gustavian court life, and thus offers the perfect conclusion to the tour.² The guide certainly recommends that the group visit the theatre shop once more to have a look at the video in which the workings of the stage machinery are demonstrated. To experience the intricate mechanisms underneath and above the stage on this tour is simply not possible – bringing a whole group through the narrow stairs and passages into the backstage areas would risk both the security of the visitors and the preservation of the delicate equipment.

The Machinery

Only on very special occasions – when a new artistic team is hired, or when scholars with a particular interest in the Gustavian era gather for a conference – is it possible to enter the stage area for a closer look (room 10). Then the artistic director or some other knowledgeable member of the crew will take visitors through the narrow door of the stage entrance. The first thing one notices is the raked floor of the stage. What looked like a slightly ascending floor from the auditorium feels quite steep in reality. The raked floor constitutes an important element in producing the overall perspective view of the stage design. From the auditorium the stage design makes a neat and compact impression whereas now the actual size of the flat wings becomes apparent.

The pair that stands closest to the proscenium measures more than five metres in height. As the floor rises, the height of the flats is gradually reduced to create the visual principle of perspectivism associated with the baroque stage. Their heights, from front to back, in metres is: 5.63, 5.10, 4.82, 4.70, 4.55, and 4.13. Depending on the set, the exact size of the flats might differ slightly from these measurements, but the principle that the last pair of flats equals 70% of the first pair remains constant. Translated to the human body, and taking into consideration the fact that people were generally shorter in the eighteenth century, it is reasonable to assume that the downstage flats were three and a half times the height of the human body, whereas the upstage flats only equalled two and a half times the height of a performer of the time. This difference in proportions between downstage and upstage had to be observed when staging actions within the perspective set. The use of children in the upstage area offers one solution to this

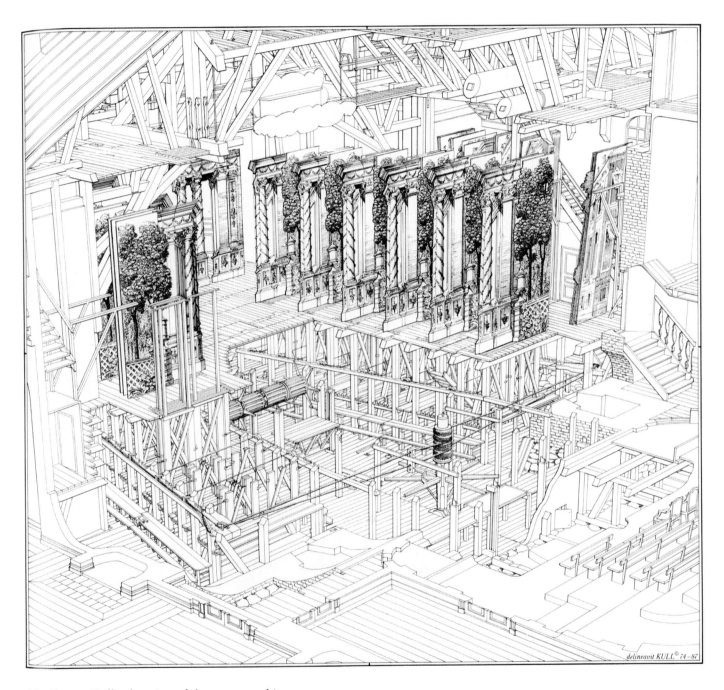

12. Gustav Kull's drawing of the stage machinery.

problem. The choice of performers' entrances and exits was another means of keeping the perspective within the frame of illusion. Movements onstage had to be carefully choreographed so as not to disturb the illusion of depth that converted these two-dimensional painted wings into a three-dimensional room or landscape.

Invisible from the auditorium, there are other flats standing behind those which create the set on display. These hidden flats come to the fore when the set is changed. Upon close examination one realises that all the flats, the visible as well as the hidden ones, are not resting on the stage floor, but instead are located within slits in the floor and are fastened to carriages underneath. For the first four pairs of flats there are four slits for each position, thus four separate decorations can be shown without lowering the curtain. There are three slits behind the fifth pair of flats, but only two slits behind the sixth pair. After the first four pairs of flats, a first backdrop can be rolled down, creating a so-called short stage for interior rooms. This first backdrop could also be cut out in such a way as to allow a view through an arch or a gallery – the downstage area would, for instance, consist of a terrace in a castle, from which a garden behind it – in the upstage area – would be visible, perhaps even including a view of the rolling sea. In other words: the downstage area offered slightly more flexibility than was available upstage; two more backdrops – in front of and behind the wave machine – increased the variations that the set designer could utilise.

Sooner or later, these privileged visitors will be told that the wings they see on stage today are not the original ones. In the 1950s the décor painters of the Royal Opera carried out the difficult task of copying the historical sets that were used in the eighteenth century. In the following decades, a number of sets that were most frequently used in modern productions were skillfully re-created on canvases, then stretched and mounted on wooden frames that were minutely reconstructed from original measurements. At the same time, the original eighteenth-century flats and backdrops were brought to a specially built barn several kilometres away from the theatre. There they are stored in an acclimatised environment, hanging from a construction which allows them to be pulled out one by one into the middle of the room for inspection. Thirty complete sets have been preserved, as well as a number of set pieces such as painted rocks, trees and benches be-

13. A painted rock on stage as used in the production of Joseph Haydn's *Orlando Paladino* in 2012. On stage Magnus Staveland and Kirsten Blaise

longing to the original décors. This collection constitutes an unusually rich source of historical material, since the eighteenth-century practice of reusing the same set in numerous productions often limited the number of sets that were available in a theatre. The same street décor might be seen in an opera, a comedy, a ballet and in a divertissement. The richness of the Drottningholm sets is the result of several factors : first of all, the theatre was a royal institution and King Gustav III engaged prominent set designers who were supposed to create new and surprising decorations; secondly, many of the sets were moved between the Royal Opera in the city and the theatre in Drottningholm; furthermore, the repertoire consisted of pieces that were set in exotic or ancient Nordic milieus which required appropriate settings. The preservation of these original set pieces is a delicate task, frequently discussed and revised, but constantly underfinanced. Experts think that the flat wings are hung too tightly, so there is a risk that the original paint will be damaged. The government, ultimately responsible for the maintenance of all the flat wings on account of their museum status, has so far not been willing to finance a new storeroom for these precious pieces. Also, ideas about how best to preserve historical décors have changed over time. Rather than restoring the flats, as was advocated in the early twentieth century, it is now considered that the paint should simply be 'conserved', i.e. the decay is stopped, but the paint is not replaced.

The copies from the 1950s and 1960s are so well-made that the unskilled eye will not notice the difference. Those old copies have already gained some patina with aging, and have become quasi-historical parts of the stage equipment of the Drottningholm Court Theatre. Thus the impression of a historical stage certainly remains, despite the fact that we do not see the original set pieces. More copies of sets are needed today, and possible ways of facilitating this task by means of computerised transfer techniques are being considered. Technically it is possible to scan the originals and to 'print' them onto canvases, but so far the process is too expensive for the management of the Drottningholm Theatre.

14. Lighting pole at the Drottningholm Court Theatre in the position of renewing the 'candles'.

In order to light the stage, including the flats, a series of lighting poles are located behind each flat. Attached to these poles, which are as high as the flats, are five reflectors. Each reflector consists of a small, open box containing two candles. A piece of metal on the inside of the box reflects the light of the candles and directs it towards the flat standing next to it. In this way each flat is illuminated by the lighting pole in front of it, although the light source remains invisible from the auditorium. The five reflectors are attached to a thin rope, which runs through a small wheel on the top of the pole. This little mechanical device – similar to a flag pole – allows for the lowering of all the reflectors so that a stagehand can easily change the candles. By pulling the rope in the other direction, the reflectors are brought back into their original positions. This is how the lighting equipment was handled during the Gustavian period, when real candles were used. Each lighting pole, just like the flat wings, extends under the stage floor from where the poles can be rotated. For that purpose, all the poles are attached to ropes that are brought together to a drum. From a 'ship's wheel' on stage, hidden just behind the proscenium arch, the drum in the basement can be steered. To make the turning of the drum easier, each pole is connected to a counterweight – a little sandbag – which pulls the poles back into their ordinary positions. By means of this clever arrangement, the light poles with their reflectors can be turned towards the stage for maximum effect, or they can be turned away from the stage to dim the illumination of the acting area, as well as to darken the flats. The light of the ten candles behind each flat can thus facilitate quite a dynamic change from bright daylight to a gloomy, menacing twilight. Besides the series of lighting poles, a row of footlights is located along the front of the stage. Thirty one reflectors, which illuminate the performers when they are downstage, extend the whole width of the stage. These reflectors are attached to boards that can be mechanically lowered so burned-out candles can be replaced underneath the stage and lifted up again at full brightness.

The artistic director guiding this privileged group of visitors certainly takes the opportunity to explain some of the problems that this delicate lighting system poses today. For safety reasons, real candles and open flames are strictly forbidden in this protected environment. Accordingly, when electricity was installed in 1921, Agne Beijer substituted yellow-coloured

15. The machinery of the theatre as used since 1766 and again since 1922: ropes and capstans moved by stage hands.

bulbs for candles and oil lamps. Initially, these electric 'candles' were thought to give a perfect illusion of the authentic illumination. But over the years, various new attempts have been made to re-create the lighting conditions of the original stage, including the computerised flickering of electric bulbs. Twentieth-century directors found imitations of the original lighting too dark for modern audiences, so they added spotlights, either as side lights beaming in between the flats or attached to the chandeliers hanging in the proscenium arch. Some even placed spotlights in the trumpet boxes. The problem with these extra light sources is not only that they are much too visible from the auditorium, but also that the flat wings are lit up so brightly that they stand out as individual set pieces. The brightness causes a complete break with the aura of the baroque stage, destroying both the unity and the harmony of the perspectival view of the stage.[3]

Members of the visiting group are most probably allowed to turn the handle of the wind machine to hear the howling storm, pull the strings of the thunder box – which cannot be viewed, because it is located in the attic of the theatre – and inspect the wave machine with its five hessian sackcloth covered beams. The kernel of the machinery is located under the stage floor. A narrow staircase with sharp turns leads down to the 'underworld' of this baroque stage equipment. The first impression is of a confusing mess of wooden constructions, beams and poles, thick ropes and thin strings, drums and capstans. Of course, this is a well-organised mess. Although it is difficult to understand the overall design at first sight, the various parts of the machinery are easy to distinguish. The most dominating feature is certainly the mechanism of the flat wings – the device that brings about the changement à vue that makes such an overwhelming impression when seen from the auditorium. The principle is simple and remained basically the same once Giacomo Torelli had introduced the technique in the Venetian opera houses in the middle of the seventeenth century. The base of each flat has two small wheels, which are carved so as to rest on a rounded rail, on which they can be pulled back and forth. The rails were made out of a special kind of oily timber, imported from Africa, to avoid squeaking sounds underneath the stage. Each carriage is connected to the main capstan by means of a rope, running over a number of small movable castors. When the capstan is moved by six stagehands, the carriage will slide backwards – out of sight of the spectators watching the changement. The disappearing carriage is connected to the next one by a short rope and a turning wheel, and the second flat is thus moved onto the stage simultaneously with the first one moving out of sight. In this way, the change of scenery only takes a matter of seconds. While the performance continues within the new perspective setting, the stage hands will have to unhook the short ropes and attach them to a third set of carriages – which has to be done by hand for each of the twelve carriages. Thus the stage will be prepared for a second changement à vue, and meanwhile other things might be happening on stage such as characters emerging through a trapdoor in the stage floor.

Seen from below, the trapdoor looks like a podium. The performer reaches the podium over some stairs and once he or she is placed firmly on it, the stagehands will turn a special, vertical capstan to pull up both podium and performer. While this happens, the equivalent section of the stage floor will be lowered just enough to be slid to one side, thus giving room for the appearance of the character from the underworld. This is executed by the same capstan and perfectly synchronised with the rising platform. In the case of a character disappearing from the stage into the underworld, the process is simply reversed. Drottningholm is equipped with three trapdoors of varying sizes, located both downstage and upstage. All of them are connected with ropes to the same capstan and can be moved at the same time or – by unhooking the ropes – one at a time. Instead of a performer, pieces of decoration such as a painted rock or a tree can also be brought on stage.

There are more capstans underneath the stage for other effects, for example operating the flies above the stage. The flies consist of painted cloth that, hung from flybars, close off the scene above the stage. When the décor changes from a room to a garden, the flies will also change from a ceiling to a sky, or maybe an overhanging leafy alley. This change is executed by six stagehands turning a capstan under the stage that is connected to a long, horizontal drum under the roof of the theatre, to which, in turn, the ropes of the flybars are attached. While one set of flybars is pulled up, the next will automatically be lowered, in synchrony with the changing of the flat wings. This synchronisation has to be achieved through the cooperation of the two crews and executed at the right moment in the stage action and the music.

17. The cloud machinery as it appeared in a rehearsal of the solo performance of the Russian soprano Julia Lezhneva in August 2013.

The attic under the roof contains devices for bringing down clouds, and there are various cloud machines that can facilitate a range of celestial displays. These particular effects are handled by pulling ropes from the side of the stage, thus controlling exactly how low the clouds will come onto the stage. Among the clouds are two cloud chariots or chars (French for triumph chariot); the great char provides room for at least two performers, the little char upstage allows only for one person. The chars are brought into motion from the side of the stage and can move both vertically and horizontally. The performers appearing on them have to climb up to the attic, via steep stairs and dangerous gantries, in order to reach these lofty swinging chariots. This is how gods enter the Drottningholm stage.

18. View of stage and auditorium from the reversed perspective – from the wave machine to the auditorium. The backdrop depicting a town square is still hanging upside-down. The false proscenium cutting off the last rows is fully visible as well as the shutters which have been painted white in the 1950s

The Dynamics of the Stage

Carefully stepping between timbered beams and crossing ropes, the artistic director will eventually ask the little group to leave this underworld through the backdoor. Climbing up a short but unstable staircase, the group now enters the backstage area. Next to the exit from the basement one can have a look into one of the larger rooms, which once served as a dining room for the artists, and which nowadays is used as a costume atelier, and during performances as a dressing room for the chorus (room 11). Here they can take a seat and put their tired feet up. The machinery under the stage floor offers a striking contrast to what one can see from the auditorium, from where the Drottningholm stage makes a rather stern and austere impression. The symmetrical perspective view of a geometrically shaped garden, or the endless columns of a hall, look formalised, unrealistic and constructed. Indeed, the baroque décor is a highly artificial construction, especially when seen during a guided tour. Only in performance can the dynamic potential of this elaborate stage machinery be experienced. Depending on how the machinery is used, the director explains, the mobility of the Drottningholm stage reveals both its horizontal and vertical dimensions.

The changing of the flats is of course the major source of the stage's horizontal dynamics. But the designer can also choose to vary the depth of the stage by means of the three positions from which the backdrops can be rolled down. The so-called short stage ends after the fourth pair of flats and provides an intimate space. This is often used for interior scenes, especially a living room or a workshop in comedies, and for tragic confrontations in the plot of many operas. Exterior scenes can also be created on the short stage, for instance a shadowy arbour for lovers. Some of the backdrops have openings such as an arched gallery, a window or even the fake mirror for Grétry's opera *Zémire et Azor* (see ill. 3). Thus, both the characters on the stage and the spectators in the auditorium can watch actions taking place in the upstage area. The deep stage extends to the sixth pair of flats and, together with backdrop, provides the 'endless' perspective of the baroque stage. The backdrops largely continue the perspectival view of the flats, but there are exceptions. For example, one backdrop depicts the Royal Palace of Drottningholm and thus suggests a meta-view of the theatre's location. In this instance it is also noteworthy that the palace is seen from a semi-frontal angle, which breaks the strict symmetry of the wings. The stage can be further extended beyond the second backdrop and give a full view of the wave machine. At this point its entire depth of nineteen metres is displayed.

Some authors of the eighteenth century, such as Friedrich Schiller and even Gustav III himself, consciously calculated the dynamic changes between the short stage and the deep stage. Together with variations between exterior and interior scenes, the construction of the plot provides ample possibilities to create a dynamic scenic rhythm. Furthermore, these changes can be supported by the manipulation of the lighting poles. The stage can be fully illuminated or it can be dimmed to give the impression of nighttime activities. For scenes that take place in daylight, the contrast between brightly illuminated and shadowed sides of a room or a garden is painted directly onto the flats. Seen from the auditorium, the light always comes from the left side, which, at Drottningholm, coincides with the west side of the building, facing the evening sun. The painted illusion of light, and the real light coming from the reflectors of the light poles, interact in a wonderful way and constitute an important aspect of the baroque illusion.

As the description of the machinery has already suggested, the dynamics of this stage are not limited to the horizontal plane. From the attic of the theatre clouds and gods might descend, and through the trapdoors characters and set pieces can appear and disappear. In the baroque world, both heaven and hell are included. These vertical dynamics offer additional potential for the entertainment of spectators, but the display of celestial characters, as well as the demons of the underworld, were also deeply rooted in the baroque imagination. The gods of antiquity which frequently appear in early operas were not merely representatives of fate, but with their human desires and virtues they symbolized aspects of life to which the inhabitants of high Olympus were equally subject with the people dwelling in the vales of the earth. Also hell is an essential part of human fears and beliefs. From the world under the stage floor, awful creatures might ascend and interfere with humans. At times, human beings might even have to descend into the underworld – this is where Orpheus finds his beloved Eurydice, and this is where Dom Juan will end his days. A baroque stage had to express the dynamics between heaven, earth and hell, and Drottningholm is fully equipped to facilitate these vertical interactions.

The dynamic potential of a baroque stage with its elaborate machinery was ultimately constructed to make the invisible visible. The aim of a stage such as the one in Drottningholm was not the realistic depiction of natural environments, but rather an artistically elevated expression of life. According to the aesthetics of the time, the stage should express profound human experiences – significant events, characters and their passions (existential as well as ridiculous ones), fate and destiny, including the other-worldly powers of gods and demons. That is why flying chares and multiple trap-doors were so important for the stage equipment of Drottningholm. Just as the music of Händel, Gluck and Mozart's operas was composed to express strong passions in harmonic melodies, so the stage was supposed to express the fictional habitat of characters in a harmonious way. That is why symmetry was so important, and why the picture the stage produced had to be framed by a proscenium arch. The technical development of the baroque stage took one hundred years – from Sebastinao Serlio's prescription of three types of scenery (1545) to Giacomo Torelli's inspired invention of carriages for flat wings running under the stage floor (1641). During these experiments, Giovan Battista Aleotti is said to have introduced the proscenium arch, which he first tried out in the Teatro Farnese in Parma (1618). Once the machinery was in place, it was copied in most European theatres until the end of the nineteenth century. Despite many variations, the principles of its construction remained intact until the advent of electric spotlights. The Drottningholm Court Theatre is one of the few places where such machinery has survived practically untouched, and where this idea of a harmonious picture within the frame of a proscenium still can be experienced. The picture has, however, to be understood as a dynamic flow on both the horizontal and the vertical planes – ultimately the purpose of this whole, intricate machinery.

Preservation

At the end of the tour the artistic director takes his visiting friends further upstairs to four small dressing rooms on either side of the stage. Some of them are wonderfully preserved (room 12). They are equipped with tiled stoves (there are altogether 24 such stoves in the various rooms of the building) and the walls are covered with beautifully designed wallpaper. These wallpapers are actually the original ones and they are marked by their age. In other rooms the wallpaper looks more fresh and colourful, but these are reprinted copies that were nailed to the walls, according to the old technique, in the twentieth century.

For non-specialists it is difficult to see immediately what remains of the original building and where later additions, reparations or 'improvements' begin. At the same time, one has to understand that a building that is about 250 years old has had to be maintained, and that every act of inference affects its overall historical status. When the theatre or the 'opera house', as it was called then, opened in 1766, construction work was not yet finished. Through the bills from carpenters, painters, stove and wallpaper makers and so on that are kept in the archive of the royal household, these building activities in and around the theatre can still be followed.[4] In the early 1770s, when no theatrical performances were given on stage, some of the living quarters upstairs were remodelled, new walls were erected and more tiled stoves paid for. When the Queen Mother handed over the building to her son Gustav III in 1778 and the theatre was once again used for performances, the stage area was widened and in consequence some of the dressing rooms were cut off from their corridors, so that artists had to get into their rooms through the chambers of their colleagues. In 1791, the Déjeuner-Salon was added to the building. Originally it was called 'Salon pour les Festins et les Ballets' and received its present name only in the nineteenth century. Designed by the stage decorator Louis Jean Desprez, it is in a more classical style than the theatre. To give easier access to this salon, the royal suite was moved from the east to the west-side, so that during the intermissions of performances, or at soirées, the king could enjoy the new building without having to pass through the auditorium. What had formerly been the king's suite was remodelled to house the architect Adelcrantz and his servant, whose small room next to the architect's was a segment of the king's antechamber, with a new wall erected to separate it from the stairs leading to the auditorium. When the tour guides bring their groups into the first room and explain that the bed belonged to Adelcrantz, this is true, but it became the architect's chamber only at the very end of the Gustavian era.[5]

During military manoeuvres in 1825, both the palace and the theatre

19. Dressing room with original wall papers as it appears today. Agne Beijer's prints illustrating theatre history have been removed.

were badly damaged, and altogether 330 window panes had to be replaced. In the middle of the nineteenth century, when the tutor of the king's sons had moved into some of the theatre's chambers, one of the rooms was turned into a kitchen with a proper stove. Later some rooms were redecorated with dark-patterned wallpapers in the style of the nineteenth century. Such was the theatre that Agne Beijer re-discovered in 1921. He did not like everything he saw. Not only was the debris removed from the auditorium, but these 'ugly' wallpapers were also replaced with reprints in the rococo style that Beijer had ordered. In other rooms, fresh paint was used to cover some of the worn-out joinery and door fittings. Considering these circumstances, the question arises as to what degree we still can speak of Drottningholm as an authentic eighteenth-century theatre building. This question triggers, at the same time, another question: what do we mean by authentic in the context of a building?

Of course, a building needs maintenance – broken windows and leaks in the roof have to be repaired simply to prevent the deterioration of the building's substance. The remodelling of the interior that was carried out during the Gustavian period seemed acceptable, whereas the refurbishing of the nineteenth century was not, at least not in Beijer's view. This was the reason why he tore down the Victorian-style wallpapers and replaced them with new ones, albeit in the style of the originals. Beijer attempted a restoration of the eighteenth-century opera house – restoration in the literal sense: to restore its original appearance even in those rooms that were not immediately connected with the stage or the auditorium. Restoring means to recreate the style of the old with new materials in order to make it look like the original. These substitutions are of course no longer authentic in the sense of historic artefacts remaining untouched, but they might very well make an authentic impression. When questions of authenticity are discussed later in this book, it will be important to keep in mind the distinction between authentic objects – the material aspect of authenticity – and the experience of something as authentic, which can be referred to as the phenomenal aspect of authenticity.

In order to give visitors the feeling of an authentic place, Agne Beijer not only removed wallpaper, but also had to install a number of modern devices to make the theatre accessible to the public. First of all, electricity was needed to bring some light into the auditorium and onto the stage. Beijer found sockets that resembled candles and yellow bulbs, which were inserted into all the places that had formerly held candles – the lamps in the auditorium, the chandeliers hanging in the proscenium arch and the reflectors on the lighting poles. The equipment was rather primitive in 1922 and had to be renewed again and again: in 1948 all the electric installations were changed, and this time even the dressing rooms got electric light; in 1962 power outlets on stage were added to facilitate additional spotlights; in the 1970s the new flickering candles – in Sweden called Drottningholm candles – were substituted for the old yellow bulbs; in 1993 all the electric equipment was renovated again, and brought up to the latest technical standard. A similar list could be established for the installation of water, sewers and fire protection. Originally, the theatre had no running water at all, and today there are lavatories as well as washing facilities for the artists. A complicated dry-sprinkler system, which would only spray water onto the location of an actual fire instead of drowning the entire building, was put in place in 1992. Prior to this new system, two big trucks were placed in front of the main entrance, each with a full escape staircase leading up to the rear windows of the auditorium, thus providing an unsightly emergency exit.

Amazingly enough, these installations have not left any visible traces in the theatre. An ordinary visitor will not notice any fire protection gear, will not see any conductors providing electricity to the lamps and can hardly find the toilets that have been squeezed into the building. All these modernisations have been carried out with the utmost care and with the ambition of preserving the Drottningholm Theatre 'as it is'. A number of authorities have been involved in this pursuit: The National Board of Public Buildings in conjunction with the Drottningholm Court Theatre Foundation (which is in charge of guided tours and the performance programme), the Office of the Governor of the Royal Palaces, the Court Architect and the Central Board of National Antiquities.[6] The preservation of an eighteenth-century building, in which both the outer appearance and the inner equipment are so well preserved, is not only a delicate process, but also an ideological question. The court architect Ove Hidemark, who was in charge of a major investigation into the demands of preservation, compared attitudes towards an old building with the way in which we treat elderly people.

> An old building resembles the body of an elderly person. It consists of memories, wrinkles, suffering from one or another ailment and therefore we should embrace them cautiously and listen to what they have to tell. One does not easily change an old person; instead one learns to be with them on their own terms.[7]

At the time of Beijer, the restoration of eighteenth-century style was important. Today, experts are less keen on changing anything and make no attempt to recreate 'original' environments. They would rather treat the building like a palimpsest, and make all of the different layers of time vis-

20. The wear and tear of history.

ible. In part, this is no longer possible since Beijer removed everything reminiscent of the nineteenth century. Meanwhile, even Agne Beijer's activities in the 1920s have become historical layers of time. In order to stop the ongoing process of deterioration, a detailed plan was developed for the preservation of the building and its architectural details. In 1980, a commission was established to investigate wear and tear upon this historical theatre. One major source of this wear and tear are human beings. They not only carry sand and gravel into the theatre, but they touch everything within reach. Fat spots on the wallpaper near doors bear witness to the urge to let one's fingers glide over ancient materials. With more than 60,000 visitors (two thirds of them on guided tours, one third attending performances) this touching wears away colours and paint. The number of visitors has been reduced, both in total and for each guided tour, and the guided tours have been shortened and made safer – for the theatre. Other measures have been taken to keep the theatre accessible to as many people as possible, and at the same time to preserve it as a witness from the past – a common problem facing historical sites as well as nature reserves : how many people can walk through a place before its uniqueness will be spoiled?

Since 2004, a small group of specialist artisans have been 'repairing' – or rather they speak of 'conserving' – everything from the paint of the window sills to analysing and mending cracks in the ceilings – not by brushing up the colours or using modern materials but, on the contrary, by striving to work as closely as possible to the original craft. Not renewing, just preserving it. These artisans are still at work as this book goes to press.

David Wiles

3. A VISIT TO THE OPERA AT DROTTNINGHOLM: FIRST IMPRESSIONS

On 1 August 2008, with little idea of what to expect, I accepted Willmar Sauter's invitation to join a group of theatre researchers investigating modern performance at Drottningholm. The journey to the Palace of Drottningholm was an integral part of our experience, creating a sense of pilgrimage. As busy academics we ignored the ferry and took the quick route: down the metro, onto the bus, over two bridges and so onto the island of Lovön. Dining on reindeer and smoked trout in the old barracks provided cultural ambience, and was followed by a stroll past the waterfront and palace. We felt cut off by water from the everyday world. Though no opera buff, I was hoping for a unique theatrical experience, and that was indeed my good fortune.

The festival programme which I read on the metro was austere. I noted the social democratic levelling of all the participants whose biographies and photographs made no distinctions of status, the Lutheran sobriety of the text on slightly yellowed paper, the pleasant absence of commercial advertising, and the UNESCO World Heritage logo. The only colour was the image of Queen Lovisa Ulrika in the guise of Minerva which would greet me again on the curtain. The theatre when I finally reached it presents a modest façade in accordance with rococo principles which prefer beauty to be hidden within. A cloakroom attendant in period costume politely confiscated my camera as I made my entry into the sacred space of this perfectly preserved eighteenth-century theatre.

21. *Return of Ulysses* on the Drottningholm stage 2008.

Monteverdi

Claudio Monteverdi's *Il ritorno d'Ulisse in patria (Return of Ulysses*, 1640) was written for an earlier age, and for an aristocratic republic rather than a monarchy, but it served its turn perfectly in demanding of the Drottningholm Theatre its pictorial magic: the bobbing boat out to sea, amid swirling waves created by gigantic horizontal corkscrews, the huge figure of Neptune rising from these far-off waters. It was clear that the star of the performance would indeed be the theatre. However saturated I may be by modern technology, how could I resist the child-like magic of puppetry, and the power of this illusionistic ocean created by painters whose craft was based on years of observation? Sensing that I was journeying into history, I felt I could understand why Lovisa Ulrika and Gustav III – modelling themselves upon Louis XIV a century earlier – devoted such resources to the manufacture of a few moments of wonder. Their aspiration was not mere conspicuous consumption, but a particular quality of aesthetic experience.

All was not well for long, sadly. After Neptune the sea-god emerged wonderfully from the distant sea, he shrank as he walked down the raked stage towards the audience, and the illusion of perspective was destroyed, along with the illusion of divinity. Deposited on the beach of his homeland of Ithaca, Ulysses likewise shed his heroism as he strode towards us. The goddess Minerva had a pleasing statuesque moment standing on top of her two-dimensional rock on the beach, but then in a kind of erotic fantasy she elected to sit on top of Ulysses, and diminished her godly stature still further by walking all the way to the front of the stage. The vice girl image made me wonder for a moment if the director was going to try something postmodern and conceptual in deliberate counterpoint to the period setting, but no such luck. The amateurism of the acting forced me eventually to close my eyes to recapture the drama of Monteverdi, voices excitingly in dialogue with instruments. Closing my eyes liberated the imagination, but alas for the poor theatre whose sumptuous pictorial sets had brought me on this pilgrimage.

The orchestra and singing were of a secure professional standard. When I reopened my eyes I observed that the instrumentalists were dressed discreetly in black, symbolically invisible, with electric lights to illuminate their scores. They played period instruments, but without any attempt to periodise their bodies. Instinctively I wished the conductor Mark Tatlow had been wearing a white wig, in order that I might have, as it were, permission to concentrate upon his relationship to the actors, and the fluid physicality of his performance. Tatlow had his back to the audience, which would have been a breach of decorum in the days when queen or king sat on the front seats, and the music was led by the player of the harpsichord. I sensed how the authority of the modern conductor substitutes today for the absence of the monarch. The theatre is articulated around a lateral oval chamber centred on the seat of the monarch who once unified the space. I was aware of the social dynamic that had vanished: the monarch now replaced by a group of anonymous spectators, the musicians pretending to be invisible, singers isolated on the stage by electric light, and feeling obliged to entertain the unseen audience with the physical business of acting.

In the modern order of priorities, it is the musical director, not the stage director, who is allowed to become artistic director of the festival. In this capacity, Tatlow proclaimed in the bilingual programme that Drottningholm is 'the only theatre in the world where you can get a fully authentic experience of early opera'. A leaflet handed out on yellowed paper and dated 1766 urged: 'You are in a living eighteenth-century environment. Treat it gently.' It repeated its request for care so 'you can experience a truly genuine 18th century environment.' Genuine and authentic? Having done my homework, I tick the checklist. The architectural décor is of course the genuine eighteenth-century article; the instruments are period-style instruments, though it is beyond my expertise to comment on the manner of their playing; the stage settings are copies of the fragile originals, but executed skilfully by hand so I'm not sure I would ever notice the difference; the operating mechanism, with replacement hemp rope, is operated by the original technology. However, the audience are people like me, observing no court protocol and making little effort to dress for conspicuous social display; the lighting is too bright because the audience want to see what they have paid good money for, though an effort has been made to create bulbs that flicker like candles; the costumes aspire to a timeless and discreet period-style, apart from those of Penelope's suitors, which in cheap, garish satin have been cut in a style that evokes more precisely the age of Monteverdi; the musicians sport the modern uniform of the tuxedo. It is also hard to find any conception of 'authenticity' in the disposition of the actors' bodies, here in this building which King Gustav once used as a place for training actors.

It is a longstanding bone of contention that operatic training subordinates acting to singing, even though the last twenty years have seen huge advances in the quality of acting within the major metropolitan opera houses. Operas are likely to be reviewed and critiqued by musicians who take scant professional interest in acting, and 'music-theatre' is only now starting to carve out a place for itself in the academic curriculum.[1] Though Drottningholm was not built primarily as an opera house, today's festival is operatic not theatrical because opera attracts affluent audiences and corporate sponsorship (Stena, Scandic Hotels, Volvo et al are mentioned in the programme.) Moreover, the operas of the eighteenth century have retained their place in the modern repertoire, while the spoken drama of the Enlightenment era has gone out of fashion. If the performer's voice is esteemed more than the performer's body at Drottningholm today, perhaps we are looking at one symptom of a wider cultural problem related to protestant anxieties about the body and a historic anti-theatrical prejudice. Such reflections occurred to me afterwards. While I watched *Ulisse*, my attention was fixed not upon the diagnosis but the result: 'acting' that lay far outside the domain of 'historical authenticity'. The mentality of the performers in front of me was abundantly clear: first you render the canonical opera, then you decorate it with that universal thing called acting. Am I, I wondered, simply looking at a rather poor performance that could be sorted out by a better stage director, or are deeper historical issues at stake? The failure of this performance exposed for me a set of structural issues that a more subtle stage director would have managed to camouflage.

In the Gustavian era, most actors straddled the three branches of sung, spoken and danced theatre, but today in the professional world of performance and in academia sharp lines have been drawn. The problem with the neglect of acting in this production in favour of music was that the performance negated the power of the space, and even its acoustic potential was unrealised when the singers were in the wrong place. Seventeenth- and eighteenth-century acting only makes sense in relation to occupation of the forestage, used to create an interactive relationship with the conductor, the instrumentalists and the audience. Footlights emphasised the mystery of the face, while the curves and harmonising asymmetries of the actor's body configured aesthetically with the rococo lines of the décor. Common rhythms united movement and space. A unique opportunity for integration has been lost in this revival of an old opera in an old building

The space of the baroque world, the world of the *ancien régime*, was not, politically, psychologically or aesthetically, the space of today's world.[2] The ideals of the baroque world were already under attack, politically and theatrically, from Enlightenment thinkers such as Diderot. But since we were in Sweden, my thoughts turned not to Diderot but to the best known Swedish theatre manifesto, Strindberg's preface to *Miss Julie*, which set out a modernist ideal for performance space. Strindberg wanted no perspectival stage flats, no rocking canvas doors, no painted pots and pans that only betray their artifice as painting, no footlights or frontal acting. Having actors turn their backs through a critical scene was still beyond his dreams, and treating the stage as a room with its fourth wall missing was going too far, he felt, but his successors had no such caution. Strindberg reinforced the sense of real space in *Miss Julie* by abolishing act breaks so clock time correlated with stage time. His desire for the solidity of real space meshed with his conception of human character as an unstable patchwork of rags and citations, with motivations influenced by the spatial environment – the smell of the flowers, for example.[3]

Today, 120 years after *Miss Julie*, despite the best efforts of post-modernism to deconstruct the real, we retain Strindberg's notion of reality as a reference point and norm. The assumptions of the baroque era were quite different. The distinction between the heroic body (Miss Julie the aristocrat) and the servile body (Jean the servant) left no room for confusion. The job of the actor, cast in a socially inflected *emploi* or role type, was to present passions to an audience, passions which assumed an interface of body and mind but separation from the setting in which the human being was located. Since the actor did not inhabit an environment but stood before a backdrop, this backdrop was free to function on a symbolic level, and in Monteverdi's day, recession towards an infinitely distant vanishing point generated a neo-Platonist sense of mystery. In the production which we saw at Drottningholm, despite the distractions of the acting, the designer gave us glimpses of the poetry of light which was the staple of baroque stagecraft.

After the suitors had assailed Penelope in an enclosed room, the rear panel opened and the arrival of the long-lost Ulysses correlated with a sunset, and when Ulysses slew the suitors the sunset turned to storm clouds. The paintings of landscape became paintings of feelings, more expressive than anything mere human actors could achieve.

These were high points. The lowest point of the production was the scene on Olympus. The rolling thunder clouds of the baroque stage once spoke of a cosmic power that humans could not control, and this cosmic power was in part a metaphor for absolutist royal power, but our Juno was a busty Wagnerian vamp henpecking her husband. It would seem that we know today, as men and women of the Baroque apparently failed to grasp, that gods cannot really influence the weather and secure a sailor's safety; and since belief in gods is manifestly daft, gods can only be played for laughs.

22. The gods in Monteverdi's *Return of Ulysses* 2008. On stage Miriam Treichl, Niklas Björling Rygert, Lukas Jakobski, Susanne Rydén.

The consequence of this secularist mentality was to reshape Monteverdi's opera into a psychological soap opera. In place of passions, we had to make do with character. The stage director allowed Penelope to be tempted by the most handsome suitor, so her reunion would have 'human' interest. This domesticated opera gave no serious thought to the horrors of a futile war, nor to the plight of a lone woman abandoned by her husband.

The opera buffa

It was useful to return next day for the comic opera, a work of 1769 ironically entitled *L'opera seria*. Here the acting and costuming displayed a basic level of professional competence, and the lack of historical engagement emerged even more starkly. Although the stage director had formerly been artistic director of the Drottningholm Festival, we observed little sensitivity to the aesthetics of the eighteenth-century stage. The programme, thankfully, was not distributed until after the performance, since the bright tones of cerise and orange would have collided horribly with the ambience of the theatre. The anomalous colour reminded us that this production was a transferrable commodity, presented by a visiting company with a home venue elsewhere. Cartoon sketches in the programme linked the characters of the drama to figures like Batman in the popular culture of today, offering a clear message: people haven't changed, actors then are just like actors now. Which of course they are not. One sign of difference is the way this piece is today marketed as a musical work by Florian Gassmann, not a drama by the celebrated librettist Ranieri de' Calzabigi set to music by Gassmann. Gassmann's *L'opera seria*, according to the official festival programme, satisfies the longing of audiences 'to know what really goes on behind the scenes as a first night approaches'. A particular discourse of authenticity was judged appropriate to the authentic environment of Drottningholm: a discourse about the timeless truth of what actors are really like backstage. I felt there was ample scope for an alternative discourse of inauthenticity, in an opera once designed to make spectators reflect upon their own experience of spectating.

I will summarise the plot-line of this little-known piece. The first act presents the rebellion of actors who are about to present a grand and 'serious' opera, the second covers preparations and the absconding of the director, while the third act presents a performance of the *opera seria*, which is booed off, allowing us to cut to dressing rooms for the finale. The theatre of Drottningholm had to be shown performing its tricks, so in the opening scene of this production the actor playing the 'director' descended on Jupiter's throne and the prima donna rose on the trap from hell without any rationale in preparations for the forthcoming show. The second act set in an elegant rehearsal room offered us a mysterious vista quite unconnected to the disappearance of the 'director'. The third act, set in an extravagant oriental wonderland, had no new resources to offer, and the opportunity for perspectival depth was wasted when a triumphal procession mime-walked towards the audience. When the 'director' planted in the audience encouraged us to boo the play-within-a-play, it seemed impolite to respond because there had been no shift of register between the grand mode of *opera seria* and the realist mode of *opera buffa*, prompting me to wonder whether it was the audience as much as the company who lacked a historically informed vocabulary of acting. The canvas flats of the dressing room wobbled in precisely the way that drove Strindberg into the arms of naturalism, defeating the sense that we had shifted from the artifice of performance into the material reality of the performers' world. The uniformly bright lighting, calculated to achieve a bright and jolly mood in the audience, compounded the sense of a homogeneous world of fiction, with no risk that theatrical play with illusion could raise troubling ontological questions.

The mentality of the company was clear. The theatre of Drottningholm is a toy, a delightful box of tricks, and excuses must be found to make the moving parts function. If the director did perceive the eighteenth-century world as different from our own in ways that extend beyond musical style and modes of dress, then he clearly felt that such differences would not interest his modern audience. I believe he was wrong here. Paradoxically, the search for otherness often results in the discovery of similarities. The opera-within-an-opera, for example, is a fantasy about seductive and enslaved oriental women, a kind of virtual sex-tourism. But the production was geared at fun, not ideas – and 'why not?' many would say. The charge can easily be made that academics like to stand on their soapboxes of principle, not compelled to deal with the exigencies of getting the show on the stage, and audience 'bums on seats'. The academic world, moreover, is not without complicity in the box-of-tricks approach we saw in this production. The weight of attention given by historians to the stage gadgetry of Drottningholm Court Theatre at the expense of its aesthetics and social meaning does much to legitimate the approach that we witnessed in both *Ulisse* and *L'opera seria*.

It became clear to me after seeing these two productions that the problem of theatrical representation at Drottningholm is systemic, a function of the cultural process in which such contemporary performances are caught up. An opera performed at Drottningholm today is part of 21st-century social and artistic life, just as Gustav's theatre was an integral part of palace life. When King Gustav made his way down the great staircase of the palace, winged goddesses flew about him just as they did on the painted scenery. He enjoyed continuities on his path to the theatre, and so do we, emerging from metropolitan public transport into a contemporary leisure amenity, not a time capsule. The audiences who come to Drottningholm are opera aficionados and tourists, broadly happy with what they see. My regrets are less for the tourists and opera-lovers of Stockholm than for the theatre at large, deprived of a living contact with theatre history. I discovered on this visit to Stockholm much about the power of perspectival theatre that I could not learn from books or computer-generated models, and I began to sense why monarchs invested so much time and money on an inflammable plaything. As a theatre researcher, I regretted in 2008 that genuine experimentation at Drottningholm seemed impossible, so we cannot learn all we might about former ways of making theatre. Drottningholm is a unique resource, and as UNESCO insists, it is part of the world's heritage and not just Sweden's. Like Ulysses wanting to rescue his Penelope from a horde of uncouth suitors, I wanted to reconnect with something that had survived against the odds.

The Debate

The production of *Ulisse* triggered a passionate debate amongst the diverse academics whom Willmar Sauter had gathered together for a symposium on performance at Drottningholm. The production's claims to historical authenticity were a red rag to all of us. The Japanese musicologist Motomi

Tsugami like me felt obliged to close her eyes if she wanted to respond to the musical or dramatic qualities of the opera, and her principal concern was a lack of fidelity to the musical 'Work'. Her critique was developed on the three levels of genre, characterisation and worldview. The production failed to recognise the generic qualities of the work as a tragedy – as defined by certain structural rules, like the distinction between genteel suitors and the comic parasite. In characterising Penelope as the archetypal silly woman, the production did no justice to her status as heroine, and thus to her rendering of the music. And in terms of cosmology, it was symbolically wrong for Jove to play on a regal, a coarse keyboard instrument, for this trivialised the world of the gods and made a nonsense of vocal distinctions used by Monteverdi to render the divine world. Although ascribing authority and authenticity to the original Monteverdian Work, Tsugami conceded that the 'Work' was not a stable concept since the earliest libretto was likely to have been divided into five acts. The Swedish theatre historian Inga Lewenhaupt, on the other hand, was preoccupied by the acting, and the failure of the cast to observe what she claimed to be the basic principles of eighteenth-century rhetorical acting necessary to create harmony with the space. Though acknowledging that eighteenth-century acting was not a constant, with ideals of the rococo curve and the sublime preceding a more austere and historicising neoclassicism, she insisted on certain underlying principles of gesture and blocking. Presentational acting on the forestage, she argued, was essential for the scenery to work its perspectival magic. In her ideal of authenticity, the reference point was not the work but the space.

This discussion set the agenda that Willmar Sauter and I decided to pursue in this book. In this miraculously preserved eighteenth-century space, what sort of 'authentic' staging is possible? And what should we understand by the notion of authenticity in this context? The question has an obvious bearing upon the 'original practices' movement in the field of Elizabethan theatre, in the field of Early Music, and the 'living history' movement in popular culture which extends to re-enactments of medieval jousts, life in reconstructed Viking villages or gladiator fights in Roman arenas. Is authentic staging a quixotic fantasy, and a goal that does not stand up to serious postmodern scrutiny? Or is it a means of transcending the limitations of language in the quest for historical empathy?

What draws me to the baroque and Gustavian eras in particular is the special pleasure those cultures took in theatricality. The performativity of the eighteenth-century world encapsulated by Drottningholm fascinates me, at a point today when human essences are mistrusted and the paradigm of 'performance' is widely invoked. We cannot get away with the pretence that people of the baroque era walked, talked and dressed like us, and in that difficulty of representation lies the fascination of seeking to understand. Since the quest for authenticity in modern life is so often a quest to escape from a feeling of alienated performativity, the ultimate challenge at Drottningholm must be to create, somehow, authentic inauthenticity.

23. The scholars discussing Monteverdi in the Drottningholm park. From left Rikard Hoogland, Willmar Sauter, Inga Lewenhaupt and Eske Tsugami. Private photo

Willmar Sauter

4. EIGHTEENTH CENTURY COURT LIFE

'The past is a foreign country: they do things differently there.' The famous opening sentence of L. P. Hartley's novel *The Go-Between* from 1953 points to an essential problem in all historiographic writing: how do we understand unfamiliar buildings and landscapes that are populated with people wearing unusual clothes and hats, moving about in peculiar environments, occupied by strange activities?[1] The past is a country that we can visit with the help of our imagination. In order to describe the Gustavian era of the late eighteenth century, I invite the reader to spend an imagined day with the court at Drottningholm. I will follow the central figure at Drottningholm, King Gustav III, from his morning rituals to his retreat to bed late at night. I hope this approach can illustrate the social and political context of the theatrical activities that were not confined to the so-called opera house at Drottningholm, but were present in much of the daily business at court. The royal activities on the particular Wednesday in August 1786 that I have chosen are not freely invented but are historically well documented, although events did not occur in exactly the chronological order I present here. And I have taken the liberty of framing the various circumstances of this day by referring to earlier and later events that can enhance our understanding of the politics of the Swedish court in the eighteenth century. Thus this Wednesday will not constitute an isolated, accidental moment in the history of Drottningholm, but a representative day – possibly slightly idealised – that suggests the flow of artistic, social and political achievements within this period.

24. The courtiers entertaining themselves at Drottningholm.

25. Gustav III overlooking Stockholm.

A Wednesday in August 1786

Gustav III was in the habit of getting up late in the morning. The royal bedroom was divided by a balustrade separating the bed, placed on an elevated podium, from the open space surrounding it. From the moment Gustav opened his eyes, he was accompanied by courtiers who executed what was called the levée. The king had imported this idea from the French court of Louis XIV who had invented this morning ritual more than a hundred years before Gustav became King of Sweden. The procedure consisted of two parts, le petit and le grand levée. To begin with, only a few of the closest and most highly ranking courtiers were allowed into the king's bedchamber. Their duty was to assist Gustav in dressing, from the underwear, the shirt, the breeches, the shoes, to the jacket and the coat. The petit levée served the purpose of transforming Gustav's body into that of the king, and could therefore only be undertaken by the noblest members of the court.

The clothing that Gustav III would have worn on this day was the standard, national dress that the king had designed for all members of the court and the nobility – the Swedish national costume. This uniform costume for the court, the nobility and also government officials belonging to state institutions was one of Gustav's state projects. In 1778, he had written *Reflections Concerning a New National Costume*, in which he declared: 'Dress yourself all in an *esprit national*, and I dare to say that a national costume will contribute more than you might believe.' Although this manifesto was enthusiastically supported by Voltaire, not everybody in Sweden was in favour of it. Those opposed to this centralised regulation, in particular certain aristocratic circles, were warned: 'You do not belong to the eighteenth century; the sound philosophy that casts light upon delusion and drives away prejudice, has not yet taken hold of you.'[2] Besides this vision of national unity, the king also argued in economic terms. The national costume was simpler and cheaper than imported French fashions, and the textiles were to be produced in Sweden. To dress in the national Swedish costume in a ceremony inspired by French court conventions did not seem to create any contradictions for the king and his circle. The standard court costume was black with bright red decorations, the festive full-dress was in white and light blue, the black coat was lined with red and equipped with a useful pocket. A round hat with plumes was prescribed for men, while women were allowed to wear whatever hat they preferred. Gustav III had actually managed to overcome initial resistance to this reform, and the national costume was to be in use long into the next century. The peasantry was not included, and the priests of the Swedish church already had their traditional outfit, so all in all about five percent of the population were to be seen in the national costume.

King Gustav's old wet-nurse kissed him welcome to the day and the physician-in-ordinary to the king confirmed his well-being. Being rather short and thin and 40 years old, Gustav's physical appearance was not impressive, but he refrained from having his waistcoat upholstered or his calves enlarged with the parchment insertion under their silk stockings that many men of his time used to achieve a more vigorous appearance. Adjusting his white wig and renewing his make-up with rouge and powder made Gustav ready for the second part of the levée. Here, it is noteworthy that the distinction between public and private was not yet recognised in Sweden, or in many other societies during this period. The sphere of the intimate was also considered to be public, both for the king and for his servants.[3] This morning, as he did every morning, Gustav stood in front of the balustrade that separated the royal bed from the hall, where he welcomed his courtiers and other nobles – and occasionally even some distinguished bourgeois who had petitioned to attend this extravagant occasion. They had all come to wish the king a good morning. The guests of the grand levée formed a semi-circle and Gustav approached each one of them for a short conversation, normally in Swedish unless the guest came from another country and spoke French. Many of the visitors had prepared a sentence or two to address to the king, but nobody could be sure that they would have a chance to utter a word about their concerns. It was all in the power of the monarch: he might simply glance at a guest, he could ask an unexpected question, or he might be willing to listen. Those who documented these royal morning encounters were most impressed by the king's quickness in improvising an appropriate response. General Skiöldebrand remembers: 'He spoke swiftly and politely so it was a pleasure to listen. Lucky those who had an answer ready, which usually provoked an – ha ha.'[4] From Skiöldebrand's remark we may also understand that everybody present in the room could hear these conversations. After these personal encounters the king would listen to military reports, and when the crowd dispersed he was eager to catch up with the latest gossip from town.

 At this point, Gustav would look out of the window to decide if the weather was fine enough for the court to spend the day playing cards and other games in the Chinese Pavilion, some hundred metres away from the palace. If the weather was too bad, the court would stay inside the palace. This morning Gustav decided that the sky was fair enough for a walk to the Chinese Pavilion, and he set up a playing card showing the King of Hearts. All members of the court were supposed to check this card that was posted outside the king's chamber, because it meant that they were allowed to wear simple country clothing. From experience, members of the court knew that the king might change his mind quickly. Clouds on the horizon could rule out the option of the Chinese Pavilion, meaning that the whole court had to change their dress to a more formal variation of the national costume.

26. Cards indicating fine or bad weather, according to Gustav III:s opinion.

This is probably what happened this morning, because the king replaced his original card with a new one, the King of Spades, telling the court to stay in the palace. Gustav had decided that he would attend a rehearsal in the opera house, i.e. the theatre at Drottningholm.

A Rehearsal at the Theatre

First of all, Gustav sent out his chamberlain to find Badin, who was instructed to come to the theatre with the six pages who had been studying dance with the ballet master of the Royal Opera. Badin had a very peculiar position at court. His real name was Gustav Couschi and he was the son of a slave from the West Indies.[5] The French nickname Badin means buffoon and he was famous at court for his pranks, but he was equally well-known as the more-or-less secret lover of many a court lady. Badin was supposed to control the young pages. Today, Gustav was curious about the dancing skills of the pages: had they learned enough from Monsieur Gallodier to dance the concluding part of the comedy *Le Philosophe sans le savoir* that the French theatre troupe would present on stage shortly?[6] Gustav's interest in the pages and the process of educating them into becoming real noblemen was obvious to his contemporaries. The choice of this comedy, however, is less easy to understand, since the piece had a rather controversial theme and a contradictory history.

Written by Michel-Jean Sedaine in the early 1760s under the title *Le Duel*, the police and the French censor had delayed the premiere of this piece since the contents of the play were seen as a defence of the prohibited habit of duelling. Sedaine rewrote the piece, changing the attitude of its protagonist, the merchant Vanderk, and adjusting the plot to include a more sentimental ending. Sedaine wrote this drama in support of Denis Diderot's programme of Enlightenment, and it has been interpreted as a response to Charles Palissot de Montenoy's fierce attacks on Diderot's play of 1758 *Le Père de famille*.[7] Sedaine's play premiered in Paris in December 1765 and, less than a year later, Lovisa Ulrika's French troupe performed the piece at the Drottningholm Theatre on the occasion of Gustav's wedding. Now, twenty years later, Gustav wanted to see it again, either for sentimental reasons or because he felt that the plot had gained some new relevance.

Sedaine's *Le Philosophe sans le savoir (Philosopher Without Knowing It)* indeed contains an amazing plot. The merchant Vanderk discovers two pistols in the possession of his son. We learn that an unknown person has made depreciatory remarks about merchants, and has therefore been challenged to a duel by Vanderk's son. We are also informed that the Vanderk senior was originally a French nobleman, who fled his own country after a duel. A Dutch merchant helped him out of his precarious situation, and subsequently Vanderk took over the business, adopting his benefactor's last name. Vanderk senior opposes the aristocratic code of honour and he delivers strong arguments, in accordance with the new thinking of the Enlightenment, against the disastrous habit of duelling, which he describes as a remnant of ancient, feudal practices. However, his aristocratic past forces him to concede: once one has thrown down the gauntlet, one has to stand up for one's honour. The son's tutor Antoine and his daughter Victorine – in love with the young Vanderk – follow to witness the duel. Meanwhile, a Monsieur d'Esparville visits Vanderk senior in order to borrow the money needed for an escape after the duel. Just as Father Vanderk begins to make the connection, Antoine and Victorine return to report the death of young Vanderk. This information proves to be false, since the two youngsters only fired their pistols in the air, and were reconciled, and the play ends on a happy note with the wedding of Vanderk's daughter, who otherwise has played no part in the plot.[8]

King Gustav obviously knew this play very well, but now, while he, his chamberlain, Badin and the pages were crossing the gravel yard towards the so-called opera house, the king was only interested in the last act. He wanted to see how the actors would execute the change from deep sorrow to overwhelming happiness. Such sentimental turns in tragic plots, in the genre known as comédie larmoyante or sentimental comedy, were fitted to the taste and the sensibility of the late eighteenth century. At the same time, Father Vanderk's appeal to reason in his speech against duels was the typical expression of an enlightened bourgeois intellectual. It is difficult to say which one of these tendencies made Gustav ask his French troupe to revive this drama, but on this particular Wednesday, he was primarily keen to observe the theatrical arrangement of the finale.

At the entrance to the theatre, the king was welcomed with a deep bow (as

27. The eminent actor Monvel. Drawing by Carl August Ehrensvärd 1782.

was fitting for a servant) by the leader of the French troupe, Monsieur Monvel or, by his full name, Jacques-Marie Boutet de Monvel. This handsome actor, 41 years old at the time, had been hired by King Gustav through his ambassador Gustaf Philip Creutz in France in 1781.[9] He came directly from the Comédie Française, where he, under the guidance of Henri Louis Lekain, had developed into a leading actor. Lekain, his teacher and model, was a master of declamation and from him the young Monvel had learned that texts have melody and rhythm, even when written in prose. This leading principle became extremely influential for the Swedish stage since Monvel, in turn, became the teacher of the first generation of professional actors in Stockholm. One of his apprentices, Lars Hjortsberg, who was only fourteen years old at the time, but who had appeared on stage since the age of six, was standing behind the entrance of the theatre to watch the king approaching. Since Monvel was quite short and thin, he was not considered to be the ideal hero on stage; instead he specialized in comedy, in particular the role of fathers. Father Vanderk with his enlightened sentiments was a role that suited him perfectly.

Monvel lived a hectic and quite varied life. Although he never married, he proved attractive to many women, not the least his female colleagues. Some years before he came to Sweden, a natural daughter was born to him who would become one of the most famous actresses at the Comédie Française, Mademoiselle Mars.[10] Monvel never liked Sweden, and perhaps his little daughter in Paris was one reason for growing desire over the years to return to France. Not even an extravagant salary could compensate him – he earned four times more than the best paid Swedish singers at the National Opera. King Gustav was worried about his French star and posted police officers outside Monvel's home to make sure the actor would not disappear to France. After the summer season of 1786, he finally received

28. A group of actors as painted by Johan Pasch on a wall of Confidensen at Ulriksdal

the king's permission to visit Paris – and he never came back! He returned to the Comédie Française, where he stayed until 1806 and among his new apprentices we find the noted actor François Joseph Talma, future colleague of Mademoiselle Mars.

When Monvel came to Sweden in 1781, he brought with him a theatre troupe of the considerable size of sixteen actresses and actors. According to the internal rules of a troupe, they all were specialists associated with certain types of roles so that they could encompass all the normal range of fathers, kings, mothers, servants, fools, etc. included within their repertoire. Some of them stayed on in Sweden and became highly influential for Swedish acting including opera and dance. During the summer of 1786, they all lived, together with their spouses and children, in the Drottningholm Theatre to serve the king's wishes at any time. Since they did not know that the king had decided to attend a special rehearsal this morning, some of them had to rush to dress properly and to reach the stage before Gustav entered the auditorium. Greeting Monvel with a gallant phrase in French, the king turned right and went to his private chamber in the theatre, while the rest of the group followed Badin to the left, through a series of rooms, to reach the auditorium. Gustav stopped briefly in his chamber and asked that the new director of the Royal Orchestra, Abbé Georg Joseph Vogler, be sent to him.

Abbé Vogler had just returned from the German speaking world and Gustav wanted to hear the news. According to Vogler, Berlin was in a sad mood when he was there, because everybody anticipated the death of the great Prussian King Friedrich, the brother of Gustav's mother. Gustav pitied him, since his uncle had become a lonely and bitter old man without children. At the court of Emperor Joseph in Vienna, things were a lot happier. The big news was that the controversial play by Pierre Augustin Caron de Beaumarchais, *The Marriage of Figaro*, had been presented as an opera in May. Well, Gustav III had seen the play twice during his visit to Paris in 1784 and had greatly appreciated it, welcoming its criticism of the aristocracy, as long as the authority of the sovereign was not questioned. The play had even been performed by the French troupe in Drottningholm earlier the same year, and when the king learned that the libretto of the opera was in Italian, he understood even better why the emperor had allowed it. The composer, a certain Wolfgang Amadeus Mozart, seemed to be very popular in Vienna, but Vogler doubted that the music would be to His Majesty's taste. It is of course difficult to know why Vogler held such an opinion, but a look into the Gustavian repertoire easily confirms his assumption – there is Gluck and Gluck and more Gluck, but no Mozart.

Alors – Gustav jumped to his feet and walked briskly towards the auditorium. At the side door members of the troupe had gathered to greet the king. He had a charming little phrase for each one of them, encouraging them, asking about their children and so forth. Gustav was known for his charm, his swift responses and his care for ordinary people. To be loved by the people was one of his innermost wishes as a monarch, and in return he treated ordinary people well. The actors returned to the stage and Gustav entered the auditorium, which was not illuminated as in performances. Only the big chandeliers in the proscenium arch were lit, and additional light came in through the windows at the rear end of the auditorium. Badin, with a friendly joke, held the chair for the king and the pages had settled further back in the darkened part of the auditorium.

Monvel explained the situation at the end of the play that they would rehearse. Father Vanderk receives the message that his son has been killed in the duel and everybody on stage expresses despair at the situation. Then the good news arrives – a complete change of mood, but displayed differently according to each character. The happiness accelerates and the dancing begins. Well, where are the youngsters who should carry out the dance? They were asked to leave the auditorium and to stand-by behind the wings. But where was ballet master Gallodier? He had not even come down to the stage! Monsieur Louis Gallodier had gained weight lately and avoided all hasty movements. Although he had been a solo dancer and choreographer under Gustav's father, now at the age of 53 he had long since stopped dancing and limited his work to staging ballets and operas. The king had ordered him to train the pages in the art of dance and court behaviour, once a week, but Gallodier was a bit nervous of these boisterous youngsters. A lackey was sent upstairs to Gallodier's room to hurry him down to the stage area.

Acting and Dancing on Stage

With everybody in place, the rehearsal could begin. Monvel as Father Vanderk positioned himself at the centre, in the middle of the proscenium arch. He was wearing his everyday coat, similar to the one he would wear in performances. The tutor Antoine, who had just delivered the fatal message, stood to his right, being next in rank. His daughter Victorine, to the left of Vanderk, expressed her grief by touching her nose with a handkerchief in a delicate movement of her arm. Monvel articulated the father's despair in a clear melodic voice. To our ears, Monvel's declamation would sound too beautiful: Vanderk is completely crushed by the news that his son has just been killed, but Gustav appreciated the fact that decorum of expression was preserved in this style of acting. Unlike audiences of the twentieth century, the Gustavian spectator did not expect a psychologically precise portrait of a unique character, but pure and strong emotions filtered through art and artistry. Fate has hit Vanderk, and Monvel created the monologue like a musical piece. The length of the vowels brought out his grief, the rising pitch at the end of a sentence expressed his desperation. Monvel had trained the members of his troupe in 'silent acting', meaning that they were not supposed just to stand on stage waiting for their cue, but play physical reactions to what happens on stage at each moment. Victorine kept to her handkerchief and Antoine pressed his hat to his breast. More was not needed since such actions were not supposed to distract the spectator from the words that were being uttered.

Monvel had instructed the performer who arrived with the happy message to enter the stage slightly before the father's lamentation had come to its end. The messenger entered from stage right, a classical tradition that goes back to the directions of city and countryside in the Athenian theatre.

29. A group of actors as painted by Johan Pasch on a wall of Confidensen at Ulriksdal

Gustav stopped the rehearsal to give the actor his personal advice: when coming out from between the flats, the actor should freeze for a moment so the audience can properly observe him before the action continues. Monvel took this opportunity to instruct his fellow actors in more detail by demonstrating to them the exact movements of their characters. To him this piece of what might today be called blocking was vital. Through these movements the tension of the situation could be clarified. Will this message worsen the desperation into which the characters are already plunged? Monvel was working towards a classical peripeteia, a turning point in the drama, prolonging the state of tragedy before it turns into a comedy. The turning point is further postponed because the gestures of the three mourners express disbelief, raising the open palms of their hands and stretching them slightly towards the other speakers. Although the message they hear gives every reason for happiness, this delay of the positive response heightens the sentimental effect of the emotional reversal.

The rehearsal resumes with the entrance of the messenger. For a moment, the messenger is visible only to the audience, before the characters in the play catch sight of him. As soon as Vanderk notes the arrival of this person, he takes a step back and, at the same time, slightly to the side. Antoine and Victorine follow him a moment later and thus open up the circle of three towards the fourth person, who takes a step towards the front of the stage. Gustav expresses his pleasure. The actions on stage continue. The son arrives, he is alive, his sister arrives and her wedding can take place as planned. More characters arrive and fill up the stage. And now is the moment for the pages to enter the stage. But what are they supposed to do? Gallodier is called upon because he has fallen asleep on a chair behind the wings. When he steps out on the boards of the stage his massive body comes alive and with quick gestures and nimble feet he instructs the young boys.

In his youth, Louis Gallodier was engaged by the *Opéra Comique* in Paris and had been privileged to dance under the guidance of Jean George Noverre, whose *Lettre sur la danse* (1760) would make him world famous in the dance world. Noverre advocated that dance should always tell stories. It might have been from Noverre that Gallodier had learned to distinguish the three kinds of ballets that characterised stage dance at the time: the noble dance such as would be executed by gods and heroes, the semi-serious dance

30. Louis Gallodier, the ballet master.

of the so-called demi-caractères for young and lively characters, and finally the comic dance for grotesque and uncivilized characters. For the final act of *Le Philosophe*, to follow the relief that the arrival of young Vanderk has just occasioned, the youngsters were to be taught a semi-serious dance in which they were supposed to express their happiness. Gallodier had been training the pages during weekly classes that the king had ordered, but these dances (such as minuets and contradances) were better suited to festive occasions at court. The pages were young nobles who were expected to rise in the ranks of the military once they reached adolescence. In this case, lively and swift movements were required, which the boys immediately exaggerated. Instead of maintaining elegance and decorum, the youngsters drifted off into grotesque and ugly movements, bending their knees and jumping high in the air. Badin laughed loudly and compared their dancing to the gambolling of goats in a meadow. Gallodier stopped the exercise and explained how the boys had to co-ordinate their feet with their arms, how they should grasp each other's hands and turn their eyes towards the couple that were about to be married. And there was another problem: when they trained in the ballroom of the palace, they danced in a circle that could be viewed from all sides of the room. Here on stage, the spectators would only view them from the direction of the auditorium, so their movements had to be arranged in such a way that the dancers kept their faces towards the audience, never turning their backs while nevertheless dancing together as an ensemble. This entailed two complications that Gallodier was working on. First of all, their entrances between the flat wings had to be executed sideways, i.e. facing the audience rather than the middle of the stage. While the pages struggled to accomplish this demand, the next problem was that they also needed to move backwards in order not to expose their backs to their noble spectators. This proved to be rather tricky. Only young Lars Hjortsberg managed to elegantly step backwards, still giving an illusion of dancing in the round with the other boys. Despite his youth, Hjortberg had long experience of appearing on stage and therefore excelled in lively steps forward, sideways and backwards. Gallodier, whose heavy body no longer allowed him to give a full demonstration, let young Lars show how one could dance in a semi-serious dance in a circle without ever looking away from the audience. Vogler took his violin and played a tune in 3/4 time, Gallodier beat time on the floor with his walking stick, while Lars Hjortsberg's twirling feet looked so simple and elegant. He combined one long step with two short touches to the floor, changed foot and repeated the movement to the 'un-deux-trois' that Gallodier was counting aloud.

Could the other boys try to imitate him, please? Their steps turned out to be clumsy and boisterous and they lost all connection with each other. They tried again, and while Gallodier got angry, Monvel and his colleagues giggled and even the king himself smiled. While they were repeating this exercise for the fifth time, a rolling of thunder in the sky caused pandemonium. The thunder was, however, not the sound of a storm outside the theatre. Badin, unnoticed, had left his place in the auditorium, sneaked up to the stage and pulled the rope of the thunder machine. Everybody laughed at the frightened pages and this brought the rehearsal to an end. Gustav quickly decided that pupils from the Royal Opera's professional dance school that Gallodier directed would have to come to Drottningholm so *Le Philosophe sans le savoir* could end on the desired sentimental note. The pages looked a bit ashamed but were relieved about the King's decision to spare them from public humiliation.

The Art of Acting

The failure of the pages to execute their joyful dances in the concluding scene points towards some central principles of baroque stage acting and dancing. These principles or rules for performers of the eighteenth century ranged from specific codes of movement to more aesthetic and philosophical principles. One overarching, absolute rule was the tribute that had to be paid to the presence of the audience. All stage actions had to be directed towards the auditorium. On today's stage it is not unusual for performers, at a dramatic moment, to turn their back to the audience, at least temporarily. In theatre history, the practice of turning away from the audience is usually attributed to the naturalism of the late nineteenth century. But when August Strindberg wrote his instructions for young actors as late as 1908, he still advised them never to turn their backs to the audience, unless it was absolutely necessary. Even for Strindberg this new fashion of facing upstage was ugly and aesthetically inappropriate.[11] Although Diderot had floated some radical propositions, a century before Strindberg, such scenic behaviour was generally regarded as unthinkable. The focus towards the auditorium had a number of consequences for positioning on stage, and the gestures, of the performers.

That Monvel in the role of the father occupied the centre of the stage was both obvious and insisted upon. The highest ranking character in a scene would be placed in the middle of the stage, with the next-ranking to the protagonist's right, the third-ranking to their left – much like the positioning of winners of gold, silver and bronze medals in the modern Olympic Games. In order to mark the direction of speech in the dialogue, actors were allowed to turn their heads (at the most) 45° towards the addressee of the utterance. That meant that the speaker's face was still fully visible to the audience, marking the dialogic nature of the exchange with only a minimal turn of the head. At the same time, the speech would be supported by gestures in such a way that the movable, pointing arm was turned towards the partner actor and kept the body in full view of the audience. For the actor standing to the right of the protagonist, this meant that he or she would gesture with his or her left arm and hand, whereas the right hand would serve only to emphasise the rhythm of the speech. This use of hands and arms derived from the traditions of rhetoric, according to which the text, rather than its content, decided the rhythm and melody of the delivery. Monvel knew very well that these rules applied not only to tragic drama and alexandrine verse, but also to the prose of comedies and comédies larmoyantes, which required a musically honed delivery of the text. It was up to a good dramatist to compose dialogues and monologues in such a way that they supported the rhetorical skills of the performers.

The gestures not only followed the rhetorical rules of the time, but were also subject to a more general decorum which insisted upon the expression of even strong feelings with certain elegance. The hands should not be raised higher than the head nor lowered beneath the hip, with the exception of comic characters, and these rules applied even to moments of strong emotional outpouring. There are many illustrations to printed dramas of the time, depicting the most dramatic turning point of the plot, in which the actors can be seen following this conventional decorum – for example a series of oil paintings in which Pehr Hilleström portrayed the courtiers

31. Actors of the Comédie Française in the 1760s. Feulie and Monvel in the comedy *Les Rendez-vous*.

who created the characters in Gustav's own play *Gustaf Adolphs ädelmod (The Magnanimity of Gustav Adoph)*.[12] Occasionally we see a person in an engraving bending down on his or her knee (usually only one knee) begging for mercy or expressing respect, but lying on the stage floor was avoided, and even a corpse would rather be placed in a chair or on a rock. Normally the actors stood with their feet neatly placed in one of the five ballet positions, which were also de rigueur in daily life. Moving the body's weight from one foot to the other provided a certain dynamic in a dialogue.

Of special importance was the entry, since it focused the attention of the spectators. The front of the performer – face, wig, dress – has to be immediately visible to the audience. This sideways entrance was a difficult exercise confronting the dancing pages, and for actresses there was practically no other way, since their crinolines could not otherwise pass through the space allowed by two flat wings. The skirt of a crinoline was extremely broad, and held up by a metal scaffold. Women in crinolines could never pass straightforwardly through an ordinary door, and it was even harder to navigate the passage between two wings in the theatre. Once fully exposed to the audience, the performer should then stop for a brief moment to display the significance of their character, before taking up position next to the footlights in front of the proscenium arch. Usually entries were made between the first pair of wings, but diagonal entries were also possible, although the diagonal was a shallow one, pointing for example from the third wing on the right to the first wing on the left. Special care had to be taken not to enter through the middle of a painted feature that joined two adjacent wings, such as a chaise longue or an open fire place. Furniture was normally painted on the flat wings and only exceptionally were a chair or a sideboard brought on stage – like the famous table for Molière's *Tartuffe* (performed later in the autumn of 1786) or a secretaire containing secret letters that were at the heart of many plots. These pieces of furniture were carried out immediately at the end of the scene in which they were used.

One particular convention was crucial for theatre troupes of this and even later periods: the division of characters into stock types.[13] Each troupe needed a certain number of specialists for standard characters: beautiful young lovers of both sexes, a hero and a heroine, a father who could also play kings and nobles, a mother and queen, servants of both sexes, an actor specialising in villains and, not least, a clown, creating the comic characters. Actors were hired according to these specialisations, which also made the distribution of roles simple, although jealous conflicts could not always be avoided. One need only think of any classical play by Shakespeare or Molière, and all these characters are in place.[14] The same system of specialisation applied to opera, where it was more complicated due to the need to find a voice consistent with the score. The success of a character on stage depended not upon casting but upon the skills, elegance and taste of the performer.

In the latter half of the eighteenth century a theoretical debate was raging concerning whether actors and actresses were supposed to express emotions according to ruling stage conventions, or whether they should rather let it be seen that they themselves felt these emotions. In practice, the perfect rendering of emotional expressiveness took precedence over any attempt at creating similitude to a living person. Today, Denis Diderot's *Paradoxe sur le comédien,* from about 1770, is regarded as an important document of the Enlightenment, but it was not published until 1830 and therefore had no influence on contemporaries. Diderot distinguishes between two kinds of acting, one of which came to be known as 'cold', emphasising rational calculated effects on an audience, and one which came to be termed 'warm' privileging emotionally driven and extemporal expressions of the performer. In the 1750s, Diderot was still advocating an emotional acting technique, but in the *Paradoxe* he preferred the cold actor and his ideal impersonator was the English actor, playwright and theatre manager David Garrick, whose demonstrations of technique took the Parisian salons by storm. Diderot was impressed by the way Garrick could transform himself into any Shakespearean character in the course of a few seconds,

Acting was much discussed during the eighteenth century, not least in handbooks for actors such as Franciscus Lang's dissertation on acting from 1727.[15] My reconstruction has been based on contemporary Swedish iconography, and on the assumption that Monvel followed the principles of his famous mentor Lekain. It is to be noted, however, that the amateur actors in Hilleström's paintings were already beginning to adapt to changing conventions and one can clearly see that Armfelt raises his hand above the level of his eyes. The complex issues around acting on the baroque stage will be taken up in more detail by David Wiles in Chapter Seven.

Whatever the nuances of changing technique, it is abundantly clear that the stage of the Drottningholm Theatre required an acting style which accorded with the conditions of this space. The unification of a play's acting with the perspective created by six pairs of wings, miscellaneous backdrops,

32. Gustav Mauritz Armfelt in a scene of Gustav III:s play *Gustaf Adolf's Magnanimity*. Painting by Pehr Hilleström.

the occasional wave machine and the raked stage floor was mandatory if aesthetic harmony was to be achieved in the moment of performance. From today's post-Freudian epoch it might appear problematic to imagine that emotions were not clearly grounded in the individual, but emanated from character-types such as gods, heroes, nobles or even the fathers and servants of comedy. It was not the given circumstances of a situation, as Stanislawski described them for actors of the twentieth century, but the plot in its entirety that determined players' actions, while convention and the societal position of each character regulated the expressivity of the player's performance.

Of course, the gods – especially in operas – could show human-like weaknesses, but they never behaved like human beings. A king could be disguised as a farmhand, but would still behave as a royal personage. The incognito deeds of Gustav II Adolph, who saved a fisherman from drowning in Gustav's play about his predecessor, were as heroic as might be expected from a nobleman, even though the stage villagers at that moment did not recognise him as the king.

The baroque stage produced performances for the nobility in the auditorium. These spectating aristocrats – including royalty – were the central focus of the performance, not the actors, singers and dancers on stage. The performers of gods and kings were nothing more than actors, and although Gustav III treated them with respect, they remained servants of the royal household. This explains, in part, why their performative actions were strictly directed towards the audience. Turning one's back on the king would have been deemed close to an act of lèse majesté. This is just one instance in theatre history which demonstrates the close ties between aesthetic principles and social codes.

Instructing the Director

Meanwhile, the chamberlain approached Gustav III to tell him that Baron Gustav Mauritz Armfelt was waiting for him in the theatre's vestibule. Having been one of Gustav's favourite courtiers for some years, Baron Armfelt could easily have sneaked into the auditorium without a reprimand from the king, had he not met one of the beauties among the ladies-in-waiting on his way to the opera house. Although happily married to Duchess Hedvig Ulrika de la Gardie, a match proposed by Gustav himself to raise Armfelt's aristocratic status, and eventually having eight children with her, Gustav or Gösta, as the king called him, was always involved in amorous adventures. His contemporaries considered him an exceptionally handsome man and his stature was impressive – he was more than 1.90 metres tall and thus made an almost comical pair together with the king, who only measured 1.67 metres. There were very close ties between these two men and now they met in the theatre's private chamber, settled on easy chairs and were served the recently imported beverage of coffee – black as night, hot as hell and sweet as love, as the saying was. Armfelt knew his master very well, so he told the king all the latest gossip from the Royal Opera in Stockholm, of which he had become the administrative director earlier the same year. The Royal Opera remains on the same site today, although replaced by a new building dating from 1898. The story Armfeld came with this morning was as follows.

Elisabeth Olin, one of King Gustav's favourite singers, was causing trouble. Gustav had used both persuasion and the gift of a golden box to make her join the Royal Opera when it opened in 1773.[16] Up until that year, Elisabeth Olin had only appeared as a concert singer – at the funeral of Gustav's

33. Kjerstin Dellert as Elisabeth Olin in front of a portrait of opera singer Elisabeth Olin.

father, Adolph Frederik, as well as at Gustav III's own coronation – but to appear upon the operatic stage was beyond a married woman's honour at the time. At the age of twenty, Elisabeth had married a lawyer and she gave birth to six children – however, rumour whispered, not all them were his. She had carried on a well-known love affair with a prominent aristocrat for some years, but at the Opera she fell in love with the singer Carl Stenborg, twelve years her junior. For years, Olin and Stenborg had been the leading singers of the Gustavian opera, and they were lovers on and off the stage, until the handsome Carl transferred his tender feelings to Elisabeth Olin's daughter Betty. Now, Armfelt reported, Elisabeth Olin refused to sing at the Opera unless both Carl Stenborg and Betty Olin were discharged. Most probably, Gustav responded with his high, giggling laughter. Neither he nor Armfelt would choose the singer, now aged 46, over her successful younger rivals. Elisabeth Olin left the Royal Opera and resumed her career as a concert singer, though she would still entertained royalty at the wedding of Gustav's son in 1797, persuaded to do so by another golden box with the royal insignia in diamonds attached to it.

The substance of Gustav and Armefelt's meeting was twofold. Their first piece of business actually concerned opera and more specifically, the revival of Gustav's own opera *Gustav Vasa*, which premiered in January the same year. Already, as crown prince, Gustav had been an admirer of Gustav Vasa, who had liberated Sweden from the Danish 'tyrant' Christian in 1521 and became the first Swedish king of the early modern era. Gustav's teacher at the time, Olof von Dalin, had written a detailed account of the achievements of the 'Father of the Swedish Empire', and eventually Gustav would make use of his historical knowledge and incorporate it into what was for a long time considered to be *the* national opera of Sweden. He had himself written the libretto, which was versified by the court poet Johan Henrik Kellgren, while the music was composed by the German Johann Gottlieb Naumann.[17] The production at the then new opera building in Stockholm was a major success, and one reason for this success was the animosity against Denmark expressed in the opera, which reflected political tensions between the neighbouring countries at the time. Gustav was very well aware of the political effect this opera had on Swedish audiences, and even on the soldiers who were recruited as extras – none of whom wanted to perform as Danes

35. *Gustav Vasa* by J. G. Naumann and Gustav III. Act I, scene 8: King Christian threatens the young Svante Sture, son of Christina Gyllenstierna.

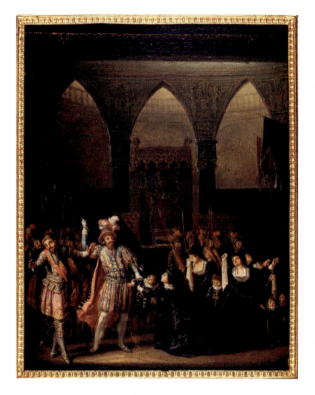

on stage! Therefore, he had been eager to bring *Gustav Vasa* back to the stage again during the autumn season. Meanwhile though, the political situation had changed and he wanted to explain his new plans to Armfelt.

In 1785, Gustav still had ambitions to provoke Denmark into a war. In the event of a victory, Sweden could then claim Danish Norway as part of the Swedish Empire. In the spring of 1786, Gustav had called for a national assembly, consisting of the four Estates: the nobility, the clergymen, the bourgeois and the yeomanry. The noblemen and the priests usually favoured the same policies, while the bourgeois took a quite liberal stand in most questions, privileging profit over ideology; the peasantry of Sweden had, throughout history, been a free class and acted upon their own rather utilitarian perspectives. In 1786, the Estates were reluctant to support any belligerent confrontations – not least because of a weak economy – so these plans had to be cancelled. Instead, Gustav tried a conciliatory approach. While he was reviewing his forces' manoeuvres in the south of Sweden in June 1786, the Danish crown prince Fredrik came to the Swedish camp for a courtesy visit. The two men reached a cordial understanding, eagerly supported by the Russian ambassador to Copenhagen, and animosity against Denmark was buried, at least temporarily. Of course, Armfelt knew all this, but he would not interrupt the king's argument. Considering these circumstances – this was the conclusion – it would not be feasible to take *Gustav Vasa* back into the repertory of the Opera. The king proposed another drama of his own authorship, also depicting a historic hero who shared his name, *Gustav Adolph and Ebba Brahe*. The opera had a folkloric tone and would suit the political situation much better than the politically incendiary *Gustav Vasa*. Betty Olin would be a wonderful Ebba Brahe, the young noblewoman who sacrifices her love to the political interests of the empire.

At this point, Armfelt saw a good opportunity to bring up a proposal of his own. Did His Majesty possibly consider it the right time to establish a dramatic theatre as a complement to the Royal Opera? There were good actors in town and the citizens of Stockholm deserved a place in which spoken drama was produced. The king listened, but did not respond directly. Armfelt went on to suggest that a Swedish troupe could alternate with Monvel's Frenchmen in the so-called Bollhuset (Ball House), built as an indoor tennis court, but for a long time now used as a theatre. Comedies performed by the personnel of the Opera had been successful, and even at court spoken drama was popular, whether performed by Monvel's troupe or by the courtiers themselves – the latter usually performing in Swedish. Armfelt had touched upon an interesting matter, because in less than a year, Gustav would grant Adolf Fredrik Ristell the right to perform 'Swedish tragedies, dramas and comedies' at the Bollhuset. When this private enterprise suffered a financial collapse, the king took over and established the Royal Dramatic Theatre in 1788 as Sweden's national theatre, an institution that is still one of the country's leading stages.

The last part of their conversation concerned a more trivial matter. Armfelt, as the Master of the Revels at court – another of his many duties – had prepared a surprise promenade for the courtiers through the French Garden at Drottningholm. As always, Gustav was well informed, even about events which were meant as a surprise to him. He always tried to obtain full control of everything happening at court. Now, at noon, he saw that the sun was shining through the windows, so this would be a fine occasion to surprise the court ladies, but since the promenade needed a number of actors, musicians and servants to be in place, Gustav was wondering whether the walk could still be organised in the course of the afternoon. Armfelt could say nothing but yes, although he knew that he would have to hire a boat from Stockholm to bring out some singers and instrumentalists to satisfy the king's wish. Since Armfelt had originated from the lower aristocracy in the province of Finland, and had risen to this privileged position at court, he would always do his utmost to live up to the king's expectations.

Armfelt – The Courtier

Armfelt was, indeed, an unusual figure at court. There were many members of the Swedish aristocracy with kings and queens in their ancestry who felt neglected by Gustav III. Now this Finnish baron was favoured and catapulted into high positions that had traditionally been reserved for more privileged members of the nobility. In this respect, Gustav was a product of the Enlightenment. He, among many other surprising moves, became the first European head of state to recognise the political independence of the United States of America. Under these circumstances, the advancement of Armfelt becomes understandable. As a young lieutenant of 23, he had met Gustav at the fashionable health resort of Spa (in today's Belgium) in 1780, and very soon a close friendship developed between the two men. To what extent the relationship between the 34 year old king and the 23 year old baron exceeded the homosocial is not known. A royal prince had been born in 1778, albeit after 12 years of marriage, but not even Gustav's own mother, Ulrika Lovisa, believed that Gustav was the father of the new-born prince, thus precipitating a life-long split between mother and son. By the time Gustav III was shot dead in March 1792, Armfelt had become one of the most influential courtiers, which laid him open to the hostility of the Swedish nobility. After the king's death he was driven into exile for ten years, sentenced to death, pardoned, sent to Vienna as Swedish ambassador, and eventually became a close friend of the Russian Tsar Alexander I; he died in 1814 in the Tsar's residence as governor of the Russian province of Finland. All this, of course, lay far ahead in time, when at Drottningholm Gustav the king, and Gustav the baron, were discussing the divertissement of the afternoon.

Just a few days earlier, on the so-called Day of the Revolution, 19 August, Armfelt had arranged the official

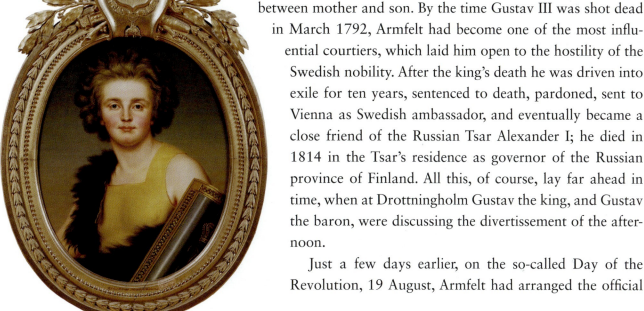

35. Gustaf Mauritz Armfelt. Portrait by Adolf Ulrik Wertmüller, pained in Paris 1784.

ceremony of laying the foundation-stone for a new palace in the park of Haga, another lush area to the north of Stockholm, near the waters of the Baltic Sea. Designed by Louis Jean Desprez, who was in charge of the décor at the Drottningholm Theatre, the building should have become another distinctive Gustavian edifice, but it was never completed. The foundation ceremony was, however, spectacular, with singers of the Opera appearing as goddesses and gods to protect the project, the ballet corps as nymphs and spirits of the place, and the military fleet, playfully representing the real power of the state, crowded into the bay of the Baltic Sea. Even Duchess Hedvig Elisabeth Charlotta, married to the king's brother Karl and usually very critical of the court in her diary, was impressed by the delicacy and elegance of this divertissement. Armfelt had obviously exploited the deep sense of rococo culture that he had developed as part of the entourage on the king's Italian journey, 1783-84. Already in 1783 he had written the first Swedish vaudeville, *Tillfälle gör tjuven*, which was first presented as a court performance at the Confidencen Theatre close to the Ulriksdal Palace.[18] Originally an equestrian training hall that Gustav's mother Ulrika

36. View of stage and auditorium of the Confidensen theatre.

Lovisa had converted into a baroque theatre, Confidencen was frequently used for the court's amateur performances. Armfelt had himself played the main role, a farm-hand in a rural setting, as he did with most first-lover parts in the performances that the court staged during Gustav's reign. Now, in 1786, he had become the director of the Royal Opera, and had recently been elected to the Swedish Academy, which Gustav had established in the spring of the same year.[19] With all these new titles, duties and honours bestowed upon him, Baron Armfelt also had important tasks to perform on this ordinary Wednesday in August 1786.

Gustav III – The Playwright

When Armfelt left the royal chamber of the theatre – and he was eager to leave, partly to arrange the afternoon's promenade, partly to find the lady-in-waiting he had spoken to before his conversation with the king – Gustav called upon his scribe to dictate dispatch and personal letters to his military confidant Johan Christopher Toll, who had assisted him in his coup d'etat back in 1772, the anniversary of which event had been celebrated at the foundation ceremony in Haga. Gustav made a clear distinction between friends and enemies and Toll, whom he had made major general earlier in 1786, definitely belonged among the military experts he trusted. He also sent some notes to members of the court and some invitations to citizens in town, who were honoured to be invited to the evening's performance of the Gluck opera in Drottningholm. He also dictated some new rules for the employment of artists at the opera, in response to the rumours about Elisabeth Olin. Gustav was very strict in organisational matters and, in the case that his directives were not followed, Armfelt was entitled to use physical punishments. Gustav then sent out the scribe and personally took over the writing desk. Nobody knew what he was working on when he was on his own. It could be a new strategic plan for an attack against Russia or it could be a concept for a new play. Gustav had at the time completed a number of plays and librettos for operas. In 1782 he wrote no fewer than five scenarios, and now he might already have thought about what was to become the last of his plays, *The Jealous Neapolitan*.

Most of Gustav's plays, librettos and scenarios were completed by one of his court poets – usually Johan Henrik Kellgren (1751-95) – in a mixture of current styles. On the one hand, the traditional Baroque style appropriate to royal heroes might prevail, the most obvious example of this heroic style being the opera *Gustav Vasa*. On the other hand, a number of new stylistic elements were beginning to appear during the latter half of the eighteenth century. While the spirit of the Enlightenment had focused more upon the individual, the age of sentiment emphasised strong emotional turning points, and an interest in the gothic past foreshadowed the Romanticism of the next century. In Gustav's play about the jealous Neapolitan, several of these elements converged.

The stage represents gothic environments. In the first act the story is set partly in a deep forest with a highway and a gothic castle in the background, partly in the interior of a hermit's cave, where a skull lies on a prayer stool and an hourglass stands opposite.[20] The second act moves to the castle, and the third act is located in its dungeon. The story is about misunderstood love and alleged unfaithfulness. Don Diego, who tortures and punishes his wife Donna Elvire and their son because of a letter he found, will perish in the end, and the hermit Theotime will save the woman and her child from starving to death in the prison. This is a tale of courtly love, mediaeval in its purity, and the chastity of the hermit is uncompromising. Of course the hermit is a nobleman who was once in love with the heroine, Donna Elvire. He shoulders his responsibility as an individual when he follows the jealous Don Diego and secures Elvire's well-being.

From a historical perspective, the stage directions that Gustav wrote are more interesting than the plot. From the French dramatist Baculard d'Arnaud, Gustav had learned to use full stops to indicate the rhythm of speech. Two dots (..) meant a longer pause than only one dot at the end of a sentence, and three dots (…) indicated a long interval before the next spoken line.[21] Gustav's play is written in prose, where the rhythmic emphasis is even more important than in French alexandrine verse. Unfinished sentences and short outcries mark important emotional moments in the manner of the Romantics. But physical movements are also described in detail. In the following, both the actions of the performers and those of the stage-hands are included:

Elvire [...]

(She falls, her face to his feet. A pause, and the long silence may take one, at most two minutes. Eventually it is interrupted by the noise of spades, pikes and iron-bars working to open the wall of the vault towards the king's side. Elvire, attentive, lifts her head and listens; she extends her arms in amazement and hope, and says:)

What strange sound breaks the silence of death that prevails under these vaults.. – Heaven, who is coming to rescue me?

A stone falls[22]

(One stone of the vault falls down – through the gap it creates, the torches of the workers throw a feeble light onto the stage :)

God, I see the light… My son, my son! You are free! – Heaven! The fresh air coming in is restoring him.

Alonzo (: regaining consciousness:) *2 stones*

My mother!

(Meanwhile the workers have broken loose several stones that have fallen down, and further stones fall from the wall in such a way that they form steps, on which Theotime easily can jump down – Elvire, when she sees the stones falling, throws herself over her son to protect him:)

Elvire *all falls*

God! The vault is falling upon us! Lord save us.. Alonzo.. I die …
(She falls across him fainting.)

Theotime (: in the opening:)

Our efforts have been rewarded – here is the vault!

(He searches with his torch in his hand and when he becomes aware of Elvire, he jumps down and throws himself at her feet ---- :)[23]

This dramatic turn in the drama of the jealous Neapolitan would be completed some years later, but Gustav had seen similar early Romantic plays in Paris during his last visit there in 1784. Romanticism had already a firm grasp on Gustav's contemporaries in Germany such as Johann Wolfgang von Goethe and Friedrich von Schiller, while the melodramas of René Ch. G. Pixérécourt, which flooded Europe after the turn of the century, were not far away. These Romantic tendencies are surprising, since Gustav generally favoured the simplicity and harmony of the neo-classical designs that Desprez offered him both on stage and in his architectural sketches – the Déjeuner-Salon being a typical example. But while the Déjeuner-Salon was being built, Gustav sat next door and wrote his Romantic, gothic drama of guilt and redemption.

Gustav's dramas tell us quite a lot about the king and the man who governed Sweden for more than twenty years. It is obvious from the printed dramas – both those which were completed by Kellgren and those that Gustav finished himself such as *The Jealous Neapolitan* – that Gustav had a profound knowledge of theatre. As the stage directions quoted above indicate, he knew what was possible and desirable on stage. The darkness, the silence, the sounds that accompany the breaking of the wall, the light of the torches – all these devices were brought together to create the best possible effects.[24] The dramaturgical devices of broken dialogue, threats and cries and fainting, added to the tension of the plot, and to the impression the drama made on its spectators. This impact on the audience was profoundly important for Gustav. In this respect Gustav was not only a dramatist interested in engaging an audience; his work also had far-reaching ideological

37. *The Jealous Neapolitan*, act III, scene 3, Gustav III:s last play.

purposes. While the glorification of the earlier kings of the name Gustav does not need much explanation, the victory to the 'good' in the *Neapolitan* is of another kind. Since 1771, Gustav had belonged, together with his brothers Karl and Fredrik Adolf, to the Freemasons. One of the tasks of Freemasons is it to guide people towards good morals without revealing the origin of these intentions. Therefore, the play's messages are wrapped in symbolic disguises such as the frequent use of the number three: three acts, three men around Elmire, three knocks upon the door of castle, three letters and so forth.[25] The drama also describes a journey from darkness to light, from captivity to liberation, from confusion to clarity, from death to rebirth. After being staged for the first time after Gustav's death, the *The Jealous Neapolitan* carried the Freemasons' ideas far into the nineteenth century.

On a more general level, Gustav's dramas also illustrate important aspects of his character, first and foremost the multiple dimensions of his personality. Any attempt to reduce Gustav to one particular characteristic trait is doomed to fail, irrespective of whether we think of his dramas, politics, people or issues. In terms of design, the Gustavian style is a typical hybrid: a bit of neo-classical rigidity, some rococo playfulness, some baroque representation, but also a portion of Romantic mysticism. Instead of describing Gustav as volatile, he might be characterized as flexible. In addition, one could emphasise two aspects of his character that proved to be very useful for him: first of all a large portion of pragmatism – especially in relation to politics – and secondly, his enormous curiosity – an eagerness to learn the latest news, from high diplomacy to the latest gossip. So it suited the king very well to receive a familiar visitor from Paris.

The name of this visitor was Axel von Fersen and he represented the highest ranks of the nobility of Sweden. In the summer of 1786, Axel von Fersen was still a relatively young man who had spent most of his life in France. He had also participated in the War of Independence in America – on the French side, coming back with a medal from General Washington – and he had bought his own French regiment, Royal Suédois. He had just returned from Paris for his annual visit to Sweden. To report to King Gustav was part of his obligations, although he was aware that the king was well informed about everything French through his new ambassador Erik Staël von Holstein. There were, however, some questions that the king could not or did not want to ask his ambassador: the affair of the royal necklace with 647 diamonds, that cost Cardinal de Rohan his privileged position, was one of the stories Gustav was keen to enquire about. It was also well known that Axel von Fersen was the lover of the French Queen Marie-Antoinette – had he anything to do with the birth of her third child last year? Although Gustav might have hinted at this intimate question, the answer would have been no! Anything else would have been suicidal, but Gustav had a fine ear and could distinguish between various kinds of 'no…'!

It was only a short step from personal conversation to diplomacy of the highest level. Since personal and political histories coincided in aristocratic Europe, an intimate knowledge of all kinds of relations was vital for foreign politics. Maria Theresa of Austria had been succeeded by Marie-Antoinette's brother, Emperor Joseph II, but would these ties between brother and sister endure the constant struggle between their respective countries over The Netherlands? And, more vital to Gustav, would France support Austrian aggression against Russia? Axel von Fersen had very good relations with the most influential circles of French politics, so it was well worth listening to his observations and opinions and they might have been sitting there for a long time, were they not most charmingly interrupted by Badin, who told his master that the afternoon's promenade was now fully prepared.

The Park of Drottningholm

The wife of Gustav's brother Karl, Hedvig Elisabeth Charlotta (usually referred to by only her final first name) wrote one of the most remarkable documents about court life in Sweden. Coming from a bishop's home in Lybeck in Germany, she was married to the Swedish prince at the age of fifteen. Due to her husband's many love affairs, their marriage did not appear to be overly happy. In 1798, at the age of 39, she gave birth to a son who, however, died the same year. Nevertheless, she is mostly described as a good-humoured woman, and she often seems to have mediated between competing factions at court. Her observations and comments she saved for her extensive diary, which she wrote from 1775, the year after her marriage, until the year before she died, 1817. The diary is written in French and

38. The Drottningholm domain. In Cecilia Uhrstedts water colour, the symetrical French park can easily be distinguished from the irregular English garden.

consists of nine volumes.[26] In one of her entries she describes a promenade through the park of Drottningholm, which we can imagine happened on this Wednesday afternoon in August 1786.

> First it was intended as a surprise for the king, but since he always is so pleased to know of all arrangements in advance, the party was said to be given in honour of the princess and myself. Since the weather was fine and all were in good spirits, the event was very successful. The king proposed to the queen and the entire court that they take a promenade in the park and right at the entrance we were met by a guitar player, who sang humorous albeit not indecent songs; after that an old woman came forward to tell me and the princess our fortunes and to say some friendly words to the queen; in a nearby grove an hermit told his story, which was especially entertaining since he referred to adventures that had recently happened. Eventually we arrived at a little platform, on which the most prominent members of the opera danced, and in a little theatre among the greenery, the French actors presented a prologue and the little play Le fou raisonable; the not so remarkable prologue contained some well-chosen compliments to the royal family. After the end of this performance the whole group moved to another grove, to a market where coffee was being served to the sounds of a pleasant and delightful serenade.[27]

Charlotta mentions a few things that are worth some comments. The king obviously presented this walk through the park as a spontaneous invitation, although everybody knew that elaborate preparations had been necessary. Had the French actors not been in Drottningholm already, and the opera artists on their way to the evening's performance, not even Armfelt could have managed to bring together all the people required for the 'improvisations' enumerated by Charlotta. The group walking through the park consisted of the king and the queen with their chamberlains, ladies-in-waiting, pages, the king's brother Karl and his wife Charlotta, maybe the king's youngest brother Fredrik Adolf and his wife, their respective entourages, Armfelt, Badin, eight year old Prince Gustav Adolf and his tutors, some of Queen Sofia Magdalena's aristocratic friends, members of the diplomatic

39. A contemporary ballet scene in the Leaf Theatre with John Massey and Solveig Åkerberg.

corps who happened to be at Drottningholm, servants carrying parasols, should these be desired, personnel preparing the coffee and so on. In total about 30 to 40 persons were wandering about the park.

Although the park is part of the world heritage site of Drottningholm, we must remember that in Gustavian times only the baroque section next to the palace was established, whereas the so-called jardin anglais, the English Park, outside the opera house did not yet exist. On the contrary, the theatre was surrounded by an ill-smelling, wet moss that was ditched out only in the year before Gustav's death. The promenade thus took place in the symmetrically shaped part of the garden facing the palace and in some adjacent groves. The theatre among the greenery that Charlotta mentions is not clearly visible in the historical ground plans of the garden, but today's copy of the perspectival stage, created through cut, living bushes, gives a lively impression of the little French play.

The guitar player that awaited the royal following was most likely Carl Michael Bellman, a Swedish singer, poet and composer, who was economically supported by the king and thus had to be available whenever the court called. Bellman had two quite different strings to his bow: partly he wrote numerous poems glorifying the king and many royal institutions, following the exact rules of contemporary rhetoric and genre conventions; but he had also composed a long series of popular songs that many Swedes still know by heart more than 200 years later. He was at home in the town's taverns as well as at Gustav's court, he appropriated well-known melodies for his poetic songs, and he created melodies that have been well-known ever since. But he was a servant and Charlotta does not bother to call him by his name.

Charlotta could in her account have mentioned that the group passed by the remains of a so-called carousel that had taken place the year before. This carousel was called *L'Entreprise de la Forêt Enchantée (The Siege of the Enchanted Forest)* and it was arranged as a tribute to Armfelt's wedding.[28] The tournament had extended over several days and included all kinds of competitions – on horseback or on foot, in groups or as single fighters, combat between men, or hitting rings or shooting at targets. These competitive elements were overshadowed by the lavish procedures around them – there was certainly more spectacle than sports. However, Charlotta still remembered that her husband, Duke Karl, had hurt his knee badly during that tournament, and that one of the pages died from an accidental pistol shot.[29]

This fascination with the Middle Ages, both its literature and stories, the clothing, equipment and weapons, and the re-construction of medieval environments and dresses en masse (up to 300 participants had been involved) was costly and – not least for foreign diplomats – quite incomprehensible. For Gustav, carousels stretched far beyond mere spectacle. He deeply involved his brothers and the wife of Duke Karl, Charlotta, performed as he heroine who was to be liberated. Liberation was a central theme in most of these carousels. Not only did such plots lend themselves to spectacular sieges and conquering battles, but liberation was also a religious-philosophical issue. The towers of the castle were obviously modelled after the Tower of the Freemasons in Paris – with its small, high-conical tops.[30] Gustav was at the time eagerly investigating the Order of the Knights Templar, to which he and his brothers belonged. While Charlotta was given the best role of the carousel, she probably knew nothing about her husband's and brothers in law's involvement in Freemasonry.

40. Painting of the carousel *The Conquest of Galtare Rock* by Pehr Hilleström from 1779. The towers of the temporary castle, built in the park for this occasion, resemble the structure of the Freemason's Temple in Paris. Spectators were placed on a particular scaffold (see detail).

Gluck's Opera

After the concluding piece performed by the French actors, the promenading group dissolved. Most of them returned to the palace where they could now spend a couple of hours at their own preferred leisure pursuit: playing cards, embroidery, reading, chatting. Not before six o'clock in the evening would they gather in the opera house of Drottningholm to enjoy the day's performance.

What opera could the audience expect this night? The early opera composers to be most successfully performed during the 21st century – Monteverdi, Händel, Mozart – were not represented at Drottningholm during the eighteenth century. Usually, historical operas were only revived with new singers if they were already in the current repertoire. To re-stage earlier operas – and music in general – first became a common practice in the nineteenth century. But why did the Gustavian court turn its back on the Viennese classicists such as Joseph Haydn, Antonio Salieri and Wolfgang Amadeus Mozart? Abbé Vogler did not think that Gustav would enjoy Mozart's *Le Nozze di Figaro* which he had seen soon after its premiere in May 1786.[31] As we remember, Gustav enjoyed the play in Paris in 1784, so it could not be the subject he objected to. In general, however, Gustav preferred more heroic operas – not least his own, set to music by German composers – and classical themes such as the ones that Christoph Willibald Gluck used for his so-called reform operas. Gluck was a pioneer in the development of integrating music and plot, and composed a number of works that demonstrated his ideas about music theatre. The earliest of them, *Orfeo ed Euridice*, first presented in Vienna in 1762, was performed in Stockholm before it reached Paris. It was, indeed, the third production of Gustav's newly established Royal Opera in 1773, and the leading parts were sung by two singers we have already heard about: Elisabeth Olin and Carl Stenborg. Gustav's Italian concert master Francesco Uttini had to transcribe the arias for the tenor Stenborg, since the part was originally written for an alto-castrate.[32] Gluck's *Iphigénie*

41. C. W. Gluck's *Orfeus and Euridice*, painted by Pehr Hillestrôm in 1773.

en Aulide followed in 1778, *Alceste* in 1781, and *Iphigénie en Tauride* in 1783 – all of them soon after their French premieres and all in Swedish translations. Only the composers André-Ernest-Modeste Grétry and Niccolò Picinni were comparable in popularity at Drottningholm. So the choice of Gluck is obvious, and since *Orfeo* was revived through a Swedish translation of the French version of *Orphée* in the year 1786 a new production of this opera had been created.

Gluck's *Orpheus och Euridice*, which concluded that Wednesday in August, followed a new trend in visual appearance on stage. These changes in performance practices were documented in two paintings by Pehr Hilleström, one referring to the production of 1773, the other one depicting the performances of 1786. These paintings reflect a major change of taste and fashion at Gustav's court. Hilleström depicted the most dramatic moment of this short opera which included only three protagonists: Orpheus, Euridice and Amor. In addition, there are large parts for a chorus (normally made up of ten men and eight women) and there are sections of music composed for the ballet corps; Gallodier had, of course, arranged the dances both in 1773 and in 1786. Hilleström's paintings show Act III, Scene 1, in which Orpheus has succeeded in leaving Hades with Euridice, while still obeying the command of the gods not to turn his face towards her.[33] In the 1773 painting, he is carrying his lyre in his right hand, and with his left hand he pulls Euridice behind him out of the cave-like opening of the underworld. According to the taste of the time, the main characters are dressed in rococo fashions. Orefeus wears a red coat over his

42. C. W. Gluck's *Orfeus and Euridice*, painted by Pehr Hilleström in 1786.

knee-long breeches, silk stockings and lace flowing out of his sleeves. On his belt, a sword hangs to indicate his dignity, emphasised by a laurel crown on his bare head. Euridice is dressed in white sateen and a chemise of Italian gauze as well as a bodice and shirt of silver cloth.[34] The picture also indicates the high speed of the actors. No matter to what extent this painting reflects the actual situation on stage, it is obvious that the two main singers, Stenborg and Olin, gave Hilleström the impression that they were escaping from hell at high speed. How much this performance impressed the royal family is documented in a letter by Carl Stenborg to the translator of the text, medical doctor Göran Rothman: Stenborg received precious gifts from both the king and from Duke Karl. And the publisher Carl Christopher Gjörwell noted that 'Herr Stenborg had played Orphée excellently, better every time, and in such a way that the King was fully pleased with him.'[35]

Gluck's *Orfeo*, i.e. in the Viennese version, was very successful in Stockholm, although less popular in most other opera houses. In 1780, seven years after its Swedish premiere and six years after Gluck's own French version, *Orfeus och Euridice* was still very much appreciated, so much so that new singers for the title roles were needed. In 1786, Johan Samuel Lalin and Sofia Franciska Stadig were ordered out to Drottningholm to perform the new translation of the Paris version of this opera. Lalin had already sung the part of Amor in 1773, but by now the staging had changed significantly. A few years earlier, the Swedish poet Anna Maria Lenngren had published some satirical verses about the singers' overburdening costumes which hardly fitted onto the narrow stage.[36] From Pehr Hilleström's new painting one can confirm that the appearance of the protagonists was now very different indeed. The new, classical Empire-style, usually associated with the Napoleonic era, had already found its way onto the Swedish stage. Orphée is dressed in an antique-looking tunic, no sword, no boots, but a bag over his shoulder and sandals on his feet. Still he carries his lyre, and has a laurel crown on his head. Euridice follows him in a simple, ankle-length dress with a belt under her bust, very much in accordance with the Empire fashions and, at the same time, imitating classical Greek costume as it was perceived at the time. The overall impression of this painting is that of neo-classical costumes for both Orphée and Euridice.

The change in the costumes also indicates that the period we conventionally call 'Gustavian' was subject to the dynamics of the time. Fashions came and went even in the two decades of the Gustavian reign. Gustav was himself fascinated by changes of fashion in Europe, and despite his invention of the national Swedish dress, he obviously wanted to see the latest costume designs in his theatre. Gluck's opera constituted an excellent opportunity to display the haute couture that had developed beyond the official aristocratic rococo dress. Such neo-classical ideals would soon be incorporated into Desprez' design for the Déjeuner-Salon that was built to extend the Drottningholm Theatre. The Gustavian era was full of stylistic surprises, and Gustav himself was the first to enjoy new approaches and artistic innovations. He left the theatre full of enthusiasm and he may very well have rewarded the singers with golden boxes and diamond rings, just as he did when he heard Gluck's wonderful music for the first time.

Evening at Drottningholm

Since Gluck's *Orfeus och Euridice* is a rather short opera there was enough time for Gustav to propose some additional entertainment. Earlier in his life, he was in the habit of having his dinner served on stage, while the court watched him and had to engage in conversations with him. When exhibiting himself in this way, he remained in the costume of the character he had been playing – so the courtiers had to guess whether they were talking to Gustav III or Voltaire's Radamiste. These dinners took place repeatedly at the court theatre in Gripsholm, which is much more intimate and was only used by the inner circles of the court. Still, the king loved to dine publically at regular intervals (and the courtiers hated it), but this evening Gustav has already returned to the palace.

If any of the princesses were having her name day, this would be an excellent opportunity to celebrate the occasion in one of the larger halls of the main building.[37] The musicians, who had just finished the opera, would move their instruments over the yard and play minuets and other dances. Now the young pages could show what they had actually had learned from their dance master Gallodier. Gustav himself rarely danced, since he had been slightly lame in one leg since birth, but he enjoyed watching others moving in intricate dancing patterns on the well-polished floor.

When the evening has become sufficiently dark – in August, daylight lasts until at least nine o'clock in Sweden – a surprise firework display might illuminate the French Garden. Everybody would rush to the windows to get a glimpse of the sparkling and splashing fire-balls that circled over the flower beds. Unlike today's fireworks, the pieces were not shot high into the air, but rather moved horizontally in straight and curved lines over the ground, forming more or less artful patterns. Therefore, the best place to watch the evening's fireworks was from the upper floors of the palace. The arrangement of such a spectacle did not demand any particular reason – it could just be one of the surprises that the king loved so much.

Another possible conclusion to this day could be less social and more business-like. Gustav might have wished to see his brothers: Karl, who was married to the diary-writing Charlotta and later, in the nineteenth century,

43. The Royal brothers: Gustav, Carl and Fredrik Adolf.

would become king of Sweden, and his youngest brother Fredrik Adolf, who had become reconciled with Gustav after the death of their mother, whom he had supported in her conflict with her eldest son. Fredrik Adolf lived outside Stockholm and visited the court at Drottningholm only occasionally. What were the three brothers talking about? In a famous painting by the Swedish artist Alexander Roslin, we see Fredrik Adolf to the right, sitting at a table measuring the distance on a map of the world; Gustav sits next to him and points to some geographical region, while he holds a book in his other hand; Karl stands behind the table stretching out the map that seems to be the focus of their conversation. Obviously they are talking politics, although the painter has depicted a moment when they all look towards the artist. Probably they were not entirely engaged in political matters this evening. We already know that Gustav was keen on hearing the latest gossip, so he might just as easily have listened to what his brothers happened to have heard.

There are many ways to imagine the evening of this Wednesday in August 1786. Since the environment of Drottningholm, with its palace, theatre, Chinese Pavilion and other buildings as well as the French Garden is so well preserved, it is in a way easy to be caught up by the imaginative power of history. An abundance of pictures, from official paintings to accidental drawings, populates the halls of the palace and the stage of the opera house. Described in diaries, memoires and notes in newspapers, these historical figures become tangible personalities. The Gustavian court remains a 'foreign country', but in our fantasies we have touched the horizon of history. Intending to provide concrete information about life and arts at Drottningholm, my imagination might at times have gone too far, in which case I sincerely apologise to the reader.

In conclusion I would say that it is beyond my imagination to claim that Gustav spent the evening with his wife, Queen Sofia Magdalena. Although their relationship had thawed since she had given birth to two princes, their daily encounters were still quite formal. It is difficult to envision King Gustav having dinner together with his family. Gustav was rarely a private person – he was the king, at day and at night. Even going to bed was formalised – the so-called couchée – though this was less spectacular than the morning ceremony of the levée. The bed was royal, and so was the man sleeping in it.

David Wiles

5. A TYPICAL 'BAROQUE' THEATRE?

Three years after my first visit, I returned to Drottningholm on foot, walking across the two modern bridges onto an island which prior to the eighteenth century could only be reached by boat. I wanted to approach the theatre by way of the palace, seeking to understand the theatre not as a hermetic space of art but as a functional part of a baroque court, a vanished social system. The label 'baroque' will need to be qualified when applied to a theatre dated as late as 1766, but sits comfortably with a palace designed in 1661 and built over the next three decades. The flamboyance and *joie de vivre* of Drottningholm have few echoes in England, with its stolid mercantile traditions. The grand politico-aesthetic ideals of the baroque - exemplified by Rubens' depiction of the Stuarts on the great ceiling of the Banqueting House in Whitehall - came to an abrupt halt with the execution of Charles I. The external style of Drottningholm is manifestly French, reflecting a long-standing political alliance. 1661 was the year when Louis XIV assumed power and started to rebuild Versailles, but the projects served quite distinct purposes. The baroque interiors of Drottningholm looked to the past, while Versailles looked forwards to a more restrained classicism, and it was the gardens rather than the interiors of Versailles that would prove a decisive influence on the layout of the Swedish palace. Paris long remained the arbiter of taste, and it was French theatre, dominated by the dramaturgy of Louis XIV's Golden Age in the 1660s and 1670s, that determined how the stage of Drottningholm would be used a century later. The theatre was built for French actors, and subsequent actors like Monvel demonstrated how the stage should be used.

    The wealth that built Drottningholm derived from the Thirty Years War, which culminated in a Swedish army plundering Prague. The Palace was built by the Queen Regent, Hedvig Eleonora, not simply as a convenient summer residence, but as a shrine to a new dynasty. Following the abdica-

44. The staircase of the Drottningholm palace.

tion of the catholic Queen Christina, last descendant of the militarily triumphant Vasas, she sought to commemorate the short reign of her husband, Karl X, and her own role as mother of Karl XI, from whom great things were expected. Britain's most celebrated baroque building, Blenheim Palace, designed by a man of the theatre, was built as a monument to victories over Louis XIV rather than as a comfortable home, and in much the same way the Palace of Drottningholm was designed in the first instance to provide the visitor with a performative experience. Like the victories of John Churchill at Blenheim, the battlefields of Karl X and Karl XI are portrayed in long galleries. Both palaces were built to be admired by strangers, and the gaze of the modern tourist sits in a line of continuity. While Blenheim is an overtly masculine space, its landscape dominated by a huge victory column, Drottningholm – as befits its name, meaning "Queen's home" – is a more feminised space. It passed directly from Hedvig Eleonora to her grand-daughter Ulrika Eleonora, and thence after a short hiatus was a wedding gift for Queen Lovisa Ulrika, who commissioned the present theatre as a space for private entertainment. The architectural emphasis of the theatre, built a century after the main palace, is upon the secret world that it encloses, and not upon the visual rhetoric of power.

Visiting the Royal Palace of Drottningholm

I enter the palace doors, and immediately I am in a kind of theatre. Before me is a trompe l'oeil perspective corridor, focused upon a statue of Hercules in the middle of the formal gardens behind the palace, serving to double the sense of distance and thus enhance the scale of the garden.[1] To climb the staircase is to climb Mount Parnassus, surrounded by statues of the Muses, as I enter a world of art and culture, while busts of Gothic kings relay a parallel narrative about dynasty. On the walls, perspectival columns frame false rooms conjured up by the court painter. Up above, on the painted ceiling which simulates the sky, an emblem of Queen Hedvig Eleonora is crowned by Apollo, on behalf of art, and by Minerva, who appears to be a cipher for the late Queen Christina. Such ceilings are a hallmark of baroque art, linking the monarch to the powers of heaven, allowing her to look down upon humble mortals like myself, who squint up with difficulty, unable to contain and control what I see in my gaze. In the modern theatre I am empowered to choose what to look at, but in this theatricalised baroque environment such control is denied me.

45. Queen Lovisa Ulrika depicted as goddess Minerva on the theatre curtain. In front of the curtain Staffan Liljas and Frida Jansson in Mozart's *Così fan tutte* 2011.

Once up the first flight of stairs, I sign up for a tour, which I find has been skilfully arranged to take me on a journey through space that is also a journey through time. Whilst English tours of country houses commonly play upon the dichotomy of upstairs and downstairs, dissolving historicity in the eternal tensions of class, the Swedish tour is more in the German tradition, taking for granted in visitors a basic stylistic vocabulary and historical orientation. Though the allegories are now hard to decipher, huge paintings on the wall dramatise for the modern tourist the journey into Hedvig Eleonora's reception chamber, just as they once did for the seventeenth-century visitor. In David Ehrenstrahl's paintings, we see the queen steering the ship of state, surrounded by figures that celebrate her patronage of the arts, while other paintings proclaim different messages about the royal line, past and future. These canvases are part of the architecture, not transferable commodities hung upon the walls, for baroque art is inseparable from relations of power. The beaux-arts framed portraits of European monarchs hung in the nineteenth century in the Hall of State offer us at the end of the tour the modern mode of viewing, presenting kings and queens as mere human individuals. Only the painted ceiling remains in the Hall of State from the baroque era, with its allegory of the four continents reflecting colonial aspirations. This is the space where temporary theatres were once set up and allegorical dramas performed, seamlessly interacting with the architecture just like Ehrenstrahl's paintings. To speak of Lovisa Ulrika building the first theatre at Drottningholm is a misnomer, and we should take care to refer only to the first *permanent* theatre. It was, nevertheless, an important historical moment when the framed space of art began to be separated off from the space of life.

Not finding any state dining room, I realise that Drottningholm was designed for encounters that transgressed the public/private boundary. The most sumptuous memorial to the baroque age is Hedvig Eleonora's bedchamber and reception room, testifying to seventeenth-century visitors that her most intimate self was bound up in her relationship to a dead husband. She wanted it to be seen that there was no division between her public and her private self. In this bedchamber Gustav III performed his levées, playing the role of a latter-day Louis XIV. Hedvig Eleonora's royal bed, as in Versailles, would originally have been in the centre of the room, underneath the ceiling which depicts the joined hands of the royal couple, but Gustav preferred proscenium theatre to theatre in the round and placed the bed in an alcove, framing it with classical columns, and closing it off with a kind of altar rail. Whilst Hedvig Eleonora positioned herself as a player in a greater cosmic drama, Gustav was a calculating scenographer in tight control of his art.

46. Hedvig Eleonora's bedchamber at Drottningholm.

Ulrika Eleonora made no significant changes when she was custodian of the palace because her husband fared badly in war and available moneys were devoted to a new palace in the city. When, in more prosperous times, the palace of Drottningholm was extended by Lovisa Ulrika, the distinction between baroque and the new rococo style is clear. The palace became her retreat after a failed coup in 1756 when she and her husband Adolph Fredrik tried to secure absolute power over parliament, at once consoling her with the decorative trappings of power, and allowing her to build the reality of cultural power. The restrained rococo style, in contrast to the sculptural, sensuous and playful decor of the previous century, transformed parts of the dynastic monument into a private home, and green silk wallpaper set off portraits of the queen's Prussian relatives. The baroque style spoke of Swedish history, but the rococo spoke of cosmopolitanism and the influence of Paris. The new Age of Reason no longer responded to the ontological uncertainty induced by trompe l'oeil effects, and emphasised the elegance of man-made form. Emblematic of the Age of Reason is Lovisa Ulrika's graceful library, reworked in the 1760s in a classicising style equivalent

47. The Baroque design of the French park emphasised by snow.

to Adamesque in an English architectural vocabulary. The modern visitor can inspect the shelves to see rows of works by Voltaire, the champion of 'enlightened' monarchy whose plays enjoyed pride of place on the queen's Drottningholm stage.[2] The visitor is, unfortunately, not permitted to see the Cabinet of Medals which still preserves the decor of 1753, and once offered to the young Gustav instructive images of great kings and emperors. These rooms were a focal point for the Academy of Letters which the erudite queen founded in 1753.[3] When Gustav eventually took over the palace from his estranged and impecunious mother, he introduced his own more masculine idiom into the decor, substituting planar classical designs for the surface extrusions and allegorical messages that texture his mother's library.

Leaving the palace, I have two more para-theatrical monuments on my itinerary before I revisit the theatre. Hidden in the baroque gardens, the 'Leaf Theatre' built of hedges evoked the theatrical environments created for Louis XIV in the gardens of Versailles. An undated sketch depicts an actual proscenium theatre erected in this garden space, while hedges planted in the form of angled flats feature in a plan of 1785.[4] At the far end of the gardens, Lovisa Ulrika's Chinese Pavilion is another kind of playhouse. The court architect, Carl Adelcrantz, built the first and then the extant pavilion at around the same times as he built the first and then the extant theatres. The pleasure of this flimsy rococo pavilion lies in its unreality, in the perception that it is surface and not substance. Here the queen could play-act membership of an exotic, bucolic and untroubled world. Adelcrantz' orientalising fantasy set up the queen as a Chinese empress, and prompts a question about the contemporaneous theatre building: in what role did Ulrika Lovisa enter the theatre? As queen regnant, fairy princess, or disciple of the French philosophers? In what sense did she assume a theatrical persona for the act of spectatorship? In what sense did she play-act her emotional responses? If they can be distinguished, what was the relationship between her public and her private selves?

The Royal Spectator

Spectatorship was a mode of performance, and there was a crucial choice to be made: where should the monarch sit in order to perform her royal role? The small theatre which Adelcrantz built for Lovisa Ulrika at Drottningolm in 1754 was laid out on the standard eighteenth-century imperial Habsburg model, exemplified today by the surviving Margravial Opera House in Bayreuth built ten years earlier for Lovisa Ulrika's elder sister, or by Český Krumlov, built in 1765/6, which like Drottningholm has preserved its stage machinery and settings. In Germanic theatres like these, a royal box or loge sat in the middle of encircling balconies to create a bipolar auditorium, the central axis leading in one direction through the proscenium to the vanishing point of the perspectival set, and in the other ending in the person of the monarch, duke or margrave framed by the box, which commanded an optimum, privileged view of the perspective scenery. A year later, Adel-

48. Section and groundplan of the 1754 Drottningholm Theatre.

49. The auditorium of Confidensen, in which the Royal box has been removed.

crantz's theatre was redesigned, with six chairs or thrones placed close to the orchestra pit in the middle of an empty central arena.[5] We have no direct information as to why this radical change was made.

The small Confidencen Theatre, attached to the Palace of Ulriksdal and built a year earlier in 1753, tells the same story. Facing the stage is a huge embrasure intended for a royal box, and the architectural inspiration is thought to have been the court theatre of Laxenburg near Vienna, but in a plan drawn up in 1783, the box has vanished.[6] The perspectival sightlines are centred on the royal box, so there is no aesthetic reason for its removal, and we must look rather to political considerations. Those responsible in recent years for restoring this beautiful theatre have elected not to restore the royal box, presumably judging that there is no way such a box could be used in today's democratic society. Dominated by such a box, a contemporary audience would feel less comfortable in its inhabiting of an 'authentic' period environment. Back in the 1750s, Lovisa Ulrika embarked on theatre building with the assumptions of a Prussian princess, but Sweden (like Britain) was a parliamentary monarchy, and the abortive coup of 1756 failed to reverse this situation. It is likely therefore, that the symbolism of an imperial box was impolitic in 1755, suggesting god-given power of an unacceptable kind. The chairs in front of the stage at Drottningholm created an opportunity for the monarch to present him- or herself informally en *déshabille*, casting of the power and dignity of office.

In terms of the classical tradition, the site of the imperial box once belonged to the goddess in the Theatre of Pompey and was used later by a deified Emperor, while chairs close to the stage recalled the position of senators as first among equals in the Roman Republic. After cautious beginnings in the Teatro Farnese of 1618, the baroque principle of enshrining in theatre architecture the monarch's claims to quasi-divine authority gradually took hold in seventeenth-century Italy.[7] In terms of cultural memory and allusion, Lovisa Ulrika's new arrangement looked to auditoria set up in the court of Louis XIV, whose aesthetic preference was for classical simplicity. This French tradition allowed the king to participate in the masque or dance, and he raised the boundary between audience and play. Although Louis viewed comedies from a royal box in his intimate Salle de Comédie in Versailles, where he needed to sit as far back as possible from the stage in order to have an adequate view of the perspective scenery, in the huge temporary garden auditoria of Versailles, and in his sumptuous Théâtre des Machines in the Tuileries Palace, auditoria with some fifteen or twenty times the capacity of the Salle de Comédie, and likewise in the Salle des Ballets at Versailles, Louis sat in the centre of the auditorium as a focus for the audience's attention.[8] In the Salle de la Comédie at Fontainebleau, used for ballets as well as comedy and tragedy, Louis again sat on a chair in the centre, and there were, unusually, no galleries, though a box was later installed for discreet viewing by his protégée the Duchess of Burgundy.[9] Louis's preferred position on the floor with communication to the stage can be traced back via the Palais-Royal, built by Richelieu in the previous reign, and to standard Renaissance practice which left a large area of floor clear for dancing or combat in front of the throne.[10] The theatre of Drottningholm was built

50. Auditorium of the theatre at Gripsholm.

51. The stage of the theatre at Gripsholm.

to house French actors, Swedish politics were consistently oriented towards a French alliance, French was the language spoken at court, and the environment of Drottningholm echoed Versailles, so there was every reason to substitute this French Golden Age model of spectatorship for the imperial Germanic model.

When Gustav created a tiny theatre in a round turret of Gripsholm Castle, he had to deal with the same issue of sightlines and protocol. The first auditorium at Gripsholm was dominated by a royal box, maximising distance from the stage within a confined space. However, the young Gustav liked to subvert baroque hierarchy by appearing himself as an actor on stage, not just a dancer like Louis XIV, so a surrogate must often have occupied his own official seat. Dissuaded from playing the actor on grounds of decorum, Gustav reworked his auditorium in the style of Renaissance Sabbioneta, probably inspired by a new small theatre built at Versailles in 1772, and responding also to the recent excavation of a theatre at Herculaneum,[11] in an egalitarian classical design soon to be imitated by his political and theatrical rival Catherine the Great at the Hermitage. The king sat in the balcony but there was no architectural marker of his special status. Unlike his mother, Gustav enjoyed the powers of an absolute monarch, and when a public theatre and opera house opened in Stockholm, he insisted on the authority of a royal box setting him apart from the regular boxes of the bourgeoisie, but in the privacy of Drottningholm and Gripsholm his performance of kingship was couched in a more egalitarian idiom.

A wall-painting attributed to Abraham Bosse represents a play performed before Charles de Valois in c.1640, probably on the occasion of his second marriage. The Duke sits on a stool directly in front of the stage, beside his wife, while his son and heir sits behind him, replicating the same sartorial fashion, upright unsupported back, and disciplined posture with the left leg forward, right leg back, attentive but studiously unemotional. A commemorative painting is not a photograph, but it does define an ideal against which deviations and relaxations of protocol could be assessed. When Lovisa Ulrika and Gustav built a French-style court in northern Europe, the physical language which they used to play out their Frenchness, their rank, their emotional restraint or engagement, and their family relationships would have been an integral part of the theatrical encounter.

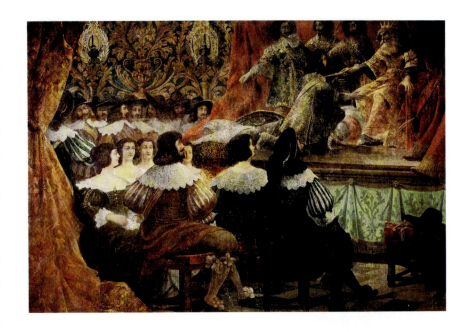

52. Charles de Valois and his family watching a play in 1640.

Gustav dubbed himself 'first citizen' in a speech to parliament upon his accession,[12] but a year later in 1772 he wrested power from the nobility and Estates in a celebrated coup that prompted Voltaire to dub him 'Saviour of a free people', saving his people from oppression by the nobility and a corrupt executive.[13] The baroque scenography of Hedvig Eleonora located her monarchy within a divinely sponsored cosmic scheme, but in the age of Enlightenment the framing of absolute kingship was less easily accomplished. For the young Gustav, the palace of Drottningholm was an extended schoolroom, defining through its books, paintings, numismatic displays and architectural vocabulary the role that he was expected to play in later life as a model king. Was the theatre to be an extension of that schoolroom, or an escape? To address this question, one can turn to a famous volume of letters addressed to the Crown Prince by his governor, Carl Gustav Tessin. Tessin's father and grandfather were the architects of Drottningholm, and his own art collection now decorated the palace, for he had financially overextended himself. He fixed up Lovisa Ulrika's marriage, and remained her fixer thereafter, advising her on her modifications to the palace, and arranging court entertainments. He fell out of favour after fixing up a future

Danish bride for his young charge. Negotiating an appropriate account of kingship was the most challenging aspect of his pedagogic assignment, since he did not share the hardline absolutist views of his patron.[14]

Tessin was happy to draw historical lessons from the paintings in the palace - respect for the peasantry, for example: acknowledging the gift of a people's hearts could be learned from one of Ehrenstrahl's paintings in the reception hall up the great staircase and on the left.[15] But the educational function of drama was less clear. Tessin urged Gustav not to grow up and become a 'theatre-king', a sham ruler manipulated by others because his sensibility had been educated at the expense of his intellect.[16] When Ulrika Eleonora thrilled the seven-year-old Gustav by inviting a troupe of French actors to play at both Ulriksdal and Drottningholm (where a temporary theatre was perhaps set up in the orangery[17]), Tessin was perplexed. As a man of the Enlightenment, he wanted education above all to be useful, and he had no romantic notions about the imagination of a child being special and different from the imagination of an adult. He himself had hitherto organised the queen's programme of entertainments, shows and dances at Drottningholm.[18] Having in mind, perhaps, the close relationship between theatre and dining at the Confidencen Theatre, he was happy to conceive theatre entertainment as 'a desert after a solid repast'. Faced with the arrival of Ulrika Lovisa's French actors, he gave his pupil an outline of the major genres, including the new sentimental bourgeois drama which he dismissed as a passing fad. He held Molière to be the greatest dramatist of the modern age because of his double identity as the 'reviver and author of good comedy', displaying originality in his reworking of a sacrosanct classical

53. Prince Gustav as a child.

tradition, and he doubtless had Shakespeare in mind when lamenting how the English stage was still infected by 'the indecent shifts of bad poets'.

As a committed historian and man of the Enlightenment, Tessin's great objection to heroic French drama was its lack of historical authenticity. Who could imagine the French stage, he asked, as a Roman Senate House? 'What spectator can so far impose upon his reason as to receive the idea of a Roman consul, from an actor in a full-bottomed wig, and a theatrical hoop?' He conceded that public theatre might be acceptable as 'a lounging place for idle folks', and so a 'rational and allowable diversion'. Moreover, he added hopefully, 'for those with sufficient sense to separate good from bad,' the stage might often prove itself 'a school of morality'. In conclusion Tessin did not recommend 'constant' attendance at the theatre, for love of shows was not numbered among the virtues of any of the emperors or kings whose images were displayed in the coin cabinets. He urged the young crown prince to 'follow the example of your ROYAL FATHER in using it with moderation'. In other words, the child should beware of Lovisa Ulrika's infatuation.[19] Tessin's successor, Scheffer, expressed something of the same alarm when he complained of how his ten year old pupil was for ever dressing up in female clothes to play the roles he had memorised.[20]

It is useful to pass from the palace to the Theatre with Tessin's arguments in mind so one can grasp the tension between the two spaces, and recognise the uncertainty characteristic of the mid-eighteenth century about what theatre meant and what it was for: a tool for education, or an escape from the tyranny of usefulness? A symbol of power, offering absolute control over a virtual world? A source of earthly pleasure, contesting the oppressive claims of religion? If the mentality behind the eighteenth-century theatre is an enigma to us today, let us not imagine that the theatre was any less of a puzzle in the 1750s and 1760s.

The Mystery of the Auditorium

In Chapter Two Willmar Sauter described the public tour that leads visitors through the ancillary spaces before they reach the climax of the auditorium. It is only on a private tour that we can go on to visit the 22 actors' dressing rooms, with exquisite vegetal designs on the hand-painted rococo wall-

54. Elisabeth Söderström in the dressing room of the primadonna. Agne Beijer's print exhibition illustrating theatre history was still on the wall.

paper. Sometimes these rooms were inhabited by professional French actors, and sometimes by courtly amateurs aping professional French actors, and later also by Swedish actors. When the professionals were in residence, one wonders in what sense these rooms constituted a private space, and in what sense just another space of performance as courtly spectators visited to conduct formulaic flirtations? When the interest of theatre lay as much in the event as in the play, scrutinising the ethics of the actors was part of the theatrical pleasure. The dichotomy between inner and outer, public and private, was much less sharp in the mid-eighteenth century.

Another privilege offered to visitors on a private tour is to inspect and play with the machinery. There was little new in this Italianate technology, which had long allowed marvels to be performed in masques and operas played before Medicean dukes, Stuart kings at Whitehall, and Louis XIV in his Salle des Machines. The meaning of the machine was changing, however. Formerly, the thaumaturgic magic of stage machinery cast the baroque monarch as a quasi divine worker of miracles, but now the machine was a metaphor and equivalence for the human individual, as set out in a notorious treatise *L'homme machine* (1748) by La Mettrie, a protégé of Lovisa Ulrika's brother Frederick the Great. From a materialist perspective of this kind, it was not the magic of Drottningholm's stage technology but the efficiency of its engineering that reflected glory upon an 'enlightened' royal patron. David Hume, another materialist, argued in 1739 that: 'the mind is a kind of theatre, where several perceptions successively make their appearance; pass, re-pass, glide away, and mingle in an infinite variety of postures and situations. There is probably no *simplicity* in it at any one time, nor *identity* in different [times].' Early baroque theatres created simplicity and identity by setting up a single authoritative viewing point in the auditorium, equivalent to the stable Cartesian ego, but that stable centre was now in question. The human being was now conceived as a more integrated and interactive mechanism. Hume clarified his metaphor by explaining that in pictures formed by the mind, unlike theatre scenery, the spectator has no sense of the actual place and fabric with which images are composed.[21] Stage machinery was losing its magic, and the political rationale for baroque stagecraft was in question. When modern visitors play with the thunder-machine and treat it as mere technology, they fail to hear its historical resonances.

55. Stucco and paint create the illusion of a column.

Entering the auditorium by the middle doors, we perceive around us the decorative vocabulary of the auditorium, and could debate whether 'rococo' or 'baroque' is the better stylistic description. The stucco motifs are all rather traditional, and there is no hint of the fashionable chinoiserie that we saw in the pavilion. The bold cartouches and the consoles supporting the boxes eliminate rectilinearity, subordinating detail to an overall formal coherence in a way that is characteristically baroque. The decorative language looks backwards rather than forwards, presenting the theatre as an appropriate place to perpetuate a performance tradition established by Corneille and Molière. The theatre was already, when first built, a statement about history – in today's jargon, its decorative detail was distinctively 'retro'.

As we enter, our eyes immediately fall upon the two modest red armchairs, which whet the historical imagination. Yet who should we imagine in these chairs? Queen Lovisa Ulrika with her shy husband, lured from the city? Gustav III, with his loyal Danish wife, no fan of the theatre, a wife with whom for many years he refused to have conjugal relations? Or mother and son, united by their passion for theatre and for radical French philosophy, but incompatible in most other respects? There is no shortage of stories that a tour guide with time to spare could weave around these two chairs. However, before our imaginations set to work placing royal posteriors, we should take stock of the boxes on either side: the King's Box on the audience's left and the Queen's Box on their right in accordance with French tradition. On the basis of the medieval theory that the monarch always had two bodies, a natural body and a political body,[22] we might conclude that there was one space at Drottningholm for the King and Queen to display themselves aloft in majesty, and another where they took on carnal form in the private environs of court society. The two boxes nearest the stage have no sight line onto the stage, and could have been used by performers, helping to create a seamless interface between stage and auditorium. A better explanation for the blind boxes lies in multipurpose usage of the theatre. Opera houses often doubled as ballrooms, and in the Residenztheater in Munich, for example, built in 1753, machinery beneath the raked auditorium allowed the floor to be elevated to the level of the stage in order to create a single unified environment.[23] There is no such machinery at Drottningholm, but the Ionic pilasters around the auditorium have pediments

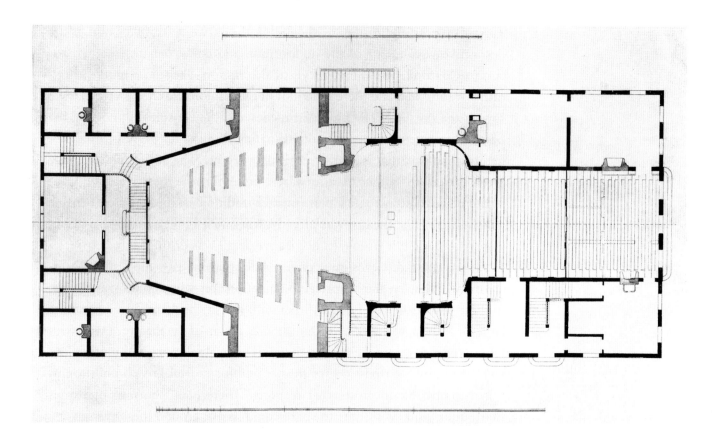

56. Groundplan of the theatre before the Déjeuner–Salon was added.

set at the appropriate height for a temporary transformation. We know that the two royal boxes were redecorated in preparation for a masquerade when Gustav took possession of the theatre in 1778,[24] and they would have served as a retreat for observing the dancing. Gustav was assassinated in the public opera house when it likewise was converted for a masquerade and the king chose to mingle with the crowd.

When we look at Adelcrantz's ground floor plan of 1765, we see that the two royal chairs were not in their present position, contiguous with the front row, but were set closer to the orchestra pit, forward of the axis line which runs through the two lateral doorways. The chairs which today form part of the audience space were in 1765 effectively part of the performance space. This repositioning of the chairs begins to alert us to the exceptional and unprecedented nature of the Drottningholm auditorium. The swelling central oval area, which results in two prominent boxes being functionally redundant though required aesthetically for their symmetry, might remind us of churches of the mid-eighteenth century Austrian and German baroque, like Ottobeuren Abbey or the Karlskirche in Vienna, where oval transepts swell out around the central domed crossing, and the choir balances the nave, leading the eye to a painting on the high altar, a mysterious vista framed by a proscenium comprised of gilded columns, sculptures and sacred objects.[25] The delight in curved forms belongs to a particular historical moment.

Willmar Sauter in Chapter Two described the symmetrical principles of the Drottningholm Theatre, whereby the front of the proscenium is set at the mid-point of the building, and the rake of the stage replicates the rake of the auditorium. Pilasters stretching up the first part of the auditorium mirror the trompe l'oeil columns of the stage set, and a flimsy curtained proscenium offers to screen off the rear, lower status rows of seating. This false proscenium framing the plebeian seats mirrors the real proscenium framing the play, and at the rear of the auditorium three windows resemble the three dooorways on a classical stage façade. The royal pair on their twin chairs, close to the orchestra pit and set apart from the rest of the audience, had the opportunity to turn around and survey their people, who were performing their roles as subjects, ranked according to social status, and perhaps wearing the traditional Swedish costume that Gustav prescribed for his courtiers.[26] The courtly behaviour of the audience was designed to replicate the theatrical performance on stage in an architectural conception that seems to be without parallel. In a letter to the boy prince on studying history, Tessin repeated the old axiom: 'What is man, but a player? and the world but a theatre?'[27] Behind Gustav's seat lay life as theatre, with governance a matter of good stage management; before him lay the stage, supposedly the mirror of life, its mechanics attesting to tradition but in need of adaptation to a new political realities and a new mode of spectatorship.

57. The Royal chairs as they are placed today, with the front benches next to it.

The third surprising feature of the auditorium – surprising in respect of baroque norms but entirely unremarkable to a modern audience – is the lack of a gallery. There is ample French precedent for straight rows of seating behind the monarch, but, Fontainebleau apart, none for a royal theatre without a gallery, and galleries were likewise a standard architectural feature of public theatres, often adapted from tennis courts. At Drottningholm, the royal pair could now weep before a sentimental drama in relative privacy with no one seeing the tears in their eyes. The uniformity of seating pre-empted competition for status and display amongst ambassadors. Most importantly, all eyes were now focused directly on the stage, not triangulated on the monarch whose responses in an Imperial auditorium would condition those of other spectators. Through creating direct sightlines upon the stage, the theatre anticipated the ideals of modernists like Wagner and Antoine, and a cinematic mode of viewing, while inhibiting social encounter. This exceptional theatre was at once retro in its decor, and a harbinger of the future.

If Drottningholm has a typical baroque stage yet is not a typical baroque theatre, perhaps this is because neither Gustav nor his mother were typical baroque monarchs. It is likely that Gustav himself in his late teens was closely involved in the design of the new theatre, as he would later participate in the design of a public opera house.[28] The new frontal design privileged vision. In Copenhagen in 1750 Holberg commented on the recent shift in Danish taste towards visuality so that even 'Molière's *Misanthrope* would scarce gain applause these days since it contains nothing for the eyes'.[29] Voltaire, admired by both mother and son, no doubt did something to inspire the new architecture. In his preface to *Semiramis* (1748), Voltaire lamented the crudeness of narrow rectilinear tennis-court theatres in Paris, far inferior to those found in England, and demanded a monumental theatre architecture suited to new plays like *Semiramis* which, though couched in an operatic idiom, were structured around stage action rather than spectacle. He sought to reconcile the Enlightenment principles of reason and plausibility with a pre-Romantic taste for ghosts and marvels. Lovisa Ulrika's French troupe brought *Semiramis* to the crude and rowdy tennis court theatre in Stockholm in 1759, and we may guess that the play also received a showing at Drottningholm, a theatre better adapted to the author's taste.

The distinctive qualities of Drottningholm owe much to the talent and Parisian training of Carl Fredrik Adelcrantz. Adelcrantz experimented with the principle of longitudinal symmetry in the Confidencen Theatre, where the huge curved frame around the royal box precisely mirrored the slightly larger frame of the proscenium. When the royal box was stripped out from the first Drottningholm theatre, six and later eight rows of straight benches were crammed into the former anteroom behind the box. In the new theatre of 1766 this arrangement was amplified and the banked curve of seats around the royal chairs was removed in order to create a rectilinear front-facing auditorium. The potential harshness of this rectilinearity was mitigated by the decorative elements and the central oval. Adelcrantz's rectilinear auditorium was both an egalitarian and a disciplined space where everyone shared the same point frontal of view, but in its central baroque oval which broke up the rectangle the monarch continued to enjoy a privileged position at the centre of a symbolic universe. Whilst the rectangle defined a demarcation line between stage and auditorium, the oval conjoined subject and object of the spectatorial gaze. It created a position of strength for the performer who stood on the forestage stage, on the perimeter of the oval. In performances at Drottningholm today, spectators conceive themselves as disembodied consciousnesses, hidden in darkness while alert to the fiction played out on the well-lit stage; but in eighteenth-century Drottningholm, stage and auditorium mirrored each other because the real drama played out in the interaction of these two worlds. Adelcrantz found a unique architectural solution to the contradictions of his age.

Gustav III

Gustav's involvement in the design of the second Drottningholm theatre might be inferred from his youthful commitment to theatre-making. A journal entry by one of his companions jotted down in 1766 documents one characteristic instance. The Orangery adjacent to the theatre was used for performances before the theatre opened.

> The Crown Prince who loves theatre passionately required us some while ago to rehearse [Voltaire's] tragedy *The Death of Caesar*. He

took the part of Caesar, Prince Karl that of Brutus... and myself Dolabella. We performed the play in the Orangery. It was well enough done, and in particular the Princes Gustav and Karl played their roles wonderfully. I may be mistaken, but I believe I grasped how the Crown Prince, who by nature loves all sorts of ceremony and the domain of performance *[représentation]*, takes a quite exceptional pleasure in declamation. In plays containing passages commensurate with the rank and character that he plays in everyday life, he may derive benefit from this talent in declamation which requires him to strike an appearance, when one day he finds he must harangue the Estates and communicate with ambassadors – in short when he has to deliver speeches in public. I suppose this is the explanation for his love of declamation, the goal he seeks to achieve. Nevertheless, I am sorely afraid that pride may be playing some part. The pleasure of imagining himself to be Caesar, speaking in haughty outrage to a senator or toadying courtier, and the pleasure of speaking words filled with pomp and ceremony, could pass beyond illusion, causing him to seek one day to make real what now is but play.[30]

The performance of Latin comedies by Terence had been used since the Renaissance as a basis for training in rhetoric and self presentation, but Gustav's apparent identification with Julius Caesar points to something different. Gustav's education had rested on classical role models. Caesar threw out the republican constitution in the name of the people, and imposed his solitary authoritarian rule upon Rome, and Gustav likewise, upon coming to the throne, threw out the quasi-republican constitution that had humiliated his parents, successfully imposing his absolute royal authority. It was on the Ides of March that he scorned rumours of an assassination plot, and he met the fate of Caesar next day. This journal entry testifies to the difficulty of reading Gustav's mind, in a milieu where it is taken for granted that he has to 'play a character' *(personnage qu'il jout)*. Was he a creature of vanity, an exponent of Realpolitik, a fanatical believer in the ideology of monarchy, or some mysterious combination of the three? The difficulty of reading Gustav's mind relates to the difficulty of understanding eighteenth-century acting, to which I shall return in Chapter Seven: was acting based upon the conscious manipulation of bodily signs, or were rhetorical techniques merely the gateway for processes of emotional identification?

In the modern imagination, thanks in part to the influence of Agne Beijer, the personality of Gustav has become intertwined with perceptions of the Drottningholm Theatre, and particularly in Sweden shapes the way the theatre has been understood. For reasons that include the politics of both nation and gender, his mother who founded the theatre has not been mythologised in the same way. The significance of Gustav in Swedish political history was undoubtedly huge. The two-directional Janus-like nature of the space relates to the ambivalence of the actor-king who sat in the seat at the centre. In his passion for theatre, was Gustav fundamentally a monomaniac like Wagner's patron, 'mad' Ludwig of Bavaria? Was he deluded by theatre, like Charles I of England whose passion for court masques supposedly diverted him from looking at the real kingdom he ruled? Or was he, like Louis XIV, a calculating impresario who used theatre and other forms of ceremony to seduce and tame a troublesome nobility? We can look at this theatre with its papier mâché mouldings as an emblem of all that was once false, a place to escape reality, or we can look at it as a political tool. We can look at Gustav as a player of empty charades, or we may conceive that when he declaimed Voltaire's alexandrines in the historicised garb of Caesar, he was able to express true and deep feelings that normally lay concealed. Drottningholm offers a context for addressing these imponderables, and debating whether the theatre auditorium was ultimately a space of ceremony, or the space where the king could most comfortably relax and be himself. The mystery of Gustav's personality is bound up with his sexuality. Was the theatre a space where he escaped an unresolved relationship with his mother, or sublimated his homosexual desires, or was it a space where he could encourage the world to acknowledge that gender is but another mode of social performance? The question of sexuality returns us to the materiality of this building: was it primarily designed to create illusory stage pictures, or to bring human flesh onto the forestage for close contemplation?

The sexual enigma shades into a political enigma, for Gustav was an apostle of tolerance in respect of private life, but an imperialistic warmonger in respect of public life. It was Gustav's tolerance of Jews and Catholics that encouraged Voltaire to praise him as a saviour, and Voltaire was doubtless flattered to know that Gustav learned by heart at the age of eleven his epic poem celebrating Henri IV as a model king and martyr to fanaticism.[31] Voltaire was a libertarian who had no truck with notions of democracy, and Gustav was caught up in these political contradictions of the Enlightenment. We can see the theatre of Drottningholm as a site where political ideologies were constructed, or we may conclude that it only provided an escape into a world of dreams. The cheap and flimsy materials of which the theatre is made offer their own challenge: an exercise in minimalism designed to create beauty, or a drain upon the public purse exemplifying insatiable royal extravagance? The past offers itself to us at Drottningholm not as a set of facts but as a set of questions.

The New Aesthetic of Desprez

We pass from the royal chairs, through the door beneath the King's box, into the Déjeuner-Salon, the foyer built for dancing and feasting, its decoration never completed because of Gustav's premature death. Twenty-five years after the construction of the original theatre, this architectural appendage belongs to another world, and makes it impossible for us to speak of Drottningholm as the product of a single historical moment. The extension turns the building into a palimpsest, and exposes the aesthetic rift that separated Lovisa Ulrika, whose French troupe was sent home by Gustav in 1771, from Gustav's own agenda when he took over the theatre in 1778. More markedly, it separates her rococo ideals from his Hellenizing programme that followed a visit to Italy in 1784. Here Gustav met and employed Louis Jean Desprez, initially as a scene painter, and subsequently as court architect. In Desprez's Déjeuner-Salon we enter a world of light, symbolic of Enlightenment rather than rococo values. Whilst the theatre feels like a highly wrought casket, designed to enclose and include, focused upon the centripetal presence of the monarch, the Déjeuner-Salon looks out upon a landscape, setting up a gap between me here and the object of my vision out there. Looking to the outside world had a correlative in Gustav's determination to take opera to the people, and the court theatre of Drottningholm lost its centrality in Swedish performance culture when Adelcrantz's monumental public Opera House opened in 1782, facing across the water the Royal Palace in the centre of the city.

58. The west facade with Louis-Jean Desprez' original design of the Déjeuner-Salon. To the right, Gustav III:s signature.

The Déjeuner-Salon looks out upon and is viewed from the 'English Park', laid out by Gustav in the English style of Capability Brown. Responding to a new idealisation of the natural world, and to a new conception of human nature as the reality beneath a surface of social forms, the English Park is a comprehensive negation of the baroque ideals expressed by the adjacent formal gardens, but sits comfortably with Desprez's graceful neo-classical structure, a seemingly natural extrusion from undespoiled turf. Scheffer, Tessin's replacement as Gustav's governor, was an enthusiastic physiocrat, teaching his protégé that agriculture and monarchy were cornerstones of a natural order.[32] The inhabitants of an idealised natural landscape surrounding the palace, the local farming community, were regularly invited by Gustav's son to breakfast in the Déjeuner-Salon, and performed their role as contented peasants beneath the gaze of the new king in the gallery above.

Gustav died before Desprez could add the planned interior swags and statuary and the exterior Parthenon-style frieze that would definitively place the foyer as a homage to Greece, and a counterpart to the redesigned theatre at Gripsholm, celebrating values of light, simplicity and verticality. The operas of Gluck, much favoured by Gustav, correlated with this Hellenised architecture, and the popularity of *costumes à la grecque* emerges from the inventory of costumes and properties used at Drottningholm in the summer of 1786. In the last chapter Willmar Sauter contrasted a painting of Orpheus and Euridice in a 1786 performance of Gluck's *Orphée* with another that depicts the same climactic moment in the public tennis court theatre thirteen years earlier [See ill. 41 and 42]. A second painting of this earlier performance also survives.[33] In the earlier paintings the gold decorative border and curved hemline of Orpheus' coat epitomise the rococo ideals of ornament and sinuous line, whilst in the later painting the simple Greek chiton reveals the natural form of the actor's body, and Euridice swaps the fashionable attire of a lady at court for a simple chiffon smock. Willmar Sauter invited us to imagine Gustav's reaction to the second production as performed at Drottningholm in 1786. The body language has been simplified vis-a-vis the earlier performance, consistent with a libretto inspired by a French rather than Italian original, and the setting is likewise simplified; the terrors of hell are communicated by real looking dogs and an owl, not by the patterning of rock formations and other marvels effected by stage machinery.

On the 21st-century stage, we are happy to see actors wearing modern costumes to depict figures from Greek mythology, and it takes an effort of the historical imagination to see how these baroque or rococo images constituted an equally natural way to bridge 'now' to 'then' in the theatre. The aspiration of the new neoclassical attire was to create timelessness and universality, in accordance with Gluck's aim to create a music for all nations. In one sense the Greek costume was timeless, but it also historicised, marking a discontinuity between antiquity and the world of the late eighteenth century. Gluck's Hellenism linked the formalism of classical French dramaturgy to the musicality of Italy, seeking an integration of music and language that was thought to have been characteristic of the Greek world. To join drama to music as a partnership of equals remains a challenge on the Drottningholm stage today. When we debate how modern work sits on this period stage, it is worth reflecting upon how Gluck's opera in 1786, characterised as a modernising piece by its rejection of musical and visual ornament, sat in a theatre marked by the beauty of its ornament as a testimony to the taste of an earlier generation. What was the relationship of old and new? Are attempts to accommodate Drottningholm to a 21st-century aesthetic doing anything inherently different?

Desprez was hired as a painter before he turned architect, and his most important contribution to Drottningholm lay in the new scenery which his Italian training allowed him to create. In lieu of a plastic baroque scenography, the excitement of which lay in its changes and movements, he substituted a painterly imagination, with detailed, carefully researched and evocative backdrops purpose-made for each individual play.[34] He could conjure up the atmosphere of the Hellenic world, the mediaeval world or the seventeenth-century world according to need. Gustav's historical operas, glorifying the exploits of his forebears, benefited from Desprez's stage pictures which persuaded the audience that this is how the past really was. The modern search for authentic historical performance practices has its roots here, in the late eighteenth-century quest for historical authenticity in stage painting, costume and narrative.[35] Whilst the Drottningholm Theatre was designed to create a fluid interchange between stage and auditorium, the new two-dimensional scenography separated the viewing subject from the viewed artistic object. The Déjeuner-Salon is essentially a facade, an imposed frontage concealing another reality behind - not a virile Palladian assertion of Renaissance power, but expressing the timeless value of art.

The Quest for Authenticity

Today, the first impulse of those wanting to authenticate and be authenticated by the historic Drottningholm stage is to look for works that were or could have been performed on this stage, but already they are caught in a contradiction. The theatre was designed on the basis of previous practices, albeit with some hazy vision of a future. Performance of a new Gustavian opera contested those previous practices, whilst performance of a comedy by Molière affirmed the continuity of tradition, and performance of a new comedy by Beaumarchais inserted the audience into the ephemeral present of Parisian fashion. The experience of now will always elude any attempt to seize it. Performances at Drottningholm in the later eighteenth century were constantly negotiating past present and future, and a 21st-century attempt to fix them in a singular historical moment negates the historical experience of witnessing or participating in those performances. To engage with the past through performance needs a more sophisticated model.

To clarify the complications, I will take the example of the musician's wig. (see ill. 66) The wig can function as a standard attribute of eighteenth-century costume drama, and a generic signifier for the eighteenth century at large, or it can be read as a contested historical sign. When in 1752 Baron d'Holbach wanted to undermine academic taste for the musical formalism of Rameau, he described 'elderly gentlemen in respectable wigs, whom long experience and the liveliness of their ears have for the past sixty years entitled to pass judgement unexamined and beyond appeal'.[36] An associate of Rousseau and a champion of the new, more spontaneous Italian music, D'Holbach constructed the wig as a sign of artifice, and no doubt sported his own natural hair covered in white powder. The wig was caught up in the ideological tensions of the moment and it is only looking back that we casually construct it as a universalising sign of eighteenth-centuriness. As worn by a modern violinist or usher in the foyer – or East European ticket tout in Vienna – the wig is part of a strategy to make us comfortable with a stable construct called the past, but actually divides us from the past. It fails to set up a dynamic between our own wigless age and an eighteenth century that progressively shed the wig.

The wig issue is symptomatic of a bigger challenge when we grasp at reconstructing an 'authentic' performance of early opera. The relationship between actors and musicians was not a steady one, but subject to constant negotiation. Lully incarnated the authority of Louis XIV when, in order to maintain absolute control over the tempo of the piece, he beat time audibly with the cane that famously killed him. Rousseau, however, observed that in Italy there seemed no need for anyone to beat time because the soul of the music lay within the performers.[37] Continuing this radical tradition in the context of the French Revolution, Grétry, several of whose operas were performed in Stockholm, argued that perfect accompaniment could only be achieved when the instrumentalists looked at the singers and took the tempo from them, rather than listen for an imposed beat.[38] In Gustav's Royal Opera House, the authoritarian spirit of the Ancien Régime prevailed when the Kapellmeister was required to beat time, albeit with attention to the needs of the actor.[39]

Rousseau in 1768 identified the damage done to opera when Music starts to walk alone and disdain Poetry. 'So the Musician, if he has more art than the Poet, obscures him and causes him to be disregarded. The Actor, seeing the Spectator sacrifice words to Music, in his turn sacrifices gesture and theatrical action before Song and vocal brilliance – which leaves the Play quite forgotten, and turns the Spectacle into what is properly a Concert.' The best music, Rousseau argued, is a music that is unnoticed because the spectator is so caught up in the dramatic situation.[40] The relationship between music and text was historically contingent and subject for negotiation, complicating any attempt to recreate a definitive eighteenth-century style. Today operatic music has become unhitched from language, and the actor is often squeezed between the demands of musicianship and the demands of a directorial mise-en-scène. When we attend performances in modern Drottningholm, it is easy to conclude that the orchestra is accomplished and secure in its technical mastery of early instruments, so the problem to be addressed must lie within the tackiness or stylistic uncertainty of the acting, when what is really at stake is the actor/musician relationship. Finding a plausible eighteenth-century style for the actors is a doomed enterprise, if the modern relations of production are simply taken for granted, relations which delimit the communication that can take place across the footlights. If the actors perform upstage in the glare of strong lighting, then whether or not the musicians wear regulation tuxedos, no amount of imposed gestural style will create a total performance in harmony with the historic space. To interrogate the relationship of actor and musician is a necessary starting point for a historical journey of rediscovery.

The Baroque

I have argued in this chapter for historical specificity and precision rather than generalisation. Historical empathy requires us to intuit the tensions and contradictions, memories and aspirations of particular historical figures, not impose received generalisations. I have placed a question mark after the headline of this chapter and interrogating the overarching label 'baroque' is part of the process of breaking down easy generalisation. Unlike the bland term 'eighteenth-century stage', the phrase 'baroque stage' raises direct questions of aesthetics. The term 'baroque' is counter-intuitive in regard to a theatre of 1766, since most musical and architectural works of reference offer 1750 as the convenient notional cut-off date for the baroque style, and it usefully evokes the retro quality of Adelcrantz's decor which inscribed the theatre within a long French tradition, and the time-honoured mechanisms used to change the scenery. The tenacity of the Parisian Comédie Française and Opéra in reperforming Molière and Lully over more than a century, a cultural practice unparalleled in Germany, Italy and England, reflected nostalgia for the Golden Age of Louis XIV, and a determination to preserve the socio-political structures that he implemented.[41] With its baroque theatre, the Swedish monarchy sought to capture that French legacy.

Coined retrospectively, the term baroque catches a set of striking continuities that joined the sixteenth to the eighteenth centuries, and it helps us focus on the interplay between text and music, architecture and acting. The term was given currency by nineteenth-century German art historians seeking to explain the apparently bizarre interlude between the prestigious Italian Renaissance and a prestigious German neo-classicism,[42] and gave focus to a particular problematic: what happened in the interim to the Graeco-Roman aesthetic principles of plausibility, imitation of nature, and economy of form? The term 'baroque' evokes a playful disruption of classical illusion, and a shaken confidence in the authority of the real, or the straight line of cause and effect. Literary scholars, particularly anglophones, are generally more hesitant than musicians and art historians to speak of the 'baroque', partly because of the challenge to literature as a category. Walter Benjamin explains that in the baroque 'the tension between the spoken word and written word is immeasurable', and it is for this reason that seventeenth-century German drama resists the label 'tragedy'; when written language is polarised against sound, and 'word-baroque' against 'image-baroque', to speak of a purely literary baroque becomes impossible.[43]

The arrival of the baroque coincides with the emergence of opera in early seventeenth-century Italy, a form that mixed elements from different arts and demanded an elaborate scenography from the outset, with the emphasis on fluidity and change. The Teatro Farnese (1618) established the normative U-shaped auditorium used by Adelcrantz in his 1754 theatre, but abandoned in 1766. Giacomo Torelli's technical innovation in the middle of the seventeenth century was the pole-and-chariot system that allowed scenic units to move fluidly up and down, in and out, manipulated by invisible stage-hands.[44] In Italy this technology allowed the rhythm of scene changes to sit comfortably with the rhythm of the drama, while the French tradition preferred scene changes to punctuate the narrative, and a demarcated act structure was interspersed by scenic marvels that echoed the classical *deus ex machina*. The settings devised by Torelli became codified, forming the basis of sets that were preserved at Drottningholm because it was thought they could be endlessly recycled.[45] Adelcrantz relied on this century-old, tried and tested system of staging, which was in turn tied to a system of acting that placed the performer on the forestage in order not to disrupt perspectival illusion. Here the actor/singer enacted a sequence of 'passions', an ideal inherited from classical treatises on rhetoric and respected in the same way by musicians. The arrival of women on stage was a critical baroque innovation, women being considered specialists in the domain of emotion, and allegory became a key idiom for serious drama, bridging Christian and classical sensibilities, and lending a cosmic context to the emotions expressed by the baroque actor.

59. *Orpheus and Euridice* at the Confidensen theatre 2009. From left: Mikael Mengarelli, Love Enström, Karolina Blixt, Sofia Niklasson, Joakim Schuster, Sandra Bundy, Tiia Kokkonen, Bétina Marcolin.

A limitation of the term 'baroque' is its inability to deal with the Italy/France divide critical to the performance of eighteenth-century opera. To refer to the tragedies of Racine as manifestations of the baroque, though admissible in period terms, seems uncomfortable in aesthetic terms. With their strict adherence to Aristotelian

133

principles, their avoidance of spectacle and scene change (with the exception of his last play *Athalie*) in favour of a fixed setting, and their performance in plain rectilinear theatres, it is hard to see how this term helps to characterise Racine's tragedies. Lovisa Ulrika built her theatre to receive a French troupe playing the classic French repertoire, and probably carrying all necessary scenery with them, yet her theatre was equipped for elaborate Italian opera. The French dramaturgical tradition which eschews display is not a happy legacy for today's users of the theatre. I pointed in Chapter Three to the problem that, in order to meet the needs of the modern theatrical consumer, a tightly scripted opera by Calzabigi and Gassmann satirising the baroque extravagance of Italian *opera seria* was nevertheless required to purvey baroque extravagance because that is a sine qua non of the modern Drottningholm product.

Critical to stylistic conceptions of the baroque is the ideal of ornament, and the primacy of the surface, 'Nature to advantage dress'd' in Alexander Pope's formulation. The ornamental idea relates both to the decorative surface of the Drottningholm Theatre, alien but appealing in a modernist era where form is supposed to equate with function, and to the trills and suspensions of singers and instrumentalists for whom the notated score furnished only a template. On a political level, the emphasis on surface related to a perception that absolute royal authority was necessary to ward off anarchy, yet could no longer be defended on intrinsic grounds of government by divine right. The trauma of the Fronde, the Thirty Years War and other wars of religion resulted in what Benjamin called a perpetual fear of 'emergency'.[46] Philosophers from Hobbes and Voltaire to Kant saw little alternative to monarchical authority, which helps to explain the paradox of Gustav seeking to be at once a reincarnation of Louis XIV and a man of the Enlightenment, owning a theatre capable of serving both aspirations. On a spiritual level, the wars of religion did not kill the transcendental impulse and suggest that there were satisfactory materialist answers to all questions, but precise dogmas about divine intervention and the afterlife were suspect, so humankind had to content itself with the surface of reality. Under the Ancien Régime the king was a surrogate but not a representative of divinity, and, as Benjamin put it, sacred myth dissolved into codified allegory. Baroque stagecraft left its audience with a teasing question about the king in his seat of honour facing the stage: was he a worker of miracles, or simply the sole individual capable of pulling the strings that controlled the machinery of state?

The concept of the baroque also relates to a particular sensory apprehension of the biological body – neither evidence of Adam's sin, nor a temple of classical perfection, nor in modern terms a substance organically connected to a spiritual selfhood and part of a unique 'me'. Rather, the surface set before the public was the person.[47] Most baroque theatres placed spectators in galleries where they could make displays to each other of gender and status, beneath fashionable and expensive clothing, make-up, perfume and wigs, with scant attention to personal hygiene. The periwig cultivated by Louis XIV was part of a policy to feminise the nobility, aided by theatre and the culture of the salon, so they would not engage in destructive masculine warfare. Although male attire became more sober, the basic baroque outfit of breeches, coat and wig, displaying a calf suited to dancing, lasted through most of the eighteenth century to be abandoned decisively at the French Revolution. The adorned body was deemed to be a civilized body and until Rousseau there was no sartorial evocation of the natural man. Gustav replicated the cultural policies of Louis XIV because he wanted to replicate his political strategy: to tame the nobility by luring them to a demilitarised court that would serve as a site for harmless diversion and display.[48]

Heritage

The concept of the baroque has a broad-brush value for the historian in portraying a conspectus of traits that differentiate representation in the seventeenth and eighteenth centuries from the representational systems of classicism and modernity. The term has always had connotations of the bizarre and of otherness, and any attempt to recreate baroque performance needs to engage with the question of today's relationship to the baroque. I began this chapter by contextualizing the Drottningholm theatre in the culture and architecture of the palace, and it is important now to investigate how modern performances on this stage sit in the context of the World Heritage site constituted by the whole palace context. I will compare the Drottningholm experience to that of Blenheim Palace, which also boasts a World Heritage logo, in order to explore how notions of heritage shape a modern spectator's experience of a baroque environment.

Louis XIV was once a dominating presence at Blenheim, and a huge captured bust of him still crowns the south facade, surrounded by symbolic spoils of battle, while the architectural layout is a tribute to Versailles.[49] For the modern visitor, the presentation of the complex as a monument to a British victory over the French is effaced, in a modern Britain bashful about its colonial impulses and reluctant to celebrate bloodshed. The tourist's experience is focused rather upon lineage, and the continuity of inheritance that leads not only to the present Duke, but also more marketably to Winston Churchill who was born, who proposed and who was buried here. A virtual eighteenth-century maidservant Grace Ridley mediates the visitor's experience, offering vernacular anecdotes that encourage the visitor to marvel at wealth. The 200 seat theatre built in 1787 in the orangery[50] – a space used today for banquets – is conjured up by Grace Ridley as a familiarisation device that allows the aristocracy to be understood as people 'like us' because they enjoy pleasures 'we' recognise. The State Rooms call scant attention to the faded trompe l'oeil architectural paintings created by Frenchmen, and focus upon portable treasures that have since been accumulated. The narrative of military triumph created by Vanburgh and the first Duke is of less interest than the colourful personality of the first Duchess, and the visitor is absorbed by the subsequent play of personalities within a master narrative of descent. The consequence is to bestow on the visitor a generalised impression of pastness that helps the palace sit as a comfortable and profitable backdrop for craft fairs, medieval jousting and vintage car rallies.

It is neither expected nor desired that modern visitors should be familiar

60. The orangery of the Blenheim palace.

with the historically specific language of architecture. This is partly because country houses prefer to organise the past around biography. But there is also a particular British unease before the baroque, with its continental and catholic associations. A Jacobite succession was still possible when Blenheim was built, and Britain had not yet definitively mapped its course as a protestant offshore island. In contrast to Drottningholm, where the new 'English Park' sat alongside the old baroque gardens, at Blenheim Capability Brown swept away the entire baroque layout, running turf up to the doors in order to reposition the palace as quintessentially English and a natural extrusion from the landscape. British attitudes to the baroque past were not replicated in Sweden, where historical ties to the Hohenzollern and Bourbons were sustained over a long period, and baroque tradition does not as in Britain fly in the face of national identity. A nationally inflected engagement with the baroque has to be borne in mind, particularly by anglophone scholars, when they think about recreating baroque performance. It is hard to imagine in Britain an equivalent to the Spanish celebration of 'baroque' performance constituted by the annual Festival Internacional de Teatro Clásico, focused on the surviving theatre of 1629 at Almagro, and the word 'classical' in English has acquired entirely different connotations. While deep passions are characteristically bound up with the exploration of Elizabethan staging practices, baroque practice is explored clinically, as though a set of codes and rules could explain why this theatre once gripped hearts and minds.

No-one has found it easy to assess what visitors 'get out of' a 'heritage' experience, though the task is perhaps no easier or harder than defining the knowledges and pleasures derived by a theatre audience. Laurajane Smith, in her extensive work on the English country house, records the visitors' experience of 'comfort' and inspired by Bourdieu she identifies a search for the distinction of middle-class identity.[51] Other studies identify an expressed desire to learn, without being able to pinpoint what is learned.[52] Other accounts, perhaps more helpfully, analyse heritage experience in terms of memory within a culture that has lost many opportunities to remember. In *Theatres of Memory*, the British Marxist historian Raphael Samuel sought to revalidate heritage as part of public history rescued from a scholarly elite.[53] A French counterpart, Pierre Nora, described the archival nature of modern memory, and distinguished semiotic *lieux de mémoire*, sites of memory, from the spontaneous and inherited *milieux de mémoire* of earlier generations joined to the past by tradition.[54] When these debates are transposed to the theatre of Drottningholm, we may start to question how and why actors, musicians and spectators seek or need cultural memory. In one of his letters to the boy Gustav on the study of history, Tessin observed that 'A comedian, who is ambitious to shine in his profession, must be well acquainted with the history of the stage: he must inform himself in what manner other actors have played, and by what means they gained applause.'[55] Not all contemporary actors would be comfortable with this proposition. Eugenio Barba described theatre history as his 'magic carpet', his 'El Dorado', while Antoine Vitez wanted his actors to bear witness to past centuries,[56] but these are not orthodox positions. If we think of performances on the Drottningholm stage not as excavations of lost objects but as exercises in the construction and exhibition of theatrical memory, we may have a better means of connecting the otherness of the baroque to the world of today. In terms of Nora's vocabulary, Drottningholm can no longer be a *milieu de mémoire* as it was for Tessin, but it may be used productively as a *lieu de mémoire*.

The heritage experience of today's Palace of Drottningholm invites the visitor to identify an evolving cultural tradition, without offering any clear bridge to modernity, for heritage experience defines itself as the antithesis of modernity. The Blenheim heritage experience, by contrast, is a smorgasbord of marvels not united by any framework of cultural history. The same choice confronts us when we look back to the baroque theatre. Does the periodising actor place him or herself within a tradition that culminates in the present, or is baroque acting conceived as one amid a multiplicity of styles from which the adventurous modern actor can select – capoeira, commedia, Topeng, biomechanics, all circulated globally by leaders of international workshops. Whilst most classical musicians place themselves within a clear line of descent, actors, less securely harnessed to a textual canon, are far more likely to globalise and dehistoricise their art – a cultural difference which today makes a conjuncture of the two disciplines in opera particularly daunting.

Eighteenth-century opera has become a troublesome and contested *lieu de mémoire*, but for that reason all the more interesting. As a committed modernist, Theodor Adorno saw no solution save the modern technology of recording.

> The music of *Figaro* is of truly incomparable quality, but every staging of *Figaro* with powdered ladies and gentlemen, with the page and the white rococo salon, resembles the praline box [with Mozart's iconic portrait on the lid], not to mention the [silver-suited] *Rosenkavalier* and the silver rose. If instead one sweeps away all the costuming and has the participants, copying the practices of contemporary dance, dressed in sweat suits or even timeless outfits, one cannot avoid asking, What's the point? Why even bother doing it on stage? One wants to spare Mozart from this.[57]

The challenge for today's historically oriented performer is to escape the chocolate-box aesthetics of costume drama, along with a dehistoricised Regietheater, and find a way of performing that in some way produces public memory, a performance that is *werktreu* in the sense of recreating the Work afresh rather than simply reproducing it.

The challenge is to connect us in the here-and-now to others in another age, rather than isolate those others behind their footlights and proscenium frame for purposes of objective scrutiny. We need to discover those others, not in their bizarre baroque weirdness nor in their inessential similarity, but in their points of connection. The theatre of Drottningholm is a spur to this task not because it is a fossilised and virginal fragment of the past but because its architecture points us so vividly to a past that was in rapid transition, conjoining value systems that are both familiar and unfamiliar to us: equality and kingship, art and courtly ritual, the scientific gaze and thaumaturgic stagecraft. The meaning and function of the Drottningholm Theatre was and continues to be determined by its users. Agne Beijer's miraculous moment of discovery, when he pulled the dustsheets off the old scenery, appeared to reveal the past as it truly was, but recovering the past 'as it really was', in Ranke's famous phrase, is no longer a philosophical option in a post-positivist age. On the other hand, Adorno's gloomy retreat into the abstract authenticity of the Work is also no longer an option. A new way forward has to be found to construct Drottningholm as a living space that enables us to remember.

Willmar Sauter

6. DROTTNINGHOLM IN THE TWENTIETH CENTURY AND BEYOND

On 3 June 1989, 200 theatre scholars took an hour-long boat trip from the City Hall in Stockholm to Drottningholm. For most of these scholars, who had travelled from over two dozen countries, this was their first visit to Drottningholm, and their first chance to see a live performance there. After the journey, which wove its way through the inland waters of Stockholm, the boat reached the island of Lovön and the jetty near the Royal Palace. The scholars walked quickly to the theatre building and found their seats, in anticipation of seeing a fully-functional baroque theatre with moveable scenery.

Practically every scholar attending the congress of the International Federation for Theatre Research (IFTR/FIRT) was aware of the historical significance of this marvel of a theatre. The performance they were about to see was Stockholm Opera's production of *Soliman II*, a 'drama with song and dance' by the eighteenth-century Swedish poet Johan Gabriel Oxenstierna (or rather a translation of Favart's piece by the same name) with music by Joseph Martin Kraus, one of Gustav's court composers. They expected to watch the changing of the wings before their eyes. They waited until the intermission, but no change of scenery had yet occurred. When the curtain rose again, the scenery had indeed been changed, but not in view of the spectators. There was no further change of scenery during the second act, and many a congress participant would have liked to strangle the director Folke Abenius, who had deprived them of the opportunity to see a real changement à vue in a theatre with functioning baroque machinery.

The desire to see this machinery working seems to have been constant, ever since its installation in 1766. Agne Beijer understood this very well when, in 1922, he presented the re-discovered theatre to celebrities and the press: the divertissement demonstrated the capacity of the theatre in

61. *Orlando Paladino* by Joseph Haydn, Drottningholm 2012. From left: Daniel Ralphson, Ditte Andersen, Pietro Spagnoli, Rikard Söderberg, Tova Svenningsen, Magnus Staveland, Kirsten Blaise.

all its technical aspects. The wish to show what the machinery can do has persisted over the decades: a demonstration of the operation of the moveable scenery seems necessary to do justice to the Drottningholm Theatre. Of course, the divertissements of the early years also contained other aesthetic pleasures and markers of period taste, but the primary goal was to demonstrate the working of the theatre.

During World War II, new ways of using the stage at Drottningholm began to emerge, despite the restrictions that the war years imposed upon Agne Beijer. In 1944, a Swedish translation of Molière's comedy *De löjliga precisiöserna (Les Précieuses ridicules)* received fourteen performances. After the war, co-operation with the Royal Opera intensified and facilitated numerous so-called 'transfers'. For many years, the artists of the Opera staged one pre-nineteenth century work in Drottningholm every summer, thereby transposing their own production style and conventions into the eighteenth-century environment of Drottningholm. These shows included guest performances that came to Sweden during this period, for example a production of *Così fan tutte* by the Vienna State Opera in 1966.

The practice of staging 'transfers' at Drottningholm does not mean that this period lacked creativity. Swedish and international singers and actors showed that performances which stayed close to an acceptable picture of the eighteenth century could still be innovative and speak to the audiences of the time. There were also a few cases in which new works were truly inspired by the practices of the eighteenth century. This 'inspiration' first appeared in the pre-Romantic dances that Mary Skeaping created (or re-created) in the 1960s. She was in charge of the Opera Ballet in Stockholm and co-operated closely with Agne Beijer to find an appropriate dancing style for Drottningholm. A similar approach characterised the 1980s, when the Early Music Movement reached Drottningholm and infused its performance traditions with greater 'playfulness', and the new team of an inspired conductor and a playful director created a cycle of Mozart operas that became legendary in the modern history of Drottningholm.

Certain directors invited to produce operas at Drottningholm explicitly ignored or purposefully resisted the scenic features of the theatre. Fearing that their work would be labelled 're-construction', these directors excelled in 'negation', refusing to embrace a sense of history at Drottningholm. It seems logical that the attitude of 'negation' should eventually have yielded to an approach that sought to 'harmonise' old and modern elements of the performance: music, singing, movement, acting and characterisation, but also the space, stage design, the difficult task of lighting, the placement of the conductor in the orchestra pit, etc. Again, the eighteenth century became a period to learn from, but what was learned had to be applied to the performances of today. More concrete examples of these attitudes will follow later.

Demonstration, transference, inspiration, playfulness, neglect, and harmonisation – I have chosen these labels to describe not particular styles, but rather distinct attitudes towards the aesthetics of the Drottningholm stage; it is a question of approach, the way in which a modern practitioner perceives the functions of this theatre. What should it illustrate, what kind of experiences should it provide for its visitors, what is so very special about this theatre? How can new performances relate to historical aesthetics – if at all?

Demonstration

I described the first divertissement of 1922 in our opening chapter. In this first 'demonstration', four décors were demonstrated:

> The scene changes which were made with the curtain up proved to everyone's general surprise to be both noiseless and quick. The highlight of the demonstration was when the theatre's 'gloire' – the expressive 18th century technical term for the cloud machinery of revelation of the gods and goddesses – slowly and ceremoniously floated down from the fly-loft and enveloped the garlanded pale pink-coloured palace decorations painted by Carlo Bibiena in 1774 with a shimmering golden wave of cloud. In its midst was suspended a special cloud carriage on which were perched two tiny rococo Cupids from the ballet school.[1]

More such divertissements were to follow in the coming years, but this demonstration of the stage mechanics without any accompanying stage ac-

62. In this photograph, taken around 1930, Agne Beijer has hand-painted some of the flies that cover the cloud machinery.

tion was only to be repeated once. What Beijer demonstrated on August 19, 1922 was the pure theatrical toy that the Drottningholm Theatre actually constitutes. In this sense, the stage at Drottningholm is comparable to the cardboard model theatres that one can buy of the Comédie Française, of the Kongelige in Copenhagen and also, on occasion, of the Drottningholm Theatre itself. Of course these models include no machinery, but some simple mechanics allow the builder of the model to also become a player. And in a playful way, Beijer's demonstration of 1922 set up the idea of Drottningholm as a toy box. Seen from a philosophical perspective, Drottningholm was a model theatre, i.e a model of the universe with its heaven, earth and hell; it echoed Greek tragedies with their Olympus and Hades, illuminated the Christian tradition of celestial beauty and tormenting limbo, or simply enhanced an audience's fantasy about what lies above the clouds and beneath the earth. In 1922, these profound thoughts were, for a brief moment, brought to light in their most abstract and, at the same time, their most playful way.

The second performance of this type took place in June 1930 on the occasion of an international congress of museums. This time, the showing of the changements was followed by arias by Händel, Uttini and Bellman. Later in the same month, a play was performed in the open-air theatre in the shrubbery of the French Garden: *Bacchus Deceived*, with a text by Gustav III. This production, with artists from the Opera and from the Royal Dramatic Theatre (both established during the reign of Gustav III), was repeated twice more.

Actors from the Comédie Française, a congress of Nordic architects, an international congress of art history, Swedish producers of vegetarian oils, the 'Autumn Sun' hostel for retired actors – these were just some of the associations and institutions that took advantage of the divertissements at Drottningholm. At this time, the Drottningholm Court Theatre was still primarily a museum. The management of this museum gained some income from the divertissements, and knowledge about this wonderful place gradually spread both nationally and internationally. Related articles were collected in the museum library. For Swedish theatre historians, the list of visiting artists during the 1930s is impressive. A wide range of actors, singers and dancers from the royal theatres contributed monologues, dialogues, arias and ensembles, freshly choreographed minuets and instrumental music from the Gustavian period. The modern programme makers did not, however, follow the Gustavian repertoire blindly. Mozart was among the first composers to be presented on the modern Drottningholm stage and he has stayed there ever since. Another early favourite was Johan Helmich Roman, whose *Drottningholm Music* had been composed for the wedding of Gustav III's mother in 1744. Giovanni Battista Pergolesi and Georg Friedrich Händel were two other composers who soon enjoyed popularity on the modern Drottningholm stage, although they had never been performed there during the Gustavian period.

The programme that was printed on the occasion of a Scandinavian theatre congress, might serve as an example of this period. The Friends of the Drottningholm Theatre had invited the congress participants to a reception in the theatre. The Association of Friends had been established in 1934 with Prince Eugene as chairman and the Friends today are still economic supporters of the activities at the theatre.[2] On 22 May 1937, The Friends invited theatre artists from Scandinavia to the following programme:

Karl Asplund – *Prologue* (read by a star actor from the Royal Dramatic Theatre)

Molière: *Tartuffe* (a single scene using two well-known actors from the same theatre)

Händel – *Bourrée* (violin)

Scarlatti – *Andante* (piano)

Kjellgren – *Poems* (in Swedish, read by the same actor as the Prologue)

Sodi – Le Charlatan

Clémens – *La Bohémienne*

Kexel – *Captain Puff or the Bigmouth* (comedy after de Boysys' *Le Babillard*; with an ensemble of eleven actors and actresses from the Royal Dramatic Theatre)

Mozart – *Ballet divertissement* (played by two leading classical ballet dancers)

Uttini – *Gavotte* (arranged by the 'house choreographer' using eight female dancers)

63. *The Birthday Celebrated in a Fisherman's Hut* by C. M. Bellman, 1936, was one of the first plays performed at the Drottningholm theatre in the modern era. On stage: Sarah Quarnström, Set Svanholm, Gunvor Olsson, Folke Sällström.

This was an unusually rich programme, probably due to the presence of so many associates, whereas other benefactors were content with simpler programmes. The combination of shorter pieces – spoken dramas or mini-operas – with tasters of other composers and poets became a convention of the early divertissements; whenever possible, a piece of ballet would be added, such as the pastoral *The Birthday Celebrated in a Fisherman's Hut* with music by Carl Michael Bellman, which kept its place in the repertoire for a long time.

The purpose of these early divertissements can be described as twofold. On the one hand, the capacity of the stage devices was demonstrated to widening audiences, offering an amazing view of a fully functioning baroque theatre. The technicians had learned to handle the complicated machinery, including the thunder, wind and wave machines. The acoustics had been tested for singing, declamation and the sound of the orchestra. A constant issue for experimentation was the illumination of the stage, a project which continues up until the present day. On the other hand, the divertissements were also a source of income that provided the financial basis for continued measures aimed at making the theatre accessible for artists and audiences. Electricity had to be installed right away in the 1920s, otherwise no activities would have been possible at all. Over the years, water pipes were introduced into the building, two tiny toilets were built in 'invisible' places, and

64. The Drottningholm Court Theatre was, until Beijer died in 1975, a museum in the first place. Pictures, furniture and costumes were among the dominating items that were exhibited in the rooms of the theatre.

147

the dressing rooms had to be equipped at least with mirrors and costume rails. Furthermore, Professor Beijer started to exhibit prints and paintings that illustrated the history of baroque theatre. Eventually, these framed pictures covered most of the walls of the public spaces of the theatre, and visiting students of theatre history had to endure detailed explanations of each one of them. Only after Beijer's death in 1975 was this exhibition relocated from the theatre itself to one of the adjoining pavilions across from the square in front of the main theatre facade.

Transference

Although Sweden was not directly involved in World War II – officially Sweden was neutral in this military and ideological conflict – the country was nevertheless affected in economic and political terms. With the neighbouring countries of Denmark and Norway occupied by Nazi armies, and with Finland at war with the Soviet Union, Sweden struggled to keep its military forces alert and to provide shelter for refugees from all over Europe. Under these conditions, it is amazing that activities at the Drottningholm Theatre continued as usual. Every summer a number of divertissements were offered, and in June 1944 a new approach was adopted. Two private acting schools in Stockholm were invited to produce Molière's *Les Précieuses ridicules* on the stage of the Drottningholm Theatre. Together, the headmasters, teachers and students of these schools produced a complete play which was performed fourteen times during that summer. The last performance on 28 August 1944 was arranged as a special event for the Friends.

In the following year, the Friends celebrated their tenth anniversary with a divertissement entirely devoted to Mozart. The orchestra of the Royal Opera under conductor Herbert Sandberg – a refugee from Germany – was brought to Drottningholm to accompany prominent singers presenting overtures, arias and ensemble scenes from *Figaro*, *Idomeneo* and *Così fan tutte*. This was a first step towards the major collaboration that the Friends would establish with the Royal Opera, and which would dominate the programmes of the Drottningholm Court Theatre during coming decades. Although, for economic reasons, the divertissements continued for many more years, what really counted were these visiting performances from the Opera.

The first major production of a full opera was A. E. M. Gretry's *Martin och Gripon*, an opéra comique composed under the title *Les Deux avares* in 1770. Fifteen performances, sung in Swedish, were given during the summer of 1946, the same year in which Agne Beijer was promoted to full professor at Stockholm University. He had conducted seminars at the university since 1940, and in the first lists of participants may be found the names of many prominent Swedish theatre personalities, including Ingmar Bergman. With the professorship followed a secretary, and permission to examine students: that was basically all that was needed to inaugurate the very first department of Theatre Studies in Scandinavia. In the 1950s, Beijer was actively engaged in the establishment of the International Federation for Theatre Research and for a time he also acted as vice-president of this organisation.[3]

Under these circumstances, it seemed reasonable to appoint an artistic director for the future programming of the Drottningholm Theatre and its operatic activities, and in 1948, Beijer's assistant Gustaf Hilleström took up this post. Distantly related to the eighteenth-century painter Pehr Hilleström, Gustaf Hilleström had an academic background and a great love for opera. He documented his time as artistic director in several books, which were less academic than polemical in character.[4] Since the first try-out of a complete Mozart opera, *Bastien och Bastienne*, in May 1947, had proved to be so successful – with fifteen subscription and six public performances – it was obvious that Hilleström would direct all his energies into the production of eighteenth-century operas. The role of Bastienne was created by a young Elisabeth Söderström, who after many performances as Bastienne and many other roles, celebrated her 50th anniversary at Drottningholm in 1997, by which time she herself had become artistic director of the theatre.

Hilleström opened his first season (1948) with two new opera productions, an opera-comique by A. E. M. Grétry, *Den talande tavlan (Le Tableau parlant)* and an opera buffa by Domenico Cimarosa, *Il matrimonio segreto* (see review in Appendix d). Since both the conductor and the director of the Cimarosa opera were Italians, the production was, exceptionally, sung in Italian. These two works were harbingers of the coming decades: Giovanni Battista Pergolesi, Alessandro and Domenico Scarlatti, Giovanni Paisiello and Domenico Cimarosa, interspersed with the odd Frenchman such as the baroque master André Campra and the more delightful Grétry, became fixtures in the Drottningholm repertoire. They were not necessarily represented by numerous works, but their works were repeated again and again just as in regular opera houses.

65. *Orlando furioso* by G. F. Händel, 1950. On stage Sven Nilsson, Leon Björker, Carl-Axel Hallgren, Lilly Furlin, Eva Prytz.

Next to these names stand three more composers: Georg Friedrich Händel, Christoph Willibald Gluck, and Wolfgang Amadeus Mozart. Händel's *Orlando furioso* had already appeared in 1950, and the staging of his works would continue with *Rodalinda* (1957) and *Ariodante* (1964). Händel, who lived between 1685 and 1759, was considered old-fashioned during Gustavian times, his operas having been composed back in the 1720s and 1730s, but he proved popular with some artistic directors of the Drottningholm

Theatre during the modern period. His *Orlando furioso* was produced again in 1968, but the real success was *Rodelinda* in 1957. Thanks to a visit from the British Queen Elizabeth II in 1956 – more about that later – the Drottningholm Theatre had become better known internationally. The staging of this musically difficult and rarely performed Händel opera in Drottningholm attracted music critics from the Swedish and international press. The Wiener Presse was enthusiastic, and the opera critic of the London Times reported:

> Rodelinda has several advantages at Drottningholm. First, both the music and the drama are more easily and appropriately projected in the intimate baroque auditorium than in the wider spaces of Sadler's Wells. Then there are the original 18th century settings, with their Romantic realism; the graveyard with its temple and Giselle-like tomb, and the ornamental garden with a grove of trees in perspective, making full use of the deep stage, are particularly effective. And the opera is sung in the original Italian, which is undeniably more beautiful than the English version and it helps that the work sounds like the Italian opera it is, and not like the English oratorio it can so easily become.
>
> This effect is also helped at Drottningholm by the energetic, lively tempi set by the conductor, Mr. Lars af Malmborg, by the use of powerful Italian-type operatic voices and, more dubiously perhaps, by dramatic cuts involving the loss of about half the opera's arias. This frankly theatrical and sometimes unorthodox approach provides an unexpectedly enjoyable performance.[5]

If we are to trust the English critic, then this report raises a number of interesting questions. The language question has been much discussed at Drottningholm, as everywhere, since the 1950s. The Royal Opera in Stockholm was still producing most operas in Swedish translation, and only changed to original languages quite late. The artistic director at Drottningholm preferred original language productions, and struggled to change the established conventions. Another issue raised by the review is its praise of Italianate operatic voices, and today, many artists and critics deprecate this type of vocalisation at Drottningholm because the sound is too loud. A third detail that the critic mentions indirectly is the length of opera performances at Drottningholm. Due to the quite uncomfortable benches it is hard for the audience to endure more than three hours at the most. Händel has remained popular at Drottningholm and his *Il pastor fido*, *Ariodante*, and *Serse* were produced in the 1960s and 1970s. Between 2005 and 2007 all new productions were devoted to Händel's work.

However, Gustav III preferred the operas of Christoph Willibald Gluck. As I noted at the end of Chapter Four, his operas were staged early on by the newly established Royal Opera, and became more successful in Stockholm

66. *Orpheus and Euridice* by C.W. Gluck, 1957. Kerstin Meyer as Orpheus, conductor Albert Wolff. The musicians are wearing wigs.

than in Vienna and Paris. Even in the modern period, no fewer than five works by Gluck have been staged at Drottningholm. The first and also the most successful production, launched in the same year as Händel's *Rodalin-*

da, 1957, was *Orfeus och Euridike*. The managing director of the Royal Opera sent his most excellent and internationally successful singers to Drottningholm: Elisabeth Söderström as Euridice, Kerstin Meyer as Orpheus and Busk Margit Jonsson as Eros. In addition, he hired the Gluck specialist Albert Wolff from Paris as conductor. Wolff was responsible for rehearsals and performances of Gluck until 1963 and thus also produced *Iphigenia på Tauris*, *Alkestis* and *Iphigénie en Aulide*. Albert Wolff was an experienced conductor with an international career which had begun in the 1920s. After spending the years of World War II in South America, he returned to Paris and became the director of the Paris Opera, 1945-50. His engagement at Drottningholm, together with the presence of world-class singers from the Opera in Stockholm, brought the Swedish Gluck tradition into high repute. Therefore it seems amazing that only *Orpheus* became successful, with more than 50 performances at Drottningholm between 1957 and 1968, whereas the later productions were only performed between three and fifteen times. For the sake of completeness, I should also mention that Gluck's short comic opera *Kinesiskorna (Le Cinesi)* was staged in 1960, but failed to raise public interest.

The dominant approach to a historical aesthetics in this period might best be labelled 'transference', and this attitude shaped the repertoire. It was the choice of works that distinguished Drottningholm from other opera houses. As long as the costumes roughly fitted a concept of rococo, and the members of the orchestra appeared in period costumes and wigs, the frame was set for Drottningholm. Audiences were enchanted, and critics celebrated the feeling of attending genuine historical performances. Listen, for instance to Glenn M. Loney who had just seen the premiere of Mozart's *Così fan tutte* at Drottningholm in 1962:

> Così fan tutte, staged with duplicates of settings once used in Mozart's own time, is an especially charming experience. The Drottningholm Court Theatre, an almost unique survival of 18th century stage architecture, has been spared war's destruction and time's decay. With a wigged and satin clad orchestra, period scenery and talents of such singers as Elisabeth Söderström, the audience is transported back across two centuries. Miss Söderström's Fiordiligi was a fine combi-

nation of seemingly effortless singing and impishly delightful acting. While the rest of the cast was very good indeed, the orchestra, under Hans Schmidt-Isserstedt, deserves special praise. Not only did these members of the Stockholm Philharmonic wear their costumes with style, they played with real enjoyment of the performance.[6]

Robert Sages from the New York Herald Tribune exclaimed: 'Pure enchantment – an experience never to be forgotten.'[7] For the vast majority of spectators, Mozart's music performed on the baroque stage at Drottningholm was a spectacular and moving experience. Eighteen performances were sold out in the summer of 1962 and the production stayed in the repertoire until 1969 (see Swedish review in Appendix e).

This was actually the second time that *Così fan tutte* had been presented at Drottningholm. In 1956, a radio production was transferred to the stage to celebrate the 200th birthday of Mozart. Ten performances in Swedish ran parallel with Mozart's youthful *La finta semplice*, given in Italian. The 1962 production was considered the 'definitive' version of *Così*, according to artistic director Hilleström. He had managed to engage the Austrian Mozart specialist Hans Schmidt-Isserstedt, who sent his son to conduct the rehearsals, but came in person to the dress rehearsal and to lead the orchestra for at least half of the season. In subsequent years the orchestra was conducted by Ferenc Koltay, who was to reappear many more times in the programme notes of Drottningholm.

A third production of *Così fan tutte* was staged by the East German director Götz Friedrich in 1972. Friedrich was at the time frequently engaged by the Stockholm Opera, where he directed Wagner and Verdi. I remember this version of *Così* only vaguely, but the main impression I retain in my retrospective vision is of a heavy, almost tragic interpretation of Mozart's playful masquerade. Of course one can interpret this opera intellectually as a struggle between the ideas of Voltaire and Rousseau, but that is not what I remember from this occasion.

The frequent choice of *Così fan tutte* for Drottningholm was made for a practical reason, at once economic and artistic: the limited cast. In 1965, the American coloratura soprano Mattiwilda Dobbs and the Finnish base Kim Borg added considerable status and pleasure to the new production, which remained in the repertoire for four years. These were, however, all the works of Mozart performed at Drottningholm before the long cycle of Mozart operas began in 1979.

I have frequently mentioned conductors who were engaged for productions at Drottningholm, either because they were particularly competent with regard to specific composers, or because they stayed over longer periods of time. To the latter category belonged Lamberto Gardelli, who conducted the Italian repertoire of the early years, and Charles Farncombe from Great Britain, who had made a name for himself with the Handel Society. The artistic directors during these years – including Bertil Bokstedt, who succeeded Hilleström and was responsible from 1968 to 1979 – were ambitious with regard to music. However, among the stage directors who took charge at Drottningholm, the names that appear were also on the payroll of the Royal

67. *Orpheus and Euridice* by C.W. Gluck, 1957. The costumes of Kerstin Meyer and Elisabeth Söderström represent classical Greek images.

Opera in Stockholm. These were solid craftsmen, including one woman, but the available documentation distinguishes no particular style or other elements that would qualify their staging as distinctively Drottningholmian.

An interesting comparison of the various Orpheus costumes is provided by the two pictures by Pehr Hilleström – one in the rococo style, the other in the neo-classical 'Empire' fashion (illustrations 41 and 42) – when these are juxtaposed with the costume that Kerstin Meyer wore in 1957. Meyer's long-sleeved tunic is reminiscent of classical Greek theatre costume (in antiquity, actors and musicians wore long sleeves in contrast to the sleeveless tunics of everyday life) and the mantle is heavily draped as if resting on a statue of a Greek goddess. This costume would have seemed normal on any opera stage of the 1950s, and lacked any affinity to the rococo world of Drottningholm. For comparison a photo from the final scene of *Die Entführung aus dem Serail* from 1965 showed the following costumes: Bassa Selim and Osmin appear in fantastical oriental outfits, Belmonte looks like

what might pass for late eighteenth-century dress, Pedrillo wears silk stockings, but a weird waistcoat, Konstanze is seemingly dressed in a rococo crinoline (contradicted by the striped breast piece), and finally Blonde has a skirt that hardly covers her knees. Again, this stylistic mishmash would have sat comfortably on any stage anywhere in the world. The costumes of the Viennese ensemble worn for their guest performance of *Così fan tutte* at Drottningholm in 1966 look very similar to those of the Swedish singers.

The positioning of the singers on stage and their expressive gestures seem more in accordance with the settings than their costumes do. The acting style on the Swedish operatic stage continued to be traditional, essentially following the rules of declamation dominant in the nineteenth century. Opera singers were not yet affected by Stanislavskian realism and psychological ideals. In other words, their manner on stage was closer to eighteenth-century behaviour than that of their counterparts in the dramatic theatre. In order to foreground the performer, opera directors were also careful not to encumber the stage with furniture. The practice of transference allowed for a steady stream of guest performances, and the year 1956 will serve as an example. The production of Pergolesi's *Il maestro di musica* from the previous year was revived, to be followed by a new production of Mozart's *La finta semplice*, and later in the summer his *Così fan tutte* also had its first night. These were the main shows, which would be kept in the repertoire for many years to come. The first guest performance was presented at the end of May by an arts association of Stockholm high schools. Under the leadership of the professional director Arne Lydén, who was a kind of specialist in amateur performances, Molière's comedy-ballet *Monsieur de Pourceaugnac* was presented. The group consisted of 21 members and five children – all huddled on the narrow stage of Drottningholm. In addition, the association's own orchestra played music especially arranged by their own maestro Åke Kullnäs. This production was only presented once. A week later, the group that called itself 'I Classici Italiani' took over the stage of Drottningholm as part of the Stockholm Festival. 'I Classici Italiani' was a group of professional Swedish actors who performed plays in Italian. Their leader was the Italian artist and scholar Giacomo Oreglia, who lived in Stockholm. Originally in charge of the Italian Cultural Institute, he later made his living as a translator and publisher. His book on Commedia dell'arte remains on

68. *Die Entführung aus dem Serail* by W. A. Mozart, 1965.

students' reading lists . His group had been guests at Drottningholm before, and in 1956 they performed Carlo Goldoni's comedy *Gl'Innamorati*, spiced with music by Cimarosa and Scarlatti. Eva Nordenfelt played the harpsichord and altogether the play was performed three times.

In September 1956, Drottningholm was visited by the Piccolo Teatro di Milano, bringing Giorgio Strehler's amazing production of Goldoni's *Il Servitore di due Padroni* with Marcello Moretti as Arlecchino. Strehler had aspired to create an authentic world of Venetian eighteenth-century performance and this is one of those instances where I long to have been there. However, I was lucky enough to see the same production with its famous masks created by Amleto Sartori in 1998, when Stockholm was proclaimed the Cultural Capital of Europe. This later guest performance took place at the National Theatre and Moretti had been replaced, so I can only imagine how the performance looked on the stage of Drottningholm. Harlequin was a popular figure in Gustavian times, so the decision to bring the Piccolo Teatro to Drottningholm was, in its way, quite logical.

During the early years of this period, the Royal Dramatic Theatre (Dramaten) regularly performed at Drottningholm, usually performing plays from the eighteenth century. They did not perform in 1956, but in the following year they presented Jean-François Regnard's *Kärlek och dårskap (Les Folies amoureuses)*, a light comedy directed by a friend of Beijer, Rune Carlsten, who was in charge of all of Dramaten's productions at Drottningholm. Other theatre groups also came to Drottningholm, not the least acting schools such as Louis Jouvet's Athénée from Paris with Molière's *Le Marriage forcé*, and the Danish Skolescene from Copenhagen, bringing their own version of Goldoni's *Il Servitore*.

The 200th Anniversary in 1966

Spoken drama was not explicitly barred from the stage at Drottningholm, but always remained an exception. Guest performances from opera companies were more frequent and more spectacular. This became particularly so during the summer of 1966, when the Drottningholm Court Theatre celebrated its 200th anniversary. The season started early on May 2 with an English company from Covent Garden in London, performing Händel's

Acis and Galatea in a production which had been specially conceived for presentation in Drottningholm (and subsequently in the court theatre of Versailles). The British guests came with four soloists, a chorus of sixteen, two dancers, and the English Chamber Orchestra comprising fourteen musicians – altogether 36 performing artists. The press was enthusiastic: 'A splendid opening for this summer,' 'a captivating, full-sounding Galatea,' 'a Polyphemus storming like a furious volcano,' etc. The director was also praised: 'There is nothing strained in John Copley's theatre of style, he does not seek restoration, but makes us feel much the same way as the audiences did then.'[8]

After four performances, an even grander spectacle took place. An ensemble from the Staatsoper in Vienna came with their version of *Così fan tutte*. The cast list of this production contained all the big names in the opera world of those days: Elisabeth Schwarzkopf, Christa Ludwig, Walter Berry, Waldemar Kmentt, Graziella Sciutti and Karl Dönch. The critics raved, again. Kerstin Linder wrote:

> At times I worried that the floor of Drottningholm's 200-year-old auditorium would break under the stamping feet and the ovations that followed every act of the Vienna ensemble's final performance of Mozart's *Così fan tutte*. But this audience had the privilege to attend a delivery worthy of this delicate and musically complex opera buffa. The Drottningholm theatre has made a bold stab with this guest performance, the second event of this anniversary year. Two packed houses have given an audible demonstration of their gratitude and appreciation.[9]

The third guest production was Gluck's *Iphigénie en Tauride* performed by the Royal Theatre of Copenhagen. This production, together with the revival of Stockholm Opera's own productions of *Orfeus och Euridike* and *Iphigénie en Aulide*, ensured that Gluck was well represented during this jubilee year. The final guests in August 1966 came from the Sommerspiele Herrenhausen in Germany, and their contribution to the festivities was Claudio Monteverdi's *Orfeo ed Euridice*. Monteverdi's 1607 opera had not been performed before at Drottningholm and became a major success. The leader and conductor of the Herrenhausen ensemble, August Wenzinger, had brought an orchestra playing on historical or more precisely on 'historically informed' instruments. A regal and a seventeenth-century organ had to be borrowed from the Music Museum in Stockholm to complete the ensemble. This was the first time that historical instruments had been used at Drottningholm, an approach which would prevail a few decades later.

69. Dancer stretching in one of the corridors of the theatre.

Inspiration

So far, I have not included dance and ballet in this account of the main aesthetic approaches taken by productions at the Drottningholm Court Theatre. The reason now to single out dance from the staging of operas and dramas is Mary Skeaping. It all began in 1956.

Mary Skeaping was a British dancer and choreographer. Beginning in the 1920s she danced with a number of international companies, between 1948 and 1951 she was ballet mistress of Sadler's Wells, and in 1953 she was engaged as the head of the Stockholm Opera Ballet, a position she held until 1962. Her main task in Stockholm was to re-establish the nineteenth-century repertoire of classical ballets, from *Giselle* to *The Sleeping Beauty*. Her interest in historical dances stretched far beyond Romantic choreography, and she had a scholarly interest in baroque dances that coincided with Beijer's passion for this era. They made contact soon after she arrived in Stockholm.

In 1956, Queen Elizabeth II was to travel from the United Kingdom to Sweden on state visit, and part of the programme was to be a gala performance at Drottningholm. What could the theatre show her? As the first part of the evening, Pergolesi's *Il maestro di musica* from the previous year was chosen – naturally, with Elisabeth Söderström as Lauretta. For the second part, Mary Skeaping was approached: could she choreograph a pre-Romantic ballet for her queen? Yes, she could, with the benign assistance of Professor Beijer.

Immediately the search began for a suitable subject. They found a printed version of a court ballet that was performed during the reign of the Swedish Queen Christina, in 1649. The text was written by the Swedish baroque poet Georg Stiernhjelm and entitled *Den fångne Cupido*, in English referred to as *Cupid Out Of His Humour*. This mythological story in a pastoral environment offered good opportunities for the Drottningholm machinery to be used to full effect. The story itself is simple. The goddess Venus is upset about the goddess Diana's refusal to submit to love, so she asks her son, Cupid, to shoot his arrow of desire into Diana's heart. Diana's brother Apollo prevents Cupid from aiming at Diana, takes away his bow and keeps Cupid captive at Diana's court, very much to the distress of Venus. Pallas Athena advises Cupid to accept Diana's state of chastity, and to listen more to reason than to passion. The story concludes with the symbolic reconciliation

70. *Cupido out of His Humor*, ballet by Mary Skeaping with music by H. Purcell, 1966. Among the dancers Catharina Ericson, Viveka Ljung and Aulis Peltonen.

of Diana and Pallas Athena – the union of thought and virginity – arranged by Jupiter, coming down from the heavens.

Considering the fact that Queen Christina, who never married, herself appeared in the role of Diana, this story had not only moral but also political implications: the queen would not be enslaved by a king or by any other man.[10] This aspect of the ballet was, however, not the point for Mary Skeaping, who was interested in the piece's dramatic potential rather than its historical politics. In the archives, she found fragments of dance notation, which gave a picture of how this ballet was executed at the time of Christina, though these were not sufficient for a full reconstruction. Moreo-

71. *Cupido out of His Humor*, ballet by Mary Skeaping 1966.

ver, her choreography was aiming at a late eighteenth-century atmosphere, and not the earlier and heavier baroque style. More research was necessary.

This is exactly the point where I would like to propose the term 'inspiration'. Mary Skeaping's ambition was not to reconstruct a piece of historical choreography – if ever such a thing could be possible – but rather to learn the conventions of the historical period in order to create something representative of the era. This learning process included exploring everything from the notation of movement to treatises about dance, including books by John Weaver and Jean-Georges Noverre.[11] In the archives she also found models for the ballet's costumes, beautiful drawings of antique dresses made for baroque performers. Again, it was not a question of copying these costumes, but of taking this inspiration to two eminent costume designers from the Royal Opera, Brita Broberg and Börje Edh. Together they created extraordinary rococo costumes which not only enchanted the audience of the first night, but were praised long after Mary Skeaping had left Stockholm.

She selected the most prominent and experienced dancers from the Opera Ballet, most of whom had danced on the slippery floor of the Drottningholm stage before. Björn Holmgren created a lively Cupid, dressed in blue with silver wings, Ellen Rasch performed the role of Diana in a red and orange gown, and Else Marie von Rosen – well known as Miss Julie in Birgit Cullberg's famous dance version of Strindberg's play – appeared as Venus. The four continents were danced by male dancers and the stage was filled with nymphs, satyrs, fauns, shepherds and shepherdesses. And then, on 14 June 1956, the stage was set to receive royal personages from all over Europe.

To understand the enormous impact of this performance, taking a peek into the guest list might be helpful.[12] Of course there was the host, the Swedish King Gustav VI Adolf and his wife Louise, sister of Lord Louis Mountbatten – it was in fact the royal couple who had commissioned this performance – and all the princes and princesses of the Swedish court together with their chamberlains and ladies-in-waiting. The principal guest Queen Elizabeth was accompanied by her husband, the Duke of Edinburgh, and by her sister Princess Margaret. The royal families of Norway, Denmark, The Netherlands, and Luxemburg were represented, and also on the list were the Duke of Gloucester, Margarethe of Bourbon, Maximilian of Baden, the Prince and Princess of Hessen und bei Rhein, the Prince Raymond della Torre e Tasse, the Duke of Beaufort and his wife, amongst others. They occupied the front rows of the auditorium, while the rear section was filled with journalists. The visit of Queen Elizabeth was widely reported in the news media all over Europe and North America, and introduced the experience of performance at Drottningholm to a general public as well as to the arts world. Drottningholm had been catapulted to the forefront of historical and political interest.

In his retrospective book about Drottningholm, Gustaf Hilleström maintains that the vast majority of the theatre's audiences were tourists, and cites the presence of 80 – 90% foreign spectators as an argument for performing operas in their original languages.[13] This book was re-published in 1980, the same year in which I conducted my first audience survey at Drottningholm. It seems to me that Hilleström significantly exaggerated the numbers of non-Swedish spectators. In my survey, only 9% of spectators were tourists from other countries, whereas the majority of the audience actually lived in Stockholm.[14] Politically, this raises an interesting issue: The Drottningholm Court Theatre is a cultural asset for the inhabitants of Stockholm, in particular those living in the very centre of the city, while the municipality of Stockholm takes no economic responsibility for the activities of the theatre.

Hilleström describes the period following his retirement in 1968 as a disaster, and his deprecatory account of the 1970s is a polemic. In fact, very little changed in comparison with previous decades. Basically the same repertoire was produced, with the same emphasis upon the attitude of 'transference', with the exception of the innovatory dance performances. Mary Skeaping was lucky to find two successors who shared her interests: Ivo Cramér and Regina Beck-Friis continued to build their choreographies upon historical research, and educated a new generation of dancers to master pre-Romantic movements. Over time, the company of the Opera Ballet developed a unique competence in dancing pre-Romantic ballets, and the classical Romantic repertoire as well as contemporary choreographies.

Playfulness

In 1980, a new constellation of young people took over the leadership of the Drottningholm Theatre. This triumvirate of conductor, director and manager had introduced themselves with a production of Mozart's *Don Giovanni* in the previous summer. The conductor Arnold Östman, who also became artistic director, had developed his interest and skills in Early Music, and in particular the Viennese classics, during his engagement at a small opera house in the North of Sweden, and also as the artistic director of the Vadstena Academy, an experimental summer festival held in the shadow of St. Birgitta's monastery at Lake Vättern. In this latter capacity he had invited Göran Järvefelt to direct a rare opera of the seventeenth century, Francesco Provenzale's *Stellidaura*. Östman had found the score in a library in Italy, and it had never been performed since its first production in 1678. Järvefelt was a young actor who had been engaged at Dramaten since he had left acting school, and for him directing opera had just been a dream. *Stellidaura* in 1974 was his first attempt. He succeeded and continued with *Salome* by Alessandro Stradella the next summer. After directing some Ibsen plays in Stockholm and Stavanger in Norway, he went to Germany to produce Verdi's *Falstaff* in Hagen and *Don Carlos* in Gelsenkirchen. From 1977 to 1979 he was 'Oberspielleiter' in Gelsenkirchen and from that time onwards he directed operas all around the world. The third person in the new leadership trio was Per Forsström who took charge of the administration, advancing to the role of managing director, and staying with the Drottningholm Theatre for the next 30 years.

All regular Drottningholm visitors remember the 1980s as the period during which Östman and Järvefelt produced their long Mozart cycle. The list is impressive. In nine years, eight Mozart operas were presented, but only five of them were actually directed by Järvefelt: *Don Giovanni* (1979), *Le nozze di Figaro* (1981), *Die Zauberflöte* (1982), *La clemenza de Tito* (1987) and *La finta gardiniera* (1988). Between 1984 and 1986, three other directors staged one Mozart opera apiece. Järvefelt's last work for Drottningholm was Gluck's *Iphigénie en Aulide* in 1989, his last production before his untimely death. Although the Royal Opera continued their engagement with Drottningholm during this period with a broad repertoire of operas and ballets, the lasting impression was made by Östman's and Järvefelt's presentations of Mozart.

Retrospectively, one wonders what made these productions so memorable – what was the special nature of their approach? First of all, Östman and Järvefelt were not working on their own. They had established a team of artists that continued to co-operate during this entire period. From Germany, Järvefelt had brought the designer Carl Friedrich Oberle who created the costumes for the entire series. Regina Beck-Friis (who took over Mary

Skeaping's mantle in the 1960s) joined them as choreographer. Finally, the lighting designer Torkel Blomkvist handled the complicated matter of lighting the Drottningholm stage. Together, they achieved a remarkable series of Mozart operas, and since the productions were kept alive through the following decade, and were televised under the careful directorship of Thomas Olofsson, their versions of Mozart became accessible to an unusually large audience.

Östman and Järvefelt presented Mozart's operas as a form of playing, i.e. with a playful attitude. This does not in any way imply a comical or unserious approach; on the contrary, they really took Mozart very seriously, and their playfulness grew out of the theatrical space itself, through their use of the machinery, of the orchestra and the entire visual and acoustic register that Drottningholm offers. Ingmar Bergman's film version of Mozart's *The Magic Flute* from 1975 was set in the Drottningholm Theatre and might have served as inspiration. In addition, Mozart had been popularised by Peter Schaffer's play *Amadeus* in 1979, and Milos Forman's film version added to the worldwide success of the Mozart story. Östman and Järvefelt were rigorous in their approach to the music, but their attitude towards Mozart informed both their working process and the results on stage.

Arnold Östman was influenced by the Early Music Movement, and applied these principles to the Drottningholm orchestra. He found musicians, often very young people, who were interested in playing historical instruments and in learning how to treat these 'old' violins, double basses, horns and clarinets. Old does not mean that these instruments were manufactured in the eighteenth century (like a Stradivarius violin), but rather that they were built according to the same principles as musical instruments from Mozart's time. Different materials were used for strings and bow, the brass of the horn was bent differently, and so forth. Rather than speaking of historical instruments, many specialists prefer to refer to these instruments as 'historically informed'. To play them requires particular skills which have to be learned, but it is not the playing alone which differentiates these instruments from their modern equivalents. The reading and interpretation of the score is also different. This was Östman's special interest, and by going back to the original scores – as far as this is possible – he was able to arrive at his own understanding of the music. With the sound of the historically informed orchestra and his new reading of the music, Östman could circumvent twentieth-century conventions of performance. Liberating himself, the orchestra and the singers from these conventions meant that Östman now could play *with* Mozart's music. His interpretations were innovative and were highly respected and praised by international critics. After his years at Drottningholm, Östman had no problem in getting engagements all over Europe, particularly when it came to interpreting Mozart.

Göran Järvefelt was an actor without any higher education in music. At the Royal Dramatic Theatre he had been lucky enough to act under such directors as Ingmar Bergman and Alf Sjöberg, which gave him insights into the skills of directing. From Sjöberg he learned how to stage panoramic plots, mass scenes and ways of developing the central conflict; in Bergman's work he could see the psychological refinement and emotional expressiveness that would help him render the intimate storylines of many operas. His lack of training in music and opera meant that he was not impeded by the traditional schemata used to stage opera. He kept his attention centred on plot and character in a way that recalls how Gluck struggled to reform the operatic genre more than 200 years previously.

Don Giovanni was Järvefelt's first production at Drottningholm, and also his first encounter with this work. He had, at the time, a very distinct view about who this Don Giovanni, sung by a youthful Håkan Hagegård, had to be:

> I gave the title figure traits from Fellini's Casanova and emphasized his destructive side. I saw him only as negative. Håkan Hagegård became quite repulsive and decadent, with French burred r-sounds. The other characters were all his victims – not in any way responsible for the events that unfolded.[15]

This sounds very serious, as befits an opera which dramatises the last 24 hours of its titular hero's life. *Don Giovanni* remained a problematic opera for Järvefelt, who subsequently restaged this work no fewer than five times. He struggled not only with the hero, but with all of the opera's characters – characters, he also directed in Molière's *Dom Juan* with Peter Stormare in the title role at Drottningholm in 1983.

Despite the seriousness of the plot we can recognize some elements of playfulness on stage from the photographic evidence. Don Giovanni, dressed in light colours and with a rapier at his side, is leaning against one of the wings. He is physically touching the illusionistic house as if it were a concrete building, while Elvira (in the person of Birgit Nordin), looks down on him from the balcony above. We as spectators know very well that a stage flat does not possess an actual balcony, certainly not one on which a performer could stand, but the positioning of the wings creates space for a podium that an actor can use to suggest a window or balcony. No realism is striven for in this scene, but rather a lively interplay between flesh and blood performers and the baroque illusion of the theatrical space. This playful attitude is further emphasised by Erik Saedén's Leporello, who watches the scene from behind the illusionistic corner of a house. Though Håkan Hagegård's tormented face reminds us of the seriousness of the plot, this picture is a good illustration of the playfulness of the staged performance.

In regard to his production of *Figaro*, Järvefelt explained the importance of doors to the plot of the comedy, listing: 'the door to the duchess' apartment, the door to the duke's bedroom, the door to the lavatory, the door to the wardrobe and a door to the pavilion. All the doors with their keys! A very important prop in the comedy.'[16] The music is described in the following way:

> Arnold Östman's reading for the Drottningholm performance was free from conventionality and was based upon the original score. The orchestra played on period instruments, which made the music sound the way Mozart heard it: vibrant, rapidly pulsating and hot. In Houston, Christoph Eschenbach emphasized the soulfulness and metaphysicality of the music.[17]

72. *Don Giovanni* by W. A. Mozart, 1979. Håkan Hagegård, Birgit Nordin and Erik Saedén.

The many doors of the set and the hot, pulsating beat of the orchestra help us imagine the tempo and playing of the performance. With the youthful, agile and quick-tongued Michael Samuelson as Figaro, the production became a major success for Drottningholm, with revivals in the years that followed.

The team continued their close co-operation in such contrasting works as Mozart's mature and sombre opera seria *La clemenza de Tito* and his youthful and light-hearted *La finta gardiniera*. The quality of playfulness persisted in their work throughout their partnership and can be studied in the documentaries made for Swedish television. Thomas Olofsson was careful to document the performances as performances at Drottningholm, including the audiences and their reactions. From these recordings, as well as from my own memory, the playfulness of these productions is easily recalled, and the delight spectators experienced became memories. Probably for this reason, those of us who were there remember the Östman-Järvefelt productions as the dominant events of the 1980s, despite the appearance of numerous productions from the Opera, continued guest performances, occasional dramatic performances and new ballets. Göran Järvefelt's death was a blow for Drottningholm (as well as for the opera world in general)

73. *The Garden* by Jonas Forssell, 1999. Loa Falkman and Ulf Montan.

and, a few years later, Arnold Östman left the theatre. After some transitional years with Elisabeth Söderström as artistic director – celebrating her 50th Drottningholm anniversary in 1997 – a new director, and new attitudes, took over the baroque theatre.

Neglect

In 1997 Per Erik Öhrn, an opera singer and stage director, became the new artistic director at Drottningholm. He had a similar background to Arnold Östman: the Vadstena Academy, the opera in Umeå in the North of Sweden, as well as numerous engagements as actor, singer and director, including performances at Drottningholm. One of his first undertakings was to commission new operas for the Drottningholm stage – something that that had not happened since the days of Gustav III. One of the new operas, Reine Jönsson's *Cecilia och apkungen* (*Cecilia and the Ape King*, 2004) was produced by the Royal Opera. The other was composed by Jonas Forssell and called *Trädgården* (*The Garden*, 1999) – an appropriate name for an opera about the botanist Carl von Linné.

The composer Jonas Forssell thought that the delicate task of writing music for an orchestra playing on period instruments was not so different from composing for a regular theatre.[18] Since practically all contemporary operas are commissioned, there are always restraints to be kept in mind: how many singers can be cast, the size of the orchestra, how many changes of the scenery are possible, etc. Each commission has its parameters and this was also the case in Drottningholm.

The initiative was taken by the stage director Åsa Meldahl and the theme of the opera was settled at an early stage: *The Garden*, a novel by the Swedish author Magnus Florin about the eighteenth-century Swedish scientist Carl von Linné, better known as Linnaeus. Although his expertise played no part in creating the beautiful gardens of Drottningholm, Linné would now appear in a theatre that he probably never attended during his life time. The libretto had to fit the theatre. Many changes of scenery when needed, the thunder machine had to have an opportunity to roll its stones, some scene on the high seas should be represented through use of the wave machine, and so forth. The theatre functioned like a toy box at this stage of the creative process. Still, there was music to be composed.

The conditions were clear: The Drottningholm Orchestra has around 20 musicians, though the number can be expanded to 28, which is the limit of the orchestra pit. The musicians play historical instruments, with all their assets and limitations. Although Jonas Forssell did not know who would be singing the various parts, he knew very well how voices sound inside this theatre. Last but not least, he also knew that three and a half hours on the hard benches of the auditorium are too much – performances should not last much over two hours.

Though the composition reflects today's musical ideas, Forssell refrained from any extreme manifestation of modernism. The theme, the theatre and the ensemble invited him to look back to the use of operatic music in the eighteenth century. Since Linné lived from 1707 until 1787, and was thus well embedded in the culture of the eighteenth century, Forssell interwove the tonal language of that century into a score from the late twentieth. The music was intended to sound modern, but the score transmitted the flavour of the place in which it was performed. The result could be described as a kind of musical historicity, i.e. music rooted in the present but inspired by and adjusted to the musical idiom of the past: an aesthetic palimpsest, in which inspiration from, and references to, the period of Gustav were allowed to blossom on his own stage.

Although this opera was very successful in 1999, the production was not kept in the repertoire, primarily for economic reasons. The cost of producing an opera at Drottningholm had increased, as it had for all theatres. One condition remained decisive for this particular house: each individual performance costs more than the total income from a full house. Between 1993 and 2008 the subsidies from the government were not adjusted for inflation, which meant that the level of subvention diminished from year to year. The wage bill for all personnel in the orchestra pit, on stage and behind the scenes is relatively high due to the large number of people needed, while ticket prices have been kept relatively low to make the theatre accessible to all segments of society. Tourists regularly tell me that the prices for tickets at Drottningholm are ridiculously low, in comparison with what they have paid at festivals such as Glyndebourne, Salzburg or Bayreuth. This pricing reflects Swedish cultural politics, but since the state insufficiently compensates the theatre for each performance, Drottningholm has been struggling to maintain continued productions.

Per Erik Öhrn was a director himself (and even became a professor of opera direction at the University College of Opera in Gothenburg), but he rarely directed any operas at Drottningholm while he was the theatre's artistic director. Instead, he engaged directors from Sweden and abroad, directors who had no relationship with Drottningholm. The results were disastrous.

The directors who staged operas at Drottningholm during this period on the whole seemed to have neither the knowledge nor the ambition to accomplish anything that could even faintly be described as a sense of historicity in stage aesthetics. This was the dominant tendency, although there were some exceptions. There is no lack of information concerning historical performers, their movements, gestures, make-up and facial expressions, their physical placing on stage, their projection of sound into the auditorium, and so forth. Yet this historical information about stage action was largely ignored by opera directors at Drottningholm during this period.

The spectator at the Drottningholm Theatre witnessed, instead, singers who appeared from the rear of the stage, distorting the proportions of the perspective set. At times, the lack of proportion between the moving figure and the wings of the set looked awkward, on other occasions it become grotesque. While a singer might appear to be one third of the size of a column at the front of the stage, that same singer was simultaneously two thirds of the size of the column painted on the last pair of wings. Such staging not only disturbed our view of the perspective on stage, but also had a negative effect upon vocal delivery, because the voice is weakened and 'swallowed' by the wings, and it is difficult to address the voice towards the audience

74. Two singers sitting on the floor – a popular position for modern directors and completely impossible in the eighteenth century. Vivianne Holmberg and Peter Mattei in concert 2013

75. *Il matrimonio segreto* by D. Cimarosa, 2013. Solid doors were placed on the floor and the flat wings turned backwards – a dubious entertainment for visitors to a historical theatre. On stage Frida Josefine Östberg, Anna Hybiner, Jens Persson.

from any point behind the third pair of wings. When performers sing upstage they are barely audible in the first row of seats, and it is amazing that directors are either unaware of this feature, or choose to ignore it.

Other strange things have happened on the stage of Drottningholm in recent years. One inventive director had the wings turned back-to-front, showing the unpainted canvases; new stage objects were constructed to fill empty space; tables and chairs were placed onstage alongside the painted furniture of the wings. The costumes were made of non-reflective textiles, which necessitated brighter lighting on stage. Frequently, stage directors at Drottningholm have let singers crawl upon the floor as soon as their character expressed exalted emotions. It is a principle of the Baroque stage that an actor should never touch the floor with more than a single knee in order to maintain the proportions of the setting and the social decorum of the characters. Although the rhetorical rules of the eighteenth century were formalised, they can still be imbued with life. To break these rules is to deny the historical aesthetics of the stage.

A reversed set of wings or a table on stage could be acceptable, if there were a genuine need to transcend the expressive limitations of the baroque stage, but this has rarely been the case, nor has it been a case of post-modernity seeking to construct a specifically anti-baroque attitude. Rather it seems that stage directors today have a limited range of devices at their disposal, and they appear, moreover, either unwilling or unable to engage with the historicity of eighteenth-century aesthetics.

Stage directors have often insisted on their wish to avoid 'reconstruction', which they consider to be of merely academic interest. This is obviously a misunderstanding of 'reconstruction', as well as 'academic interest'. As most people recognise, there is not even a theoretical possibility of actually reconstructing historical performances, either on stage or on paper. So what have directors been afraid of? Their own limitations?

It is possible to elaborate a very elegant directorial concept, as was convincingly demonstrated in the 2008 production of Josef Hayden's *Life on the Moon*. At one moment in the fantastic plot of that opera, two daughters are locked into their father's garden. Lamenting their ill fate, they sing a duet, which ultimately leads to a high coloratura aria. While they are singing, the director had them play badminton on stage. Badminton or 'feather ball' was a popular sport during the eighteenth century, and fitted the two girls' situation well. Their playing was perfectly co-ordinated with their singing – for every high note, the ball flew higher and higher, and the audience was stunned by that vision before it rewarded the actors/singers with roaring applause. In other words: there are ways of using historical elements to entertain today's audiences, but this requires a combination of imagination and historical knowledge.

Another well-received example of a stage production that succeeded by applying eighteenth-century aesthetics to blocking and movement came, ironically enough, in a guest performance at Drottningholm. Georg Friedrich Händel's *Orlando* was originally produced for the Internationale Händel-Festspiele Göttingen in Germany, and was only performed three times at Drottningholm in August 2009. Nevertheless, the production seemed to have been directed with the Swedish court theatre in mind. Not only were the flats in full use, incorporating changements à vue, but the movements of the singers were in harmony with the aesthetics of the eighteenth century. The director and choreographer Catherine Turcoy had made sure that the singers could express their characters' strong emotions while standing upright, and at most they went down on their knees. Even when Dorinda fainted, she only reached a decorative sitting position on the boards of the stage. This part was executed by the Swedish specialist in early opera, Susanne Rydén. Obviously this artist was very well able to express herself while leaning towards a historical aesthetics, and avoiding anachronistic movements. The conductor positioned himself to the right of the orchestra space, as was customary during the Gustavian period, thus avoiding showing his back to the audience, although the chair of the king happened to be empty during this performance.

One might wonder why stage direction should be excluded from a historical aesthetics. Since audiences can obviously listen to early opera music, executed on instruments built in accordance with historical practices, and can view a stage design which retains the flats of the baroque stage, these same audiences do not need to be entertained by modern acting tricks such as rolling on the stage floor or turning the performer's back to the auditorium. If such staging were acceptable, then the music might as well be played on synthesisers instead of historical instruments.

The audiences at Drottningholm are, in the main, fascinated by the theatre's overall environment and atmosphere. They certainly appreciate productions inspired by the historicity of the theatre's aesthetic framing. Not all spectators are historically knowledgeable, but this does not imply that they are not capable of appreciating historically informed performances. Stage directors need to reach the same degree of education and practice already achieved by musicians and dancers. But this requires a continuity of experience on the stage of Drottningholm which has not yet been available to either directors or singers. Drottningholm in truth needs an ensemble of performing artists capable of reflecting upon their source material in order to create a playful appropriation of the rococo sense of the stage, of the repertoire, of music and of stage action.

Harmony

It is, of course, very difficult to maintain a scholarly attitude towards events and tendencies in one's own environment. Agne Beijer believed that research can only be carried out in regard to the history of theatre, and not its present. For twenty years he wrote theatre reviews for a newspaper, but

76. Maria Sanner's Jason attacks the 'bull' in Cavallis *Il Giasone* 2012, performed by Joseph MacRae Ballantyne on stilts.

to incorporate the repertoire of his own time into his scholarship would have been unthinkable. We might think differently about performance analysis today, but the difficulty of relating to the immediate present remains. When I speak of the next artistic director Mark Tatlow, the reader should be aware that at the time of writing, in 2014, he has just finished his term of office and I can at least use the past tense.

Mark Tatlow has a long history with the Drottningholm Court Theatre. He worked there as a repetiteur under Arnold Östman in the 1980s, and he conducted numerous operas during Per Erik Öhrn's time, before he himself became artistic director in 2007. Tatlow is devoted to Early Music and in particular to early opera, and as far as musical development is concerned, he has been a true trustee of the tradition that began with Östman. He has patiently worked to raise the artistic level of the orchestra, and as a professor at the University College of Opera in Stockholm, he has also had the opportunity to foster a younger generation of baroque singers.

During his first three years, he devoted his main efforts to Monteverdi. Then, in 2010, Mozart's *Don Giovanni* once again appeared on the stage of Drottningholm, the title role performed by Loa Falkman, a singer who first earned international fame as José in Peter Brook's production of *Car-*

men in the 1980s. This *Don Giovanni* was revived in 2011. Parallel to these productions, every spring students from the University College of Opera in Stockholm presented an opera production. Under the guidance of Tatlow, these young singers have performed in operas by Händel, Hayden, Mozart and Cavalli, operas selected according to the availability of certain voices and talents. This cooperation with the College was made economically possible thanks to a considerable contribution from the Friends of the Drottningholm Court Theatre.

For all these productions, Tatlow worked out painstaking musical schemes to recreate a historical sound in today's Drottningholm Theatre. But for the staging of these works, he retained the same directors who had been engaged by the former management. There was an often irritating gap between what one heard from the orchestra pit and what one saw on stage. David Wiles describes his impressions of one of these performances in Chapter Three, and I very much shared his view. Although audiences seemed to appreciate this production, Mark Tatlow – now responsible for the entire production, and not just the musical part of it – started to look for alternative ideas with regard to stage direction.

Although the Drottningholm Court Theatre is a well preserved physical structure, this does not imply that a visitor can step directly back into history. Even this solid construction of stone, wood, plaster and canvas cannot provide more than a glimpse of the past. We can observe how the style of classical rococo is present in all its major features, and the aesthetic of the late eighteenth-century is immediately recognisable. All restorations and the addition of supporting facilities have been carried out with the utmost care so as not to disturb the overall feel of the building. What the visitor encounters in the Drottningholm Theatre might be called the historicity of eighteenth-century architectural and theatrical aesthetics. Historicity is helpfully conceived by Frederic Jameson as a relationship with the past, not a thing or material object but a split between past and present. He explores the difference, or gap, between historical phenomena and our understanding of them.[19] What seems important in the context of Drottningholm is precisely the relationship between the past function of a rococo aesthetics, and the way in which we respond emotionally to that aesthetic today. We should regard the eighteenth-century theatre building as the architectural

77. *La clemenza di Tito* by W. A. Mozart, 2013. The Roman theme of the opera inspired a mixture of costume styles. On stage: Annemarie Kremer, Markus Schwartz, Luciana Mancini.

home for a certain type of modern theatre, providing the environment and technology for experiencing performances set in the baroque/rococo period. It is an absolute proviso of our democratic age that the theatre should be accessible to all social classes, provided the visitor is prepared to pay for a ticket.

Historicity should not be confused with the historiographic approach normally known as 'historicism'. Historicism implies that the practices and ideas of the late eighteenth century should be copied in today's productions. This historicist concept of reconstruction would, at best, result in a mechanical reproduction of past styles, whereas the concept of the historicity of aesthetics invites us to understand historical forms as modes of communication which can be made use of in today's artistic creativity.

Historicity as a theoretical principle stresses how we can only observe from today's position, and focuses on the relationship between our now and our then. The German philosopher Hans-Georg Gadamer speaks of a 'melting together' between two horizons: the horizon of the present, within which the scholar and the artist is enclosed, reaches out to touch the horizon of the past that cannot be fully recovered. In our historical con-

78. *Orlando paladino* by J. Haydn, 2012. Magnus Staveland and Kirsten Blaise in the foreground.

sciousness, the traditions and strategies of the past mingle with our own life experiences, but unless we attempt to understand material historical conditions and their significance for a historical period, our interpretations remain speculative and are doomed to miss the sense of historical objects or events. In Gadamer's view, we cannot fully appreciate a historical text in the way its contemporaries did, but we can enlarge and deepen our own understanding through knowledge and study of the past.[20] Gadamer's metaphor of the two horizons provides a model for the creative encounter with, and the contemporary perceptions of, an aesthetics of the past.

The harmonisation of all parts of an opera performance within the framework of a historicity of space requires directors interested in such an approach and prepared to experiment in accordance with it. Mark Tatlow found these directors: Sigrid T'Hooft from Belgium and Deda Cristina Colonna from Italy. Like Catherine Turcoy, who had directed the Göttingen *Orlando*, both of these directors came from the field of dance, with a particular interest in pre-Romantic dancing. Gesture and positioning are of course central to dancers, and the question had to be asked: to what extent can an eighteenth-century gestural language be imparted to modern singers. Sigrid T'Hooft directed *Così fan tutte* with students from the College of Opera in 2011, and Hayden's *Orlando paladino* with a professional cast in 2012. Deda Cristina Colonna took charge of the College students in 2012 and produced Francesco Cavalli's 1649 opera *Il Giasone*. This was a coherent project, and several critics gratefully appreciated the difference. Karin Helander, for example, observed the new style in *Così fan tutte*:

> Most striking is the gestural style of acting. The music provides continuous impulses for elastic undulating movements of the arms, fluttering hands and pliable fingers. The gestures are coded and carry significance, but are more dance-like than illustrative. Props such as waving handkerchiefs, trembling fans, spinning parasols and swaying flowers prolong the movements. Facial expressions and grouping recall eighteenth-century dance, and a rhythm or musical phrase is accentuated by combinations of steps. There is a playfulness in the fine exaggerations and subtle accentuations. The decor is balanced and harmonious. The movement sequences are not easy to master and the singers have differing levels of attainment, but overall the ensemble creates an impression of coherence. [21]

The headline over a review of *Orlando paladino* proclaimed that this was 'the best production for many years' and the critics went on to say about the director T'Hooft:

> As a specialist of the period she let gestures dominate, but only in order to let the physical action flow unimpeded just like the playing of the orchestra. That one of the backdrops threatened to get stuck half way down merely added to the charm of the performance. "Orlando paladino" was not a sensation but nevertheless it was one of Drottningholm's most consistent and accomplished productions for many years.[22]

Mark Tatlow also arranged a series of seminars and workshops with students, international scholars and interested members of the public. The ambition is to cover new ground, to experiment in order to see what the harmonious integration of elements in these opera performances can add to our understanding of the beloved classics, alongside the lost treasures of early opera. In my view, these most recent productions have changed the spectators' experience at Drottningholm. Although many share this view, not everybody has appreciated this new style on the stage of the court theatre. We will return to the recent performances of *Così fan tutte* and *Il Giasone* in the chapters that follow.

The year 2013 concluded Mark Tatlow's period as artistic director. What will be offered by the next artistic director? At the time of writing, we only know that there are many different ways to use the theatre at Drottningholm. In 2016, the theatre's 250th anniversary will be celebrated, and for this occasion, the Friends are already collecting donations in order to commission a new opera. What else will be produced, and who will be invited to work within the building, we do not yet know. Drottningholm is a history book whose pages remain open.

David Wiles

7. EIGHTEENTH-CENTURY ACTING: THE SEARCH FOR AUTHENTICITY

My second visit to Drottningholm led me, by way of the palace and the empty theatre, to a performance of Mozart's *Così fan tutte* (1790). The performance was given by students at the University College of Opera, with stage direction by a Belgian specialist in baroque gesture, Sigrid T'Hooft. In the programme, T'Hooft set out her paradoxical aim of 'trying *not to stage*' – creating a gestural language that would seem natural rather than stagey in relation to the music. She noted that: 'For more than 200 years, a consistent set of rules and traditions allowed singers, irrespective of nationality, to perform harmoniously together without a stage director, be it in Milan, Paris, London… or Drottningholm.' Miscellaneous acting manuals, preserved buildings, costume designs, prompt books, etc. make it possible for us, she maintained, to restore more or less accurate stage directions. Alluding to productions like Arnold Östman's televised *Così fan tutte*, performed at Drottningholm in 1984 in period costume,[1] she lamented that 'although modern singers may wear the costume of the time, they rarely adopt the acting style and gestures that belong to the period of historical dress'. Instead, this style involved actors

79. *Così fan tutte* by W. A. Mozart, 2011. From left: Frida Jansson, Katja Zhylevich, Sara Widén.

constantly gesticulating as if their hands were a second voice, turning their faces to the public rather than to their partners on stage, avoiding showing their backs to the audience, not leaning against the sets or lying on the floor, *painting* their passions with face and eyes rather than *becoming* them… That's why, for me, the libretto is my first and most important motivator in staging *Così fan tutte*. The *dramma giocoso* must move across the orchestra pit, the play must captivate the audience not only through singing and music, but through good acting.

In a workshop given to the actors the previous December, she elaborated on this philosophy, speaking of 'historically informed performance' rather than 'authenticity', and arguing that acting was an inherent part of the artistic Work. In symbiosis with the music, baroque acting could charm the audience and allow them to be 'transported into another world which lifts them sometimes into corners of emotional impact that they were not aware of [as] possible with that music.' She sought a baroque means of directing character that would help the young actors comport themselves, knowing what to do with their eyes and hands, while the musicians would feel more involved in the performance as a whole. It was her contention that audiences were often 'emotionalised' by baroque gestural language while critics lacked the tools to evaluate what they were experiencing.[2]

Così fan tutte – A 'Historically Informed' Production

In these student actors, despite T'Hooft's best efforts, a sense of mechanical technique remained, and the impulse to close my eyes in order to focus upon the music, which is to say the drama, was again often hard to resist. T'Hooft had concentrated her directorial efforts upon the language of gesture. A palpable advantage of working with students is their malleability, since the young are less constrained by old habits, but at the same time these students had not had time in their careers to inhabit and feel comfortable with baroque gesture, nor had they acquired the discipline to hold onto instruction rigorously.[3] In judging this project, it is worth bearing in mind Henry Siddons's words of caution when following a German manual of 1785 that set out a system of classical acting:

> You tell me, that everything which is executed by *prescribed rules* will be *formal*, *stiff*, *embarrassed*, and *precise*. You will please to observe how I endeavour to answer this objection. While the rule is perpetually present to the mind of the scholar, he will, perhaps, be awkward and confused in all his gestures, and the fear of making constant mistakes will render him more constrained and irresolute than if he were to give way to his habitual actions. I will grant you thus much with great willingness, but you will in return allow *me* one grand and gen-

eral position, viz. that use is a second nature. A man when he first learns to *dance*, moves with the solemnity which approaches the ridiculous; but this solemnity in time wears off, and his step becomes not only more majestic, but more sure, more free, and more unembarrassed than his who has never practised that accomplishment.[4]

In T'Hooft's own metaphor, rules are like a corset; surrendering to restriction results in an ability to express emotion more freely.[5] Despite obvious limitations, her experiment seemed valuable in the questions that it opened up: can the obvious limitations we observed be attributed to the actors' inexperience, relatively short training period and lack of rehearsal access to the theatre? could creative freedom potentially and in the longer term be created within the discipline of this form, as in the extreme cases of Noh theatre or classical ballet for example? or were the limitations of the production an inevitable consequence of the premise that lay behind the exercise?

80. *Così fan tutte* by W. A. Mozart, 2011. On stage: Joel Anmo, Sara Widén, Staffan Liljas, Katja Zhylevich, Luthando Qave.

The work on gesture was productive in a crude sense in that it helped the actors to stand with presence, fill their lungs and sing out towards the audience. Beyond that, the gestures often felt imposed, and the result of trying too hard, working in competition with the music rather than in partnership. The actress playing Despina came closest to finding movements that flowed easily with the music, and it is no coincidence that this was the role of the servant unconstrained by the bodily disciplines of class. The other strong performance was that of Don Alfonso, the Voltairean philosopher whose ironic detachment echoed that of the modern spectator, looking upon the strangeness of human artifice. The chief difficulty lay with the four lovers, whose deeds and emotions lie at the centre of the story, and whose imposed gestural style had a homogenising force, making it hard to distinguish visually, for example, between Fiordiligi, who is slow to be seduced, and her more giddy sister. Mozart's subtlety of characterisation clearly witnesses a post-baroque sensibility. The formality of the gestural style was nevertheless helpful in pre-empting too much psychological characterisation, leaving open the ambiguity of the denouement whereby the socially prescribed pairings may or may not coincide with natural emotional pairings. Each student actor focused upon their learned depiction of the specific passion appropriate to a given scene, making it difficult for them to interact, and they were clearly more comfortable within the autonomy of the aria. A self-oriented bodily focus did little to help the actors engage with the geometry of the stage, and the blocking bore the imprint of the rehearsal room. The homogenising force of the imposed baroque body language was most problematic when the two young male leads disguise themselves as Albanians, Rousseauesque figures liberated from the norms of Viennese or (in the fiction of the piece) Neapolitan court behaviour, in order that each may seduce the fiancée of the other. The dramatic situation requires the male actors to find a register that communicates release of the natural sexual male alongside parody of Italianate *opera seria*. T'Hooft's generic trans-historical baroque style flattened out the nature/culture dichotomy that might have made us take this Enlightenment story seriously.

Beauty, feeling, story and moral comment all seemed in short supply. T'Hooft's own training is in dance, but creating graceful beauty of movement would have required more than the few months dedicated to learning coded gestures. Her subsequent production of *La Clemenza di Tito* in 2013 with a professional cast would prove much more graceful and fluid. The challenge of this student project was to find a bodily expression able to unite the poignancy of the music at once to the delicate rococo surface of the plot and to the underlying rationale of the story which proposes that beneath the veneer of civilisation humans are animals driven by instinct. By 1790 the relationship between music and verbal text has become more ambivalent than it was in the time of Monteverdi, when it might be said that music simply expressed and amplified what was found in the text. Feeling is now at some odds with language. The decision to invite a talented specialist in baroque choreography to direct an opera of the late Enlightenment began to seem increasingly problematic. The decision turned on the assumption that a certain mode of acting would allow the text to speak for itself, without any directorial stance on what the libretto is *about*, or any serious attention to the problematics of storytelling. Gestural demonstrations of feeling did not derive from any recognition that this might be a drama about desire, jealousy, loss and the limits of rationality, connecting to feelings that the actors might have had in their own lives. Though T'Hooft had proclaimed her commitment to the libretto, the actors seemed to feel this was a cheerful story that every opera-goer already knew, and not one that should occasion perplexity in a modern audience. Largely dismissed as immoral in the 19th century, the libretto clearly failed to disturb these 21st-century performers. The overlay of period style, along with the accompanying baggage of 20th-century tradition, sanitised this *Così fan tutte*, and served as a barrier to prevent its human, philosophical and political concerns from touching the 21st-century audience. An idealised eighteenth century did not connect to that century as physically embodied and lived. The two sisters in the opera come from Ferrara because Da Ponte wrote the libretto as a vehicle for his adulterous Ferrarese mistress and her sister,[6] but the Drottningholm audience had no such bridge to the carnality of the embodied actor, and there was a disconnect between actor and role.

Baroque Acting

T'Hooft's method of using gesture to enhance emotion and join acting to music universalised the baroque, and lifted it out of the flux of history. There were in fact important counter currents in the development of eighteenth-century acting. A generation before Mozart, in an article published in Diderot's radical *Encyclopaedia* in 1757, the librettist Louis de Cahusac attacked frontal baroque acting, and in doing so identified a perennial problem of operatic performance.

> Mellifluous sounds reach my ears. I look upon a setting adorned by all that could gratify the eyes of a spectator, radiant with light such as I imagine in the exquisite gardens of Olympus. My eyes then fall on a personage whose appearance, in its grace and majesty, should have completed the vision that had heretofore seduced me. Yet what I look upon is a clumsy figure walking with an affected gait, randomly swinging two long arms propelled by a tedious pendulum; I lose concentration, a chill comes over me, all charm has evaporated - and I perceive merely a silly parody of some male or female divinity in lieu of the imposing figure promised by so fine a prelude.

The grandeur of the concept and design fails to connect with the materiality of the body. The man of the Enlightenment has become resistant to the artifice of baroque gesture, modified in mid century by a taste for pantomimic illustration. In principle the limbs should have been subservient to the face, the major signifier of emotion, but on the operatic stage, Cahusac claims,

> It often happens that the most excellent of actors can abandon their ruling purpose, and play upon words, or paint images that contradict what they are singing. We sometimes watch actors make brooks babble down in the orchestra pit, pointing them out with eyes and hand, or they may discover breezes and echoes in galleries and stage boxes where such things could not be - while ignoring for the whole long passage of their lovely arias the bowers and open water offered by the wings and backdrop of the stage, failing to bestow any sign of life upon them.

Cahusac bears witness here to a new sense of theatrical space, whereby actors should site themselves in the interior of a fictional environment rather than reach across the footlights to the auditorium. The language of the body, Cahusac argued, should be rooted in feeling, not in learned codes of gesture.

> The actor who has no feeling, but who studies gestures in others, believes that he can at least prove their equal, through positioning the arm just so, taking one step forward them mechanically back – in short through those lazy awkward tricks that chill the play and make the acting intolerable. Never in these tiresome automata is activity set in motion by the soul, which remains buried in torpor. Routine and memory become linchpins for the machine that acts and speaks.[7]

The problematic which Cahusac articulates – how to avoid the perils of mechanical acting in the interests of theatrical life - continues to resonate today, and I have cited him at length because he demonstrates how acting style, in the Drottningholm era, was not a given but was contested on aesthetic and ideological grounds. Historical acting is not a simple datum which the informed expert can reconstruct.

T'Hooft belongs to a recognisable school in her approach to baroque acting, and the Bible for this school is often taken to be Dene Barnett's 1987 *Art of Gesture*. In a comprehensive programme of research, Barnett assembled all available manuals, treatises and prompt books in order to furnish a systematic account of theatrical gesture in eighteenth-century Europe, and described a vocabulary of gestures so tightly linked to text that 'it is possible for the modern actor to learn the art of fitting the appropriate gesture to the word or words he declaims'. He catalogued expressive gestures of the hands and arms appropriate to the different emotions defined by the classical and Cartesian tradition, and explained how movements of the eyes precede those of the hand. In accordance with a baroque principle of beauty whereby the body should form graceful curves and balanced asymmetries while avoiding straight lines, he describes the semicircular form taken by stage groupings, with precedence of rank given to figures on stage right. This is a self-contained and eminently teachable system, which pays no heed to the question of dramatic context. Barnett merely refers his reader to the compendious theatre history assembled by his Austrian mentor Heinz Kindermann. The agenda behind Barnett's account of a timeless and placeless artistic sphere is a conservative one, seeking to conserve a lost world rather than build a new one, and perpetuating a particular ideal of the body beautiful.[8]

Challenging Rhetoric

Towards the end of his introduction, Barnett cites with approval the actor Jean Poisson, writing in 1717. 'All the rules of Cicero, of Quintilian, and of the Illustrious Moderns who might have written on Declamation, are useless to the writer if he does not follow the first, which is, to clearly understand what he is saying and feel it strongly himself, in order to make it perceptible to the Listener.'[9] In the production of *Così fan tutte*, it was hard to conceive that the actors felt strongly *for themselves* the emotions they had been taught to portray. The principle that the actor needs to feel was no Romantic innovation introduced in the age of Rousseau, but reaches back to the heart of the classical tradition. Cicero, for example, comparing the orator to the actor, explained how a performer needs to feel the grief that he represents, Aulus Gellius told of how the Greek actor Polus brought the ashes of his own son onto the stage when playing Electra's lament, and according to Plutarch Aesopus was so carried away by emotion in his role as Atreus that he killed a slave with the violence of his gesture. Quintilian wrote about the need to use the imagination in order to transform the mind and not simply appearance: just as actors are seen still to be weeping after removing their masks, so he as an orator in court is observed to be pallid and weeping.[10] Though Barnett has no interest in discussing the matter, empathetic feeling was widely regarded as indispensable in the eighteenth century. As in the Stanislavskian tradition, there were competing views about working from inside to out or outside to in.

At a symposium convened in association with the production of *Così fan tutte*, Jed Wentz, a Dutch specialist in early flute, gave a rendition of Brutus's funeral speech in *Julius Caesar*, illustrating how the correlation of Shakespearean language and gesture had been meticulously notated by Gilbert Austin in 1806. Wentz was vastly more accomplished than the Stockholm students in demonstrating grace of movement and fluent synthesis of gesture with text. Barnett's generalising method, according to Wentz, has too often diverted performers from attending to nuances of language and emotion and from recognising that, even if the human body is a kind of machine, each of those machines is complex and unique. Actors with their bodily instruments need to be as subtle as instrumentalists in the orchestra. More alert than Barnett to the centrality of emotion, Wentz stresses the contagious nature of emotion in the theatre, and argues that in baroque opera it is ultimately the emotions of the actor-singer rather than the score or the conductor that should determine the tempo for the orchestra.[11] This is a much more dynamic conception of eighteenth-century gesture, though it does not address the problem of how in practice the actor-singer should summon up the necessary level of emotion in order to energise gestural forms. A striking feature of Wentz's demonstration was the way one gesture rippled into another, and involved a rebalancing of the whole body. To divide a movement sequence into its component gestures is rather like dividing music into its component notes, necessary for analytic and compositional purposes, but misleading as to the overall experience of flow. Wentz offers a better touchstone than Barnett or a student production when we seek to evaluate the possibilities of historically informed performance.

81. Jed Wentz in a demonstration of a historically informed speech.

I pointed out after the demonstration that, in playing the generic personal emotions of Brutus, Wentz had not recognised the political emotions that must once have been engendered by this celebrated republican speech in a revolutionary age.[12] It is very clear in the context of the French Enlightenment that when Cahusac, Diderot or Rousseau expressed views about acting, those views were tied to a broader philosophical and political agenda. Likewise Kemble's arguments with Sheridan can be related to political tensions between a neo-classical Tory aesthetic and a bourgeois Whig view of the world.[13] The argument between Carlo Gozzi and Carlo Goldoni about conserving the traditions of the commedia dell'arte reflects a similar tension between aristocratic and bourgeois principles.[14] Ever since Louis XIV made theatre an instrument of state, a politics of aesthetic form was always at stake, and rules in a sense existed precisely because they could be contested. In its article on 'Declamation', the *Encyclopédie* insisted on classical principles, but qualified these with the remarks of Michel Baron, creator of many original roles for Molière and Racine: 'The rules prohibit raising the arms above the head; but if passion carries them there, they will do

193

well: passion knows more about it than rules.'[15] Pushing at the boundaries of seventeenth-century gestural decorum was a physical expression of the push given by Molière and Racine to the boundaries of received morality. In a seminal essay on eighteenth-century performance, Alan Downer identified the paradox whereby: 'The art of acting is traditional, conventional, hereditary, yet the art of the individual actor is a constant revolt against tradition, convention, heredity.'[16] The liveness and excitement of theatre has always depended upon contesting or transcending what has been done before and finding a new way. That was the case in the eighteenth-century as much as it is in the twenty-first. It is a paradox that 21st-century 'historically informed' actors push against contemporary bodily habits in order to replicate eighteenth-century codes, while in the eighteenth century these same bodily codes were the habits against which actors pushed in order to create the tension of live theatre. 'Historically informed' performance is energised today by the way it contests the norms of modernity. If we strive to fix the past in aspic, then the search for how the past was becomes nothing more than a rejection of the present.

Published two years before Barnett's manual, but the product of a new intellectual era, Joseph Roach's *The Player's Passion* seems to me the most important modern study of eighteenth-century acting. As his title implies, Roach concentrates upon the emotions rather than signifying systems of the actor and Wentz approves Roach's conception of rhetorical gesture as a mould into which molten passion can be poured.[17] Roach uses the history of science to trace a shifting phenomenology of the body, exploring how in practice the actor experienced the passions which Descartes distinguished and codified in 1649. While humoral theory constructed the mind-body as a kind of sponge that tended to absorb fluids unevenly, the Cartesian animal spirits operated on a hydraulic principle, pumping impulses to the surface, or retreating to leave the actor frozen in stillness at moments of astonishment or fear. The command centre shifted from a gaseous soul to the heart which pumped out vital heat, and thence to a dematerialised location in the centre of the brain, which facilitated rapid access to the muscles of the face. As a mechanical instrument, the body could never finally be separated from the player of that instrument, prior to the invention of a romantic self and a psychoanalytic unconscious. As a machine for generating heat, the body supposedly transmitted through the eyes rays that inflamed the audience. Recovering this phenomenology of the body is much harder today than recovering a set of formal rules for bodily decorum, yet without such a psychosomatic apprehension of what an emotion is, it is hard for the modern actor to make a set of gestures signifying emotion seem anything more than a mechanical operation.

82. Scene from Gustav III:s historical drama *Helmfelt*.

Inspired by Foucault, Roach identifies sharp epistemic changes within the seventeenth- and eighteenth-century period which Barnett wants to locate as a constant. Amongst English theatre historians, a Whiggish narrative of steady historical change is commonplace when mapping interpretations of Shakespeare - from a restrained Betterton still in touch with pre-Commonwealth traditions, to the heroics and declamatory acting of Quin, then the lower key vocalisation and physical fluidity of Garrick, and on to the formalism of Kemble in an enlarged Covent Garden. In the language of architecture, these transitions roughly correspond to the terms vernacular, baroque, rococo and neo-classical. Under the French Ancien Régime, where the reperformance of classic plays was subject to stricter rules of declamation and bodily comportment, evolutionary change is less apparent, despite the polemics of radical philosophers. Julia Gros de Gasquet argues that the fundamental eighteenth-century change was the '*irruption*' of the actor's own body, what Voltaire called with a smile 'le diable du corps' – that devil of a body. For most Anglophone historians,

Shakespearean acting is an index of the times that serves as proof of Shakespeare's universality, a view which sits comfortably with the assumption that operatic acting partook of an imposed and thus reproducible continental tradition.

Director's Theatre – the Case of Bayreuth

In his introduction to the 2011 Festival programme, perhaps responding to the agitation of Willmar Sauter as well as his own desire to develop academic activity around the Festival, Mark Tatlow dropped his seductive promise of 'a fully authentic experience of early opera' and undertook more cautiously that *Così fan tutte* would offer 'a thoroughly believable 18th-century world', introducing Sigrid T'Hooft as a creator of 'historically-informed productions'. T'Hooft in turn made it clear in the programme that she had no intention of 'trying to recreate the past "as it was"', and explained that she was using contemporary tools to bring the opera to life. She was after all a director, a figure unknown in the eighteenth century. She wanted sound and stage to 'speak the same aesthetic and dramaturgical language', and described how 'The music inspires me when moulding the amplitude, the rhythm and the course of the gestures.' Her contemporary job is to mould the show. In 21st-century practice, instrumentalists and actors are subservient to an interpretation of the Work imposed by a conductor or director, rather than autonomous artists charged with responding to each other across the footlights. A material record of this lost engagement is the bench that runs along the back of the pit in the Gustavian theatre of Gripsholm, which once allowed the musicians to face the stage.

Regietheater – director's theatre – is the norm in modern theatre.[18] Flying out to Stockholm on my first visit to Drottningholm, I picked up on the plane an *International Herald Tribune* displaying a prominent review of a 'visually sensual, and scenically enthralling' *Parsifal* at Bayreuth. The Bayreuth Festival remains in the international eye because it attracts some of the world's most celebrated and inventive stage directors. The Festival is historically 'authentic' in its use of a theatre building designed by Wagner, occupying a time-honoured slot in the calendar, administered by descendants of Wagner, and playing Wagner's musical Works as they were notated –

83. From this bench at the Gripsholm Theatre the musicians could see and be seen by the actors on the forestage.

and this 'authenticity' plainly lends power and excitement to the event. The attempt to use Wagner's own stage settings was abandoned at the time of the Third Reich, and assertively modernist stagings became the norm from the 1950s. I read in the plane about an innovative *Parsifal* which tracked modern German history, and implicitly reflected upon the festival's past association with fascism in order to open up a gap between past and present. This conceptual complexity was possible because the hidden orchestra pit and layered proscenium were designed, in Wagner's words, 'to separate reality from ideality':

> Having taken his seat, the spectator now finds himself in a veritable theatron, in other words, in a space that exists for no other purpose than for looking, and looking, moreover, in the direction in which his seat points him. Between him and the picture that he is to look at, nothing is plainly discernible except for a sense of distance held, as it were, in a state of suspension due to the architectural relationship between the two proscenia, the stage picture appearing in consequence to be located in the unapproachable world of dreams, while the music, rising up spectrally from the 'mystic abyss' and as such resembling the vapours ascending from Gaia's sacred primeval womb beneath the Pythia's tripod, transports him to that inspired state of clairvoyance in which the stage picture that he sees before him becomes the truest reflection of life itself.[19]

Though Wagner's Delphic metaphor has dated, his assumption that the spectator should be focused upon the stage and not upon fellow spectators, that the music should induce a heightened and meditative state, and that the stage picture should offer a reflection of truth (the truth of German history in this instance) are today still widely shared. Wagner's messianic belief that he was engaged in creating artworks of the future helps legitimate Bayreuth's cult of modernity. In Drottningholm, by contrast, the architecture insists upon tradition. Although the concentration of sightlines on the stage rather than the auditorium anticipates Wagner's Theatre in Bayreuth, the visible presence of the orchestra, the richness of ornament, the symmetrical front-back orientation and the actors' place in front of the proscenium discourage any transporting of the spectator/listener into clairvoyance and the world of dreams, demanding an awareness of self and other in the here-and-now of the performance. Radical directorial interpretations are not an option in this environment, because the stage is not a self-contained world. How to create the cultural dynamism of Bayreuth without taking the modernist road of *Regietheater* remains an unsolved problem.

84. The auditorium of Richard Wagner's Festspielhaus in Baureuth.

It is interesting to speculate what the Bayreuth Festival would be like today if the Third Reich had not created a historical rupture, and if hand-painted replicas of the old stage settings had been used as at Drottningholm to support a continuous tradition of Wagnerian acting. Would the music be able to sustain itself, or would it become, as it were, set in stone like Wagner's nearby tomb on which pilgrims still lay flowers? In the context of a nineteenth-century acting style, the music would cease to appear timeless and universal, and would seem a product of its era. The sight of 21st-century bodies struggling to adopt the emotionality and monumentality of Wagnerian gesture would, I surmise, be judged both an aesthetic offence and a distraction from the music. To make Wagner live in the context of his nineteenth-century historicity seems like an insurmountable challenge. Richard Taruskin argues that 'authentistic' performance is actually a manifestation of modernity because, in generating differentness, it answers to modernity's desire for novelty at the expense of tradition,[20] and Bayreuth is the perfect illustration of his case.

Authenticity

In order to explore the complex concept of authenticity, I will begin by distinguishing the ideal of historical authenticity from that of personal or creative authenticity.[21] The desire for historical authenticity, recreating the past as we assume it actually was, characterises amateur re-enactment groups involved with tournaments, living museums and the like in the domain of 'heritage', and catches up in its contradictions many academic theatre historians concerned with original staging practices. Theatre historians have all too often come into conflict with artists whom they thought were committed to a journey of historical discovery. My colleague Dick McCaw, for example, who co-founded a company called The Mediaeval Players in 1974, reports ongoing contention about historical accuracy with his academic sponsor and mentor Meg Twycross at the University of Lancaster. At Drottningholm in 1966, on the 200th anniversary of the opening of the building, an attempt to revive an obscure Gustavian mixed opera called *Soliman II* resulted in the resignation of the advisory working group of scholars, disillusioned by the insistence of professional practitioners on making the show work in the present, while the practitioners were plainly impatient with what they saw as the pedantry of scholars.[22]

Artists tend to honour a different sort of authenticity, defined in experiential rather than scientific terms. In his *Confessions*, a landmark work defining the modern ideal of truth to self, Jean-Jacques Rousseau undertook to describe his actions and feelings as honestly as he could, and his account of visiting the Venetian opera in 1743/4 illustrates this new commitment to authenticity of experience. Reared on the formality of French music, he responded to the emotional spontaneity of Italian music, and avoiding the company of others he placed himself in a box on his own, transforming his visit to the opera from a social experience into an individualised artistic experience. In a meditative state he dozed off and then awoke.

> What an awakening, what bliss, what ecstasy when I opened my ears and my eyes together! My first thought was that I was in Paradise. This ravishing piece, which I still remember and shall never forget so long as I live, began like this: '*Conservami la bella/ Che si m'accende il cor...*' ['Keep me the beauty who lights up my heart...'] I decided to get the music, and did so. I kept it for a long time, but on paper it was not the same thing as in my memory. The notes were the same, but it was not the same thing. That divine aria can be performed nowhere but in my head, as indeed it was on the day when it awoke me.[23]

Rousseau initially seeks to find the authenticity of the Work within the score, but discovers that the experience which set his heart on fire lay in the performance, or more precisely in his personal experience and recall of the performance. Wagner would have understood perfectly this account of a unique personal experience induced by music, impossible to analyse in scientific language and demanding a quasi-religious vocabulary.

Practitioners regularly evaluate the quality of their art by using phenomenological language of this kind. Mark Tatlow, in an introduction to *Così fan tutte*, expressed his hope that Drottningholm would 'once again become a fascinating laboratory for the exploration of theatrical expression'[24], but the language of science when used by artists in this way struggles to engender testable hypotheses. At the symposium held in connection with *Così fan tutte*, Suzanne Rydén (who played the part of Minerva in the 2008 *Ulysses*) used the language of an artist when she talked eloquently about how the theatre of Drottningholm 'speaks' to her if she 'listens', and how as a performer she strives to do 'what the theatre wants'. She explained likewise how the substitution of baroque for modern gestures affects the tempo and volume that she as a singer *feels to be right*. Ultimately she defined music as a form of communication, thus not a thing to be analysed in and of itself, and she welcomed the opportunity offered by baroque music to add ornament in spontaneous response to a particular given audience. In a metaphorical sense the theatre served for Ryden as a laboratory, but turning her propositions into verifiable experiments is difficult, for the experiences that she sought to describe would have been killed stone dead by any attempt at scientific testing.

The two notions of historical and personal authenticity converge in Walter Benjamin's account of 'authenticity' as a response to the alienation characteristic of an age of mechanical reproduction. Benjamin argues that perceptions of 'authenticity' and 'authority' derive alike from historical testimonies which can be tracked back to a point of origin. He is ambivalent about the shattering of tradition which mechanical reproduction entails, and contrasts theatre with the reproductive medium of cinema, where, in the words of Pirandello, the film actor 'feels inexplicable emptiness: his body loses its corporeality, it evaporates, it is deprived of reality, life, voice, and the noises caused by his moving about, in order to be changed into a mute image'. The film actor has to forego aura, for: 'aura is tied to his presence; there can be no replica of it. The aura which, on the stage, emanates from Macbeth, cannot be separated for the spectators from that of the actor.'[25] Of course, we may well feel today, in a digital age, that a long dead actress in a grainy black-and-white movie is well endowed with Benjaminian aura. Reproduction is at the heart of the issue we need to resolve. Drottningholm

85. Suzanne Rydén in the guest performance of *Orlando* 2009.

is perceived as an authentic and authoritative eighteenth-century environment because the testimony of conservators and scholars assures us that it cannot be reproduced; yet any attempt to render original staging practices is precisely an attempt at reproduction. The aura of Drottningholm must somehow be reconciled with the aura sought by a live performer. Benjamin makes it clear that 'authenticity' is inseverable from 'aura', and is not the precondition but the product of a historian's work.

Academic historians are often dismissive of amateur re-enactment practices, and Laurajane Smith complains that re-enactors are often patronised by academics whose 'discourse of "inauthenticity"… is inevitably entered into as a means to maintain the authority and gravity of expert knowledge.'[26] In her recent *Performing Remains*, the postmodern performance theoretician Rebecca Schneider refuses to see popular re-enactments of the American Civil War as an activity inherently different in kind from theatre, and turns around old modernist assumptions about theatre's need to keep on endlessly innovating. She challenges the idea that theatre is distinguished by its liveness and inherent ephemerality, and argues in a reversal of received common sense that live performance should rather be seen as a quasi-archival record of something previously set down. In the culture of re-enactment, she describes how 'The hauntingness of history, its literal in-bodied articulation, the boisterous and rattling ghosts of ancestors, and the queasy "something living" of the past, return us to the transmission of affect in the jumping and sticky viscosity of time.'[27] Schneider points us to a helpful way of looking at modern performance on the Drottningholm stage, as a kind of re-enactment focused upon material traces of the past, and driven by a sense of loss and a concern with ancestors. She points us to the affect that lies behind any attempt to make the past live again.[28]

Original Practices at 'Shakespeare's Globe'

The quest for eighteenth-century authenticity at Drottningholm poses specific challenges which we can appreciate more clearly in light of the recent history of performance at Shakespeare's Globe on London's South Bank since 1996. Under the artistic directorship of Mark Rylance, which ended in 2005, the theatre at regular intervals adopted what are generally known as 'original practices'.[29] Unlike Drottningholm, Shakespeare's Globe can only offer itself as a reconstruction, based on the best evidence available at the start of the 1990s, though it lays a certain claim to authenticity by virtue of its location yards away from vestigial foundations of the original. It embodies a coherent scholarly idea, without the quirks and enigmas of the extant space of Drottningholm. Various devices have proved effective in the creation of aura, helping the theatre increasingly with the years to feel like a preserved piece of English heritage. Structural timbers, for example, that in 1599 would have been painted over are left bare in accordance with twentieth-century popular conceptions of the Elizabethan style. The exposed oak provides visible evidence of the 'authentic' materials and traditional craft processes deployed in the manufacture of the building.[30] The inspiration for Shakespeare's Globe came from the American Sam Wanamaker, and the theatre has been concerned to fend off the charge of Disneyfication, evoked by English critics eager to challenge a perceived American desire to reclaim Shakespeare on behalf of ordinary people.[31] In order to create its aura of English authenticity, what the Globe needs is historical testimony that provides a direct line to a point of origin, and for this reason there has been a symbiotic relationship between practitioners and academic historians. Shakespeare's Globe is enmeshed in a wider debate about 'heritage' and commercialism. Raphael Samuel is a representative English voice in this debate with his insistence upon the longevity of popular memory, while in the USA Barbara Kirshenblatt-Gimblett prefers to emphasise that 'Heritage is a mode of cultural production *in the present* that has recourse to the past'.[32] Drottningholm is not immune to these competing pressures. Through its studious avoidance of vulgar razzmatazz, it touts a cultural authority which lends 'added value' to performances upon its stage.

When launching the Globe project, Mark Rylance – himself preeminently an actor – saw no easy alternative to the regime of the director, but qualified his policy by remarking: 'Fortunately in the theatre climate of the nineties it feels as if there has been a swing in the conception of the director's role. Many more directors are now interested in freedom of communication between actors and audience. For a director to control this communication at the Globe will be, in any case, impossible.'[33] The need to control a commercially valuable product and the lack of a long-term resident company meant that the directorial function was in practice indispensable, even though the director had a restricted range of scenographic options. John Russell Brown's *Free Shakespeare*, published in 1974, was an early manifesto seeking to provide 'a tool to liberate the works of Shakespeare from directors and academics who seek to impose their ideas upon the plays', and argued for control of the performance by actors.[34] Brown's idea that the play could somehow be freed from imposed interpretations and restored to a lost innocence did not commend itself to most academics and professional practitioners, but it addressed a widely felt frustration.

Patrick Tucker in England and Ralph Cohen at the reconstructed Blackfriars theatre in Virginia, broadly following Brown's principles, developed working practices emulating but not replicating those of the Shakespearean world. Today in the world of classical music it remains normal for instrumentalists and soloists in oratorios to study their parts in isolation and meet for a single rehearsal, but the idea that actors should follow the Elizabethan model and function in the same way continues to seem bizarre.[35] I saw in 2012 a production of *Hamlet* by Tim Carroll, an experienced Globe director, in the found space of a bookshop on a stage set up to evoke Elizabethan practice. The text was played with fidelity, but the precise casting was determined by a random spectator at the start of the performance, and the stage action was built around props brought in by the spectators.[36] The director here reverted to the role of facilitator, successfully passing much creative control to the actors, but it would be hard to replicate such spontaneity at the Globe because the space appears to impose too many rules.

Carroll's actors were free to play in their everyday clothes because they were using a found space that was always known to be a bookshop. The use of modern costumes in the context of the Globe necessarily creates an aesthetic dissonance with the period environment.[37] This is a practical conundrum for anyone attempting to replicate Elizabethan staging practices at the Globe – or indeed baroque practices at Drottningholm. Elizabethan and baroque actors wore the same costumes as their audience, modified slightly to suggest a classical or exotic context. This allowed for an ease of interaction that becomes much harder to achieve today when actors are historicised and distanced by wearing period costumes that set them apart from contemporary spectators. One logical solution is of course to periodise the audience, so they become fellow performers in a joint journey of historical discovery. George Pierce Baker attempted to go down this road at Harvard at the end of the nineteenth century, but he relied upon well educated student participants.[38] The practical difficulties and aesthetic risks of this route have subsequently been thought too great.

It is a truism but also an oversimplification to say that one cannot recreate the historical audience. Penelope Woods argues that Shakespeare's Globe is as much an imitation or mimesis as it is a 'reconstruction' and argues that 'audiences assist in the labour of imitation', engaged in a 'social practice of historical imagining'.[39] Mark Rylance noticed that after 1995 'the audience was learning how to be in the Globe just as we actors were learning', and Tim Carroll commented on 'the audience's ability to play the role required of it'.[40] Although 'we' can never behave or see like Elizabethans, a number of biological universals condition audience response at the Globe. Standing rather than sitting creates a higher level of alertness and ability to respond quickly; daylight affects the human metabolism; and, more contentiously, Mark Rylance argues that the perfect and harmonious 'sacred geometry of the architecture generates a particular collective spirit in the people gathered.'[41] Cultural specifics, whatever the effect of geometry and proportion may be, are inescapable. The two extant visual representations of an Elizabethan actor-audience relationship call attention to the spectators seated in

86. An audience dressed in Rococo costumes during a television recording in 1955.

the Lords' Room behind the stage, but this space is not used by spectators at Shakespeare's Globe today because a modern preference for democratic relationships has intervened. When these seats were placed on sale in the early days, they proved hard to sell.[42] We noted a similar reluctance at Ulriksdal to reconstruct the Royal Box for today's more egalitarian audience. Since the role played by modern spectators at Drottningholm is not and cannot be a neutral one, it follows that they need to be embraced in some way as makers rather than mere consumers of the theatrical experience.

Acting is nevertheless the core of the problem at Drottningholm. In an analysis of the pedagogic practices that lie behind modern Shakespearean acting, W.B.Worthen cites a representative statement that 'Shakespeare wanted real and organic emotions from his actors, so we handle the emotional work in his plays the same way we do in contemporary plays'; and he contrasts this with another remark that, because Molière's work is taken to be rooted in the seventeenth century, 'Molière is played in very stylised ways today'.[43] Claims about the universality of Shakespeare are bound up with a refusal to delimit his 'style'. The old formalist argument of Alfred Harbage and Stephen Joseph that Elizabethan acting could be approached through rhetorical gesture, as set out in manuals like *Bulwer's Chironomia* (1644), fell out of fashion after the 1950s, and a pragmatic approach has subsequently prevailed, focused upon the material conditions of performance.[44] Mark Rylance was emphatic in his refusal to bother about style. 'Original practices', Rylance insisted, 'was an enormous release because the world we were concerned with was the Globe Theatre and we did not need to worry about style, the style was the relationship between audience and actor in that building. Our building was demanding our style of play whether we liked it or not because our style was to hold an audience's heart and mind for a few hours in that space.'[45] Rylance assumes here that universal human responses to the specific properties of the material environment and of the Shakespearean text will generate the necessary style – whilst in fact what we witness are responses conditioned by the modern idiom of representation, an idiom that perforce seems natural to today's audience.

What prevails at Shakespeare's Globe is a contemporary ideology which Woods identifies as an ethic of 'honesty' cognate with the aesthetic appeal of stripped timber, and associated with the privileged 'intimacy' of the actor-audience relationship.⁴⁶ It is hard to apply such an ethic to the baroque, where so obviously ethics and aesthetics converge and form equates with content. As Helen Hills puts it when describing how folds of clothing are used by baroque painters to convey the spiritual force exerted on the body, 'the surface is the matter'.⁴⁷ In Drottningholm an aesthetic of ornament needs to find its modern (or postmodern) ethical correlative if it is to connect with contemporary emotions that reach beneath the clichés of period costume drama. The dichotomy whereby *our* Shakespeare is organic, intimate and universal, but the foreign Molière is distant, stylised and temporally remote, needs to be confronted and challenged. Shakespeare was after all a dramatist of the baroque period, while Molière was an advocate of 'natural' acting.⁴⁸

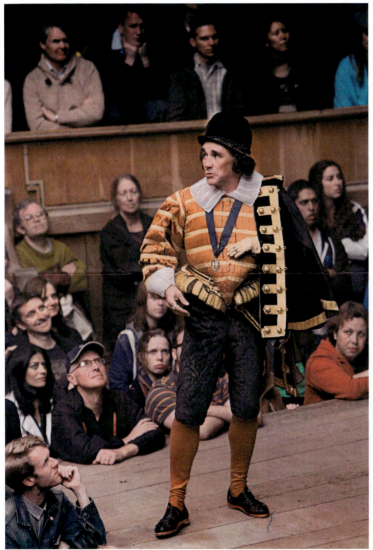

87. Mark Rylance as *Richard III* by W. Shakespeare at the Globe Theatre in London.

The Globe theatre building is often described as an instrument for which Shakespeare wrote, used to sound the music of his text by actors who aspire to a kind of neutral agency.⁴⁹ Worthen cites an advocate of 'natural' Shakespearean acting who claims in a similar vein: '[T]he playwright writes for an instrument – just as Mozart wrote for the Stradivarius – the actor's body, voice, legs, arms, torso, hair, hands, feet, etc. These have their own physical vocabulary of potentiality. The way in which they are used will of course differ in different times and according to the demands of different styles; but the instrument hasn't changed…'⁵⁰ Worthen challenges the widespread assumption, implicit in this dismissal of musicianship as merely a style, that a changeless and universal body can be a conduit for

207

the changeless and universal properties of the spoken Shakespearean text.

On the Drottningholm stage we cannot escape the simple historical fact that bodies change, for they have got bigger, and may easily seem out of proportion to the painted settings. Jed Wentz remarked to me about the development of the baroque calf, habituated to dance and emphasised by male stockings. Bodies are products of habits, and acquired bodily instincts teach actors to use the stage in different ways. At Drottningholm there is a remorseless modern tendency to move up stage in order to inhabit a naturalistic environment, whilst in the Globe, as Woods points out, performers manifest a desire to move into the yard and mingle with the audience in the centre of the architectural circle.[51] These habits can be described as manifes-

88. The walls of the banqueting hall in the castle of Český Krumlov are decorated with figures from the Commedia dell'Arte. In front of the painted Pantalone a performer imitates the gesture depicted on the wall

tations of a modern *homo democraticus*, a term that I borrow from Jacques Rancière.[52] This 'democratic human being' may be distinguished from the Renaissance and baroque figure characterised by Richard Lanham as *homo rhetoricus*. 'Rhetorical man', Lanham writes, 'is an actor, his reality public, dramatic. His sense of identity, his self, depends on the reassurance of daily histrionic re-enactment.'[53] Rhetorical man, trained to present himself frontally to onlookers with close attention to verbal and bodily style, was much happier to command the forestage than *homo democraticus*, whose body instinctively pulls him or her towards the centre, the site of balance and equality. While *Homo democraticus* cherishes interiority, *homo rhetoricus* delighted rather in surface and presentation.

The postulate of *homo rhetoricus* takes us back to the debate about rhetorical acting. Though it is impossible to describe exactly how Shakespeare's plays were acted, we can at least identify the tensions and cultural pressures within which acting sat. The famous 1615 description of 'an excellent actor', a text that sought to differentiate common actors from those in the service of the Crown, began with the declaration that 'Whatsoever is commendable in the grave orator is most exquisitely perfect in him.'[54] By the same token, Hamlet describes a modest and 'reformed' style of acting based on the classical principle of mimesis which will be targeted at the 'judicious' spectator rather than the 'groundlings' or the 'unskilful' who might potentially comprise 'a whole theatre'.[55] When Hamlet demonstrates the sawing of the air with his hand, he may allude to the rhetorical principle set out by Quintilian and familiar to an educated elite that the arm should not rise above eye level or below the chest or sideways beyond the opposite shoulder.[56] Rhetoric was central to the Elizabethan system of education, and for the educated there was no escaping the performative issues with which rhetoric confronted them.[57]

In Shakespeare's Globe the question of a historical acting style is cheerfully set aside on account of a strong ideological compulsion to insist on the natural body as vehicle for a sacred, canonical text. In Drottningholm, the same canonical status is given to the music of Mozart, Monteverdi or Gluck. As the mental product of an artistic genius, the 'music' can be more or less identified with the manuscript or published score, whilst the verbal text is commoner stuff, the product of a mere librettist, and susceptible of translation either in performance or in surtitles. We see the same ideological compulsion as at the Globe to cast the historicity of the body aside in order to foreground the sacred and timeless status of the Work. However, at Drottningholm that compulsion has to compete with a need to capture the bodily style of the period in order to avoid a mismatch with the period setting, whilst in the English context the bare open stage of the Globe and the deep familiarity of Elizabethan period costume make this demand less pressing.

Both Drottningholm and Shakespeare's Globe are functions of a contemporary cultural environment. The Globe offered an important challenge to the Royal Shakespeare Company, where the play has long been subject to the authority of a director functioning as a surrogate author of the Work performed on what was until 2006 a picture-frame stage. The success of Shakespeare's Globe challenged the RSC's claim to hereditary ownership of Shakespeare, and a reconfiguration of the Stratford stage became necessary. Jeremy Lopez has remarked on how the 'original practices' cultivated on the Globe stage served to re-empower ordinary readers and performers of Shakespeare, eager for the plays to speak more directly to them, and to be freed from the tyranny of political relevance imposed by a directorial interpretation.[58] Acting style is socially inflected today just as it was in the world of Hamlet, and Drottningholm is no less isolated from battles for cultural status. An Italian treatise on stagecraft commented in c.1630 'that just as some few connoisseurs of music have in the main appreciated excellent singers however cold their acting, so common spectators have found most satisfaction in perfect actors with mediocre voice and musical skill.'[59] In today's Drottningholm, the privileging of musical skill over theatrical skill reflects a social distinction that was also a feature of the early baroque period, and the revaluation of acting in metropolitan opera houses is related to desire to make the genre of opera less perceptibly elitist. Whilst the Drottningholm opera season seeks to emulate more prestigious international festivals elsewhere, it is also under political pressure to make itself more accessible, reflected in 2013 by the introduction of a family day at the start of the season.

***

It is clear in the context of Shakespearean performance that authenticity is a recurrent aspiration. Each generation finds its own way of representing what it takes to be the real Shakespeare, in accordance with its current tastes and conception of what it takes to be 'natural' acting.[60] Shakespeare's Globe is a manifestation of a centuries-old process. We must approach Drottningholm no less aware that each generation constructs the past in its own image, in a process of cultural renewal that should be embraced rather than scorned. Scholarly dedication to historical truth has always been part of this process of renewal.

Drottningholm survives as a vivid material trace of the historical past because of a moment of rupture. The normal organic life-cycle of pre-modern theatres involved being remodelled, accidentally burnt to the ground, and rebuilt again, but this cycle was brought to an abrupt halt with the assassination of Gustav III and the abdication of his son in the revolutionary period, a period we might call the crucible of modernity. Instead of constructing the past as a lost golden age of stability, I prefer to focus on the process of rupture which caused the theatre of Drottningholm to become frozen in time. The arrival of modernity defines our separation from the baroque era, and there are countless aspects of that separation for us to explore. Nostalgia and the quest for heritage may not be the most productive drivers of such exploration. The theatre building is itself a palimpsest and reflects competing architectural ideals. Performances given on the stage necessarily postdated the architecture, and attempts to reconstruct 'authentic' Gustavian performances have to take stock of the fact that the theatre was already out of date by the time Gustav came to the throne. There is no stable originary moment for us to reclaim.

Watching T'Hooft's production of *Così fan tutte*, my immediate impulse was to lament that the students were not performing in their everyday jeans and T-shirts. This would have allowed me to focus on the nature of the dramatic experiment, and to see how contemporary bodies were striving to engage with historic patterns of movement, including the performance of gender. This was an aesthetic rather than an academic response on my part. I would not have felt subject to any inference that Mozartian opera once really looked like this, and in consequence I would have found the performance more emotionally engaging, more possessed of dramatic tension. The image of actors in jeans performing baroque gesture lingers in my mind because modern actors' workshops normally take the world of Stanislavski and Meyerhold as the point of origin for today's craft of acting. The techniques of pre-twentieth-century acting appear, superficially, to have no relevance to the present, yet those modern masters did not start from a blank slate, and it was in the eighteenth century that acting came to be defined and analysed as an art form independent of oratory.[61] To address this Enlightenment revolution within the transmitted craft of acting and discover a new genealogy seems a useful undertaking.

I discussed in Chapter Five Pierre Nora's investigation of the link between history and memory. Nora identified the revolutionary moment in French life when historiography ran 'a knife between the tree of memory and the bark of history'.[62] Drottningholm is in Nora's sense an exemplary *lieu de mémoire*, a material, functional and symbolic site established explicitly in order that the past may be remembered. The actors who played before Lovisa Ulrika and Gustav operated within a *milieu de mémoire*, an environment of memory where oral tradition and the continuity of spatial forms joined contemporary innovation directly onto the world of Molière and Lully. Though we cannot today escape philosophical doubts about the knowability of the past, we nevertheless need such *lieux de mémoire* in order to place ourselves in time and make sense of the contemporary world we inhabit. To think of Drottningholm as a site of memory rather than a site for the creation of new art may paradoxically offer the best means of renewal. As a site of memory, we may find that the theatre becomes something more than an inert container within which we perform, watch and conduct historical experiments. The theatre rather than ourselves may finally become the performer.

From a theatrical perspective, in the way it refracts upon our present, the baroque world has become a useful world to remember. Neurologically informed accounts of a performative, fragmented, and social self are generating new approaches to emotion that yield techniques like 'alba emoting' redolent of baroque practice, while cross-cultural comparisons with Asian theatre make us less dismissive of coded systems of gesture.[63] The interdisciplinary training of baroque actors in dance, singing and speech seems more pertinent when naturalist theatre gives way to forms like music-theatre and physical theatre. We inhabit a culture obsessed with presentation, a world where materialist accounts of reality have begun to seem inadequate. The inevitability of progress has ceased to be an article of faith, and our society has become more divided and less mobile. In respect of features such as these, the world of baroque theatre is a useful world to remember.

Willmar Sauter & David Wiles:

8. TOWARDS THE FUTURE

In this book we have led you the reader on a series of journeys. First we have undertaken a journey through time: a journey through the twentieth century (Chapter Six) and through the second half of the eighteenth century (Chapter Five and elsewhere). Secondly, we have taken you on journeys through space: a celebrated journey of rediscovery made in 1921 (Chapter One); the journey of a modern visitor approaching the theatre for the first time (Chapter Two); and a studious revisit via the baroque palace (Chapter Five), on a tour that seeks to analyse the building's architecture in its context in eighteenth-century life. Our tours have also included an imaginary journey through the course of a day and around the Drottningholm estate in the late eighteenth century (Chapter Four). The visitor's physical journey to the theatre today determines how the theatre will be viewed: as an atmospheric opera venue inconveniently located on the outskirts of the Stockholm metropolis, or part of a unique summer palace, which can be apprehended as a mere delight to the eye, the culmination of scenic boat trip, or as the material trace of a lost way of life. We have also sought to take you the reader with us on our own journey of understanding as historians and interpreters of theatre. We have tried to describe how this unique space has in recent times been animated by performers, performers engaged in creating an encounter between the present day and the theatrical/musical culture of the eighteenth century. It may appear today that music and theatre are distinct branches of culture, but the eighteenth century constantly resists the distinction between singers and actors. We hope that our journey into pre-modernity will point practitioners towards ways of working that could be a release from the straitjacket of contemporary norms.

The writing of this book has unfolded during Mark Tatlow's tenure as artistic director of the Drottningholm Festival, which came to an end in August 2013. It is likely that this will be viewed in retrospect as a time of

89. Drottningholm Palace in 1697.

experiment, driven by Tatlow's passion for the historical authenticity of Early Music, a drive respected by ourselves but perhaps not by all opera aficionados. In Tatlow's penultimate season, students of the University College of Opera put on a once popular baroque opera, *Il Giasone*, marketed in Venice in 1649 as a 'Drama Musicale' by the dramatist G.A. Cicognini, but presented in June 2012 under the title '*Jason & Medea*', an opera by the composer Francesco Cavalli; and in 2013, the student company presented another once popular but much later Italian piece, *Il matrimonio secreto* (1792) – a 'Dramma giocoso' by the imperial court poet Giovanni Bertati, with music by Domenico Cimarosa. The stage director for both productions was Deda Cristina Colonna, an Italian specialist in baroque dance also trained in Stanislawskian theatre. In the summer of 2013, Sigrid T'Hooft di-

90. *La clemenza di Tito* by W. A. Mozart, 2013. From left Elena Galitzkaya, Annemarie Kremer and Katja Dragojevic.

rected a professional cast performing Mozart's 'serious' opera *La Clemenza di Tito*. The relationship between Tatlow and these two stage directors was a happy one. Tatlow appreciated the way Colonna and T'Hooft worked from the music, and felt that the attempt at baroque acting supported the singing and musicality of the performance. Working with a student cast offered more possibility for experiment in so far as the performers did not have to be paid and were more malleable, but in *La Clemenza* the performance of Annio revealed the great advantage of working with a disciplined professional who had early experience of baroque techniques.

In a vigourous manifesto in the 2012 programme, Tatlow argued against using 'today's social parameters in our creative endeavours'. His work, like that of so many exponents of Early Music and other forms of re-enactment, seems fired by a rejection of modernity. In his view:

> The Drottningholm theatre has other wisdom to impart: that what is old can be made new; that what is old and hidden in the past simply needs to be freed from its historical constraints and enabled to live once more; that the past can even speak to us of the future by reminding us of things we once knew but have long since forgotten… [A] little-known 17th century opera brings us face to face with another era and another culture; but one where we nonetheless find strong reflections of our contemporary selves and concerns. Cavalli's theatrical conventions are not our own, but they are no more difficult to grasp than those of other non-realistic drama. By choosing to put on Cavalli's *Il Giasone* we can bring you the whole gamut of human emotion, powerfully expressed by a wide range of characters using the music of the mid 17th century, and in a mixture of styles from the serious to the comical.

If we scrutinise this manifesto, we uncover three fundamental propositions.

First, there is the idea that the art of the past exists somewhere out there waiting to be recovered, if we can but free it of its historical constraints and strip off the excrescences of modernity. John Russell Brown's *Free Shakespeare* (1974) articulated the same ideal in regard to Shakespeare, aspiring to rescue a virginal text from the interpretative impositions of modernist directors and academics, and hand it back to the actors. This notion is philosophically problematic, and we find ourselves more sympathetic to the notion of cultural memory, recalling that which has been 'forgotten'. There can be no pretence that memories are ever objective.

Secondly, there is the idea that in this opera one comes 'face to face with another era and another culture' in which one sees oneself 'reflected'. This sense of cultural otherness reminds us of Brecht, interpreted by Jameson as an advocate of 'historicity'. Historicity defamiliarises the present by looking at the past as that which created the present and made the present something new. We want to resist the idea that we simply find ourselves and our problems 'reflected' in the otherness of the past because all too easily we create the past as a reflection of ourselves and our present tastes. The past does not exist as a given. As historians, we prefer to concentrate on the task of tracing a route back from 'now' to 'then', and locating our present culture within the continuum of history.

Thirdly, Tatlow proposes that beneath the overlay of 'historical convention' we can uncover a set of universal and shared emotions. How far emotions are biological human universals remains an open question, but it is never easy to separate emotion from convention. It is certainly a convention of modern Stanislavskian theatre that the actor should concentrate on motives, objectives or tasks rather than emotions, while it was the standard practice of the baroque stage that the actor must begin by directly analysing the emotions that had to be represented. Modern appeals to universal emotion tend to involve depoliticisation. *La Clemenza di Tito*, for example, was written for a royal coronation in Prague, and the intense political emotions this piece once aroused are not easy to replicate. There is too easy a slippage from the ideal of 'universal emotion' to a modern fixation on interpersonal emotion.

Beneath Tatlow's attractive rhetoric, questions remain unresolved, and these relate to our own mixed feelings about Colonna's experiments. *Il Giasone*, set in the world of Greek myth, seemed an entertaining piece of storytelling that moved in a Shakespearean manner between comedy and tragedy, and exploited the scenographic resources of the theatre. However, Colonna appeared to have little trust in the seventeenth-century narrative, and judged its themes to be out of date. The audience were inducted into the otherness of the past by Cupid, who spoke the prologue wearing dark glasses and dressed in bright red synthetic fluff; a winged god, he was nevertheless made to step clumsily over a cut-out cloud that rested on the stage. This deliberate anti-illusionism denied the magic of flying through the sky, and elicited an easy laugh of agreement that baroque gods are unredeemedly silly. The image led us not towards the past but away from it. Modern allusions replaced a commitment to the otherness of the past and the moral challenges of the text. Medea's nurse was played as a drag role, and laughter at his/her classless gender-reversal diverted attention from the baroque character's pragmatic attitude to sex which derived from servant status. The production did not engage with the hierarchical nature of baroque society because we live today in a more democratic age. It may be a historical fact that the part of the nurse was originally played by a male, but there was no historicity in the interpretation.

To engage emotionally in the drama of *Jason & Medea*, it was often easier to close one's eyes. When we did so, the baroque dance rhythms compelled our bodies to participate in the structure of the stage action, a physical animation which vanished as soon as we opened our eyes, because the movements of the performers were informed by analytic thought and not by a more instinctive response to the music. When, however, we focused our eyes on Mark Tatlow helping the performers to vocalise, something else was apparent: a complete harmony of body and music. Tatlow's involvement in the music took complete possession of his body in a way that eluded the singers, preoccupied by the comic business they had learned to perform in parallel to their singing. Tatlow has remarked on how he needs to become the character on stage; if he closes off the emotion in himself, he can no longer perform his musical tasks.[1]

In her 2013 production of *Il matrimonio secreto*, Colonna addressed many of these problems, focusing on the acting at the expense of scenography, and bringing her dance training to bear on the project. In an opera that belonged to the rational Enlightenment, and had no use for the magic of scene changes, she made the focus of her experiment provocatively clear by using blank reversed stage flats for her scenery. As a reviewer remarked, 'you might think this quite shoddy if you had forked out 800 kroner for a seat in this World Heritage theatre'.[2] She sought to develop a mode of acting that was rooted in the flow of the body rather than the mechanics of gesture, and therefore capable of converging with the music. In rehearsal, she asked the actors to improvise and find the gestures that they made instinctively to express emotion, and then used these improvisations as a bridge to create a universal language of baroque or neo-classical gesture. Searching for universal emotions, she left herself little scope to explore the social framing of emotion. The animal emotions of the rape scene were

91. *Il matrimonio segreto* by D. Cimarosa, 2013. From left Sofie Asplund, Richard Hamrin and Anna Hybiner.

strong, but the love scenes were weak, because the expression of love in the eighteenth century rested upon social convention. This was a valuable experiment, but the missing ingredient was the Theatre of Drottningholm. The acting took place up-stage as if in a nineteenth-century proscenium theatre, and it was lit from the side rather than by footlights, creating little scope for engagement with the audience. Drottningholm was merely the excuse for a valuable experiment.

The lack of engagement with the space in both of Colonna's productions is symptomatic of the fact that all the creative development work took place in a studio in Stockholm. The fragility of the fabric of the theatre means that only a minimum of rehearsal can take place on the stage, and there is no opportunity for performers and director to get to know the space, bond with it and explore its possibilities. Unlike Tatlow who has spent many years getting to know the building, stage directors only have brief encounters and therefore inevitably tend to insert productions into the space rather than realise the aesthetic and historical identity of the space by making the space perform. Sigrid T'Hooft likens the task of actors in this theatre to that of an instrumentalist asked to learn a wooden flute and after four weeks play on it as if they had played all their lives.[3] Return visits have allowed Colonna and T'Hooft to address some of the challenges of the Drottningholm stage, and it would have been fascinating to have seen what could have been achieved by an ensemble of actors/singers comparable to Tatlow's established orchestral ensemble.

Working with students, Colonna was able in some small way to challenge the orthodoxies of the modern operatic production process. According to that process, the repetiteur is always the first person whom an opera singer encounters when studying a new part. When the musical rehearsals are almost finished, movements are superimposed, and at the very end of the process, movements that seem right in the rehearsal room have to be transposed to the stage and to an encounter with a full orchestra. Acting is something added to the singing rather than inherent in the singing. In the Gustavian period, the operas performed were normally new works rather than interpretations of classics, and the actor-singer worked within a received tradition of representation that assumed certain correspondences between emotion and gesture, movement and character. The geography and acoustics of the stage environment were part of the performer's daily professional experience. The composer or librettist would be involved from the outset. If Drottningholm forces performers to rethink the historicity of the creative process, then it is a theatre 'laboratory' of no small significance.

The modern operatic festival at Drottningholm entails not only a modern production process, but also a twentieth-century mode of viewing on the part of critics and aficionados, for whom an opera consists primarily of the score and the voices. The Händel and Monteverdi cycles at Drottningholm attracted 'real' baroque music lovers who claimed to know everything worth knowing about these composers. The critics offered long explanations about the original productions of these operas, and singers responsible for classic recordings, and they wrote paragraphs about the interpretation of certain roles, but were conspicuously uninterested in the stage or the stage action. Reviews have often failed to mention that the performance took place at Drottningholm. This critical reception has made it acceptable for artistic directors at Drottningholm to conceive the stage action of an operatic work as ornament rather than substance.

Audience surveys were carried out at Drottningholm in 1980, 1996 and 2008 under the aegis of Stockholm University.[4] The number of spectators

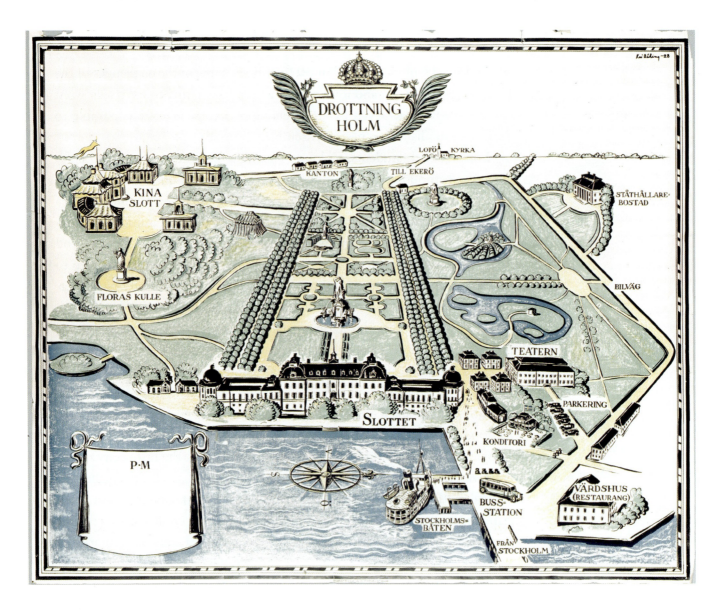

92. The domain of Drottningholm according to a tourist brochure from the 1920s.

older than 60 years doubled between first and last survey and this older age group now comprises the majority of the audience. Sadly, this is not an age profile that encourages experimentation. In interviews associated with these surveys, two categories of spectator emerged. The first and smaller category is the aficionado who comes to *hear* a performance and who does not care much about what happens on stage, while the second type comes to Drottningholm to experience the atmosphere of the theatre. For them, Drottningholm is a total experience that starts in the park before the performance and reaches its high point in the dimly lit auditorium, with the music, the costumes, the sliding wings. It is the encounter with history, not the particularities of a certain opera that these spectators enjoy. Repeatedly, the same refrain was heard: the most important aspect of the performance was the atmosphere and the privilege of being there. The majority of spectators come from Stockholm, the city and the surrounding regions, and most have been to Drottningholm before, returning again and again to make contact with history.

In 1991, the World Heritage Committee of the United Nations Educational, Scientific and Cultural Organization (UNESCO) adopted the Royal Domain of Drottningholm as a World Heritage Site. Drottningholm was registered under category C iv, meaning 'an outstanding example of a type of building, architectural or technological ensemble or landscape which illustrates (a) significant stage(s) of human history."[5] It is emphasized that the World Heritage Site includes the entire palace complex. 'The ensemble of Drottningholm - castle, theatre, Chinese pavilion and gardens - is the best example of a royal residence built in the 18th century in Sweden and is representative of all European architecture of that period, heir to the influences exerted by the Château de Versailles on the construction of royal residences in western, central and northern Europe.'[6] There is a mismatch between the World Heritage frame which places the theatre as part of the palace complex, and the festival frame which places the opera performance as part of a national and international arts scene, without reference to the Heritage location.

World Heritage status confers certain obligations on the Swedish state. According to UNESCO's 'Convention Concerning the Protection of the World Cultural and Natural Heritage' of 1972, each member state has 'to give the cultural and natural heritage a function in the life of the community and to integrate the protection of that heritage into comprehensive planning programmes.'[7] The Swedish state honoured its obligation to protect by limiting the number of performances to 40 per year in order to minimise damage to the theatre's interior fabric. Today there are fewer performances than this because of economic constraints but in the 1960s there were sometimes as many as 70 performances in a season, including divertissements and concerts. The obligation to give the theatre a place in the life of the community was conferred on the Drottningholm Court Theatre

Foundation, established in 1970 with a small subsidy from the state. This 'function in the life of the community' could be construed as the simple act of popularisation and drawing bodies into the theatre, but in our view it should involve drawing people into a reflective engagement with their 'heritage'.

No interest has been shown in another UNESCO category. According to UNESCO, the category of 'Intangible Cultural Heritage' is also to be valued.

> Cultural heritage does not end at monuments and collections of objects. It also includes traditions or living expressions inherited from our ancestors and passed on to our descendants, such as oral traditions, performing arts, social practices, rituals, festive events, knowledge and practices concerning nature and the universe or the knowledge and skills to produce traditional crafts. While fragile, intangible cultural heritage is an important factor in maintaining cultural diversity in the face of growing globalization. An understanding of the intangible cultural heritage of different communities helps with intercultural dialogue, and encourages mutual respect for other ways of life.[8]

There has not been sufficient line of continuity for baroque performers to think of applying to join the 250 or so international practices so far formally recognised. Nevertheless, the concept of 'intangible heritage' offers a different way to think about the artistic activity associated with this eighteenth-century cultural monument. The build-up of expertise in the performance of early opera constitutes a tiny fragment of intangible cultural heritage, all too easily jettisoned. It can be argued that cultural diversity means bringing a more mixed social profile into the theatre; but there is a counter argument that theatrical and operatic practice has become homogenised and globalised, and needs the injection of 'cultural' diversity afforded by historically distinct modes of performing.

The theatre is constrained by its status as a monument, and is not available for experimentation in the same way as, for example, the restored Confidencen Theatre in the palace complex of Ulriksdal. Agne Beijer had to content himself at Drottningholm with small, yellow electric bulbs, which

93. *The Magic Flute* by W. A. Mozart, performed at Confidencen at Ulriksdal in 2013 with live candle light. On stage Randi Røssaak.

offered the best approximation at the time to living candle light, and technological refinements emerged in the 1960s and again in the digital 1990s. In Confidencen, however, more relaxed fire regulations allow experiment with the 'authentic' visual and sensory qualities of candlelight. Though Confidencen offers such opportunities, as a restored space it lacks the eccentricities and challenges of Drottningholm. It lacks the atmosphere that derives from contact with the fragile, tactile substance of the past, marked by generations of usage.

At the other extreme, the Gustavian theatre perfectly preserved in a turret of Gripsholm Castle is now maintained purely as a museum piece to be glanced at alongside a gallery of period portraits, and it is hard for the visitor to get any feel of what it once felt like to perform in that space. It is a privilege and a responsibility to perform at Drottningholm. This privilege should entail not only technical mastery of the machinery, but also aesthetic knowledge about the techniques of communication proper to the building.

In the context of performance, we do not find the notion of 'heritage' offensive. The theatre constitutes heritage in two principal respects. It is part of Sweden's national heritage because of the complex place that Gustav III occupies in the nation's cultural memory: the paradoxical figure of a social liberal and political autocrat, a warmonger who cherished most forms of artistic culture and brought Sweden into closer contact with a modernising Europe. Yet the theatre of Drottningholm is also a piece of World Heritage because it is a unique survival, offering a potential tool for performers to learn about the history of their art. The usefulness of UNESCO World Heritage status, globally speaking, is that it flags the exceptional worth of that which from a purely local perspective may appear commonplace.

The theatre of Drottningholm is a special kind of museum, and we are not ashamed to say that we like museums, which - one might plausibly claim - form a more dynamic part of the modern cultural sector than theatre, animated by the challenge to find new ways to display artefacts from the recent and distant past in the context of a dramatic growth in visitor numbers. In a world of cyber realities and insulated, air-conditioned travel, it is the contact with material objects that gives museums their appeal. Museums do not just contain physical bits of the past, they give objects meaning through their modes of display. The past does not exist as a given, it always has to be displayed – by somebody, for somebody. In the theatre likewise we have to keep finding different ways of displaying the past, reading it, viewing it, performing it, and we have to keep asking new questions of what lies before us. There is no limit to experiment in the theatre of Drottningholm, because each generation comes to the past with new questions.

In regard to the future use of this theatre, and aware that a new artistic regime is about to commence, we end with three related axioms that derive from the perspectives and arguments which we have developed in this book.

> Firstly, what we hear and see in Drottningholm should only be audible and visible in this particular, unique space, and such should be the goal of any artistic director and the legitimate demand of any spectator. Of course, creative work that emerges from this engagement may well have a second and different life elsewhere, and work that has emerged elsewhere may reconfigure itself in Drottningholm in a new way.
>
> Secondly, performers should not conceive of themselves as putting their performance into a space, but as endowing the space with meaning. The theatre should never be conceived as an inert container into which a show can be slotted.
>
> Thirdly, performers should not think of the past as a fixed and separate thing, but as part of themselves, something inherited or re-

membered, something that has made them what they are. It seems easier for musicians than for actors to think along these lines.

Wishful thinking or useful strategies – the Drottningholm Court Theatre remains a challenge for future generations of creative artists, reflective historians and responsive audiences.

94. Arlecchino and Columbine in the ballet *Arlecchino – the Sorcerer of Love*, performed by Madeleine Onne and Mikael Mengarelli, 1996.

APPENDICES a-f:
DOCUMENTS FROM THE 18TH CENTURY AND REVIEWS FROM THE 20TH CENTURY

Translated by Samuel Edwards

a. Supplement to the regulations of the Royal Theatre.
Written by H. F. von Düben at Drottningholm, 8 August 1779[1]

As soon as his Royal Majesty graciously announces to the director of the orchestra and playhouse that all or some of those people under the director's charge shall present themselves for service at any of the royal pleasure palaces, it becomes the director's responsibility to arrange, in a timely manner, return journeys for them all, as well as any other necessary transportation, through requisitions to the royal stables, the shipyard, or the mayor's or superintendent's office, in all cases that require such. These unavoidable journeys are paid for from the royal purse but, by the same token, it is His Royal Majesty's earnest wish that all such transportations of people and goods, whenever possible, are to be undertaken by boat, in order to avoid unnecessary costs and the burdening of His Royal Majesty's own purse. To that end we are strictly forbidden to approve waggons for anyone other than orchestra and ballet masters, as well as the theatre's lead actors and principal dancers, or those who through established contracts already have such rights.

Those people who have room and board will each receive for their room, as is customary, one yellow wax candle for one or two days according to the season.

To all other theatre personnel occupying rooms, two are given for a larger room and, for a smaller room, a single tallow candle, either daily or every other day according to the season (namely the days of opera performances, as well as for other pre-agreed dates).

Furthermore, as is customary, lights for the theatre, the auditorium, boxes, and workshops, for which (in consideration of various needs) no certain number can be specified; likewise firewood, when needed.

All of the aforementioned expenses and needs are to be met by the royal court; however, since the court is not to be unnecessarily burdened, more than three dress rehearsals of a new theatre piece are not permitted; and, for a piece which has not been performed for a long time, only one rehearsal is allowed, unless His Royal Majesty on special occasions graciously ordains otherwise.

Lead and supporting actors and actresses, and principal dancers and danseuses are allowed, as before, to arrive the day before a performance even if no rehearsals are held; but they will receive board only for the evening.

b. Duchess Hedvig Elisbath Charlotta's[2] letter (in French) to Princess Sofia Albertina[3] concerning amusements at Drottningholm (among other matters):

Drottningholm, July 24, 1783

I would now like to tell you what has happened during the week that I have been here. On Friday eight days ago, the King travelled here with the court, but because I had only arrived in Stockholm that same day, I did not arrive here until Saturday evening. That day, nothing else happened beyond the King sitting and talking with us for a while. The following day was the French performance; they played "Democrite à la cour" and "Les précieuses ridicules." Although these pieces have been performed many times and have worn very thin, I found it all quite amusing since I have not seen any good actors in a long time, and I almost think that I prefer the King's troupe over Mr. Seuerling's, with all its scenic qualities.[4] Indeed variety is the spice of life. On Sunday, *Alceste* was performed in all its glory; never has Mrs. Müller played so well and everything gone so splendidly. Though somewhat cold, Stenborg was excellent; and Mademoiselle Bassi, the new danseuse, showed us her talent. You cannot imagine how she was applauded: it was such that you could not even have heard a thunderclap whenever she appeared. I must also admit that she has a look *à croquer*: She appears at the theatre to be about the same height as the Countess von Höken; she moves her body and carries her head exceptionally well; and when she dances, her arms remind you of Countess Löwenhielm's. Oh you could you ever forget them! Once you have seen them, you will recall Augusta's graceful arms. She rises and makes an *entrechat à six* without the slightest difficulty (I can almost believe that she made an *à huit*). The remarkable thing, however, is that she moves neither her head nor her arms when she leaps, nor twists her body in any direction. Perhaps one might think this would look stiff, but this is by no means the case; she shows no bashfulness and has nobility in her movements. Her feet carry her marvellously, even if they are perhaps slightly too long; her legs are well developed; and she is small-waisted. Though not truly a beauty, she has a cheerful and agreeable countenance when she appears on the stage; her eyes are unusually beautiful but her skin is slightly yellow as is the case with all Italians and many French people.

Nothing happened on Monday; all the actors, actresses, dancers, and danseuses were given time to prepare for the following day. The King, who suffers great pain in his shoulder (he no longer complains about his arm), was in bed most of the day. Throughout this week we had not had any readings until yesterday, then Desroches came here and read aloud from *Adèle et Théodore*, while Mr. Höjer painted the king's portrait, which already after the first sitting seems to be quite accurate.

I need not describe to you all the usual ceremonies on Tuesday, with cannon shots in the morning and illuminations at night, but wish only to concern myself with the evening's theatrical performance as it was most interesting. Two plays were performed as well as an "Intermède" in Swedish. The longer play was *Jean de Montfort*, which you might remember since you heard it read aloud last year. It is quite well written, and the King was particularly pleased with the performance. Sainte-Croix[5] criticised it quite sharply and, for my part, I agree with the general consensus that it certainly contains many beautiful ideas and lofty sentiments, but that its development is highly peculiar.

The "Intermède" was excellent. Mrs. Müller represented Euterpe, who complained that she had been robbed of her right to praise the Queen. There was notably one expression – "How can you tolerate a tragedy in prose?" – which spurred merriment, though mainly among those who did not like the performance.

Mlle Bassi, Mme Alix, her brother (Bournonville), and Marcadet were very successful in a *pas de quatre*; it is great fun to watch all four of them dance. The shorter piece was *Le galant jardinier*, which you possibly recall was intended to be staged at Gripsholm, and I already knew parts of Mathurine's role.

---

c. C. F. ADELCRANTZ' Memorandum concerning debts incurred as a result of the construction of the Drottningholm Theatre and the French troupe's dismissal

This memorandum was attached to a letter to President Reuterholm, dated Stockholm, 14 February 1794 (National Archive signature: EA: G.A. Reuterholms brevväxling, 1773-1801, Riksarkivet)

With blessed King Adolphus Frederick's fatal demise, I found myself in troublesome circumstances, both as custodian of the royal buildings, and as director of the playhouse.

The first difficulty consisted of the fact that during the construction of the Drottningholm Theatre, for which funds should have been taken from the King's purse, and due to a lack of assets therein, I had, in the years 1765 and 1766, borrowed against my own credit and the mortgage of my property a sum of money with a promise to repay it within a number of years. But with the blessed King's demise there remained an unpaid balance of 103,116 copper daler.[6]

As the director of the playhouse, I was also responsible for an unavoidable expense created through a royal order from the blessed King Gustavus III – who at the time lived in Paris – declaring that the French troupe would immediately be discharged, which could not be done without paying outstanding wages to the actors, as well as to those without a contractually stipulated travel allowance. Although those funds should have been taken from the royal purse, the gentlemen of the Council of the Realm, who were responsible for the estate inventory, determined that they were not authorised to meet such expenditure, and I had no other option than to borrow money again which, together with the previous advance amounted to 112,916 copper daler.

During the years 1771 and 1772 some of these debts were paid off, but at the beginning of the year 1775 – according to the attached certified transcript of His Excellency Count Beckfrijse's personal note of January 30 in the same year – there remained a claim against me of 104,215 copper daler.

Ever since that time, I have been unable to pay back the least part of this debt, and yet for nearly 30 years have had to pay the interest, the total of which is nearly twice the amount of the entire borrowed sum.

In order to pay the interest, I have not only been compelled to sell my property, both in town and in the country, but I have also accrued several thousand riksdaler of further debt, a burden from which I see no escape, unless His Royal Majesty intends to compensate me for my plight, which is no fault of my own, from public funds.

Two objections, however, could be raised against this case: the first, that the theatre construction is bound to the blessed King's own purse and that the debt cannot therefore be paid out of any fund other than this: and the second, that such considerable expenditure as this would burden the state too far in its current situation.

Concerning the first, the theatre construction debt is of a completely different nature to the King's personal debts incurred for the blessed King's own needs and enjoyment. When the construction of a theatre was declared an imperative need at Drottningholm Palace – where a theatre is, in conjunction with celebrations and court days, indispensable – and when all other buildings at Drottningholm Palace have been constructed using funds allocated by the state, there is hardly any valid reason why this alone should be paid out of a fund that no longer exists.

Concerning the burden that this expense would cause the state, I appeal to your Royal Majesty's gracious and sound discretion – in case the entire claim cannot be granted – to reduce the same to an amount that can be accommodated by existing assets; as well as to divide payment into so many annual payments that the repayment causes no suffering to the state.

In addition, I hold His Royal Majesty's magnanimity in such high regard that I imagine he cannot with pleasure watch plays at a theatre that for so long has remained unpaid for, and at the cost of a faithful subject's worldly well-being.

C. F. Adelcrantz

d. Summer Festival at Drottningholm
Review in Uppsala Nya Tidning 7 August 1948, by Richard Engländer

It is not impossible that, in the future, the Drottningholm Court Theatre will play the same role as Glyndebourne near London, or Munich's Residenztheater, with its summer pageants. One prerequisite is to develop an appropriate organisational form and a definite line in terms of repertoire. It is also to be hoped that this treasure will be fully discovered by the people of Stockholm themselves.

With Domenico Cimarosa's *Il Matrimonio Segreto* (*The Secret Marriage*), the opera being performed there offers more than a mere taste of theatre history. This captivating work, which had its first performance in Vienna a year after Mozart's death, has remained in the repertoire in Italy to this day, and has even appeared elsewhere, including Leipzig's municipal theatre around 1930. And that is quite understandable; people enjoy this kind of bourgeois rococo most, when one is reminded of Mozart as little as possible in spite of all the Mozartisms. In their comic opera, Italians demand above all else the typical scenarios of situation comedy as theatrical entertainment. In this respect, Giovanni Bertati's text is already ideal, not least due to its naturalness and a certain balance. One noticed this even more yesterday, as the Italian guest director Riccardo Picozzi - along with conductor Lamberto Gardelli - accomplished an ensemble effect of the highest order. It was a joy to confirm the strength of our opera singers in their certainty of gesture, their linguistic prowess – you heard excellent Italian the entire evening – and their song-like charm.

There was, playing the proper comedic type,

Sven-Erik Jacobsson, in the role of deaf merchant Geronimo, who dreams of noble sons-in-law; then the elegant young Earl Robinson, (a role which might have been created for Åke Collett); the proud, ambitious, and beautiful Elisetta (Lilly Furlin); set on marriage, the wealthy widow Fidalma (a priceless study by Benna Lemon-Brundin); and the faithful, loving couple Carolina - Paolino (Eva Prytz, Arne Ohlsson). The latter's secret marriage is the source of constant concern, comic entanglements and, last but not least, beautiful music.

Eva Prytz and Arne Ohlsson's arias and their duet at the beginning of the opera, along with the famous finale of the second act, were the musical highlights. Birger Bergling as set-designer has fitted the three rival ladies with individually coloured crinolines, and positioned himself as a quasi-contemporary of Cimarosa. Also, the gentlemen in the orchestra under Zamberti's vibrant leadership were dressed in period costume. Was the orchestra's sound also original? It is difficult to say. It might have been more transparent here and there. Sometimes it seemed almost as if the house's peculiar acoustics (more accustomed to Gluck's pathetic tones) worked against so many gleeful melodies and the opera buffa's rapid pace. Be that as it may, in any case we experienced a delightful afternoon, which we can regard as a crucial step towards Drottningholm becoming a major hub for summer festival performances.

Richard Engländer

e. Wonderfully Vibrant *Cosi fan Tutte*
Review in Stockholms Tidningen 2 July 1962, by Leif Aare

Mozart's characters are psychologically as complex as Shakespeare's. Putting on an opera buffa such as *Cosi fan Tutte* must be one of the most difficult tasks a director can attempt.

The situation comedy can be quite wonderful. But the comedy never turns to farce because humanity is always the focus. Mozart's music gives us a sense of every emotion, every slightest impulse of the characters. And yet there is nothing heavy in *Cosi fan Tutte*; it dances with unearthly grace and spirituality.

Yes, *Cosi fan Tutte* is truly difficult for the director. But at the same time it is easy. There is no opera composer who gives the stage director as much help as Mozart; everything is there in the music, one just has to listen. This, by all means, is not necessarily simple and requires the greatest of sensibility, as well as a suitable temperament for translating whatever the music specifies into the theatrical dimension.

It seems to me that the man behind The Drottningholm Theatre's Sunday premiere of *Cosi fan Tutte* – Danish director Holger Boland – possesses the right sensibility and, to a great extent, the temperament.

Not everything is ready. Boland is said to have had an unusually short time for rehearsal work. But the performance as a whole is spectacular.

Boland succeeds particularly well in suggesting, tightening and emphasising in the opera's movements what the music is saying. At times he grasps stylisation with excellent effect. When one of the girls is in the midst of succumbing, accompanied by a swelling and sensual violin arabesque, she moves towards her new love in a way that resembles a dance.

Even the character direction seemed inspired in

most instances. The two girls are sung by Margot Rödin and Elisabeth Söderström. Once again, Ms. Rödin establishes herself as one of our most interesting and intelligent young opera singers. As the more libidinous of the two sisters, she is quite wonderful when she passionately defends her old love. At the same time she cleverly reveals to the audience that her new love has come into full bloom. Vocally, this difficult part fits perfectly with Margot Rödin's exquisitely honed voice.

The more faithful and more dramatic Elisabeth Söderström (Fiordiligi) balances her fiery sister with mature womanhood. She simply becomes a reluctant victim of circumstance. Through Elisabeth Söderström's vocally brilliant interpretation we learn that lust is not synonymous with love.

The courting gentlemen are sung by Carl-Axel Hallgren and Kåge Jehrlander. Hallgren makes an artistically balanced study. Jehrlander is fine as long as he gets to play comedy. But suddenly, the music intensifies and we no longer know whether Mozart is being playful or serious. Jehrlander then continues to clown- which is wrong. I really like Jehrlander's vocal timbre, a rare thing in our country.

Exquisitely malicious is the piece's cynical philosopher portrayed by Erik Sundquist. His accomplice in the plot, the chambermaid, is sung by the coquettish Karin Langebo.

I cannot in truth accept the undeniably beautiful 1700s décor; it fits well with the classicist style of Gluck but not with Mozart's psychological comedy.

Hans Schmidt-Isserstedt conducts and he is obviously enraptured by the task; I have never heard Schmidt-Isserstedt conduct in a manner so wonderfully vibrant, subtle, and penetrating. It is simply masterful.

Leif Aare

f. Mozart: Earthy and Brilliant
Review in Svenska Dagbladet 4 August 1979, by Carl-Gunnar Åhlén

OPERA

The Drottningholm Theatre: Don Giovanni by WA Mozart & L. da Ponte. Director: Göran Järvefelt. Conductor: Arnold Östman. Choreography: Mats Isaksson. Costumes: Brita Broberg, Börje Edh. Lighting: Torkel Blomkvist. Cast: Helena Döse, Birgit Nordin, Anita Soldh, Håkan Hagegård, Bengt Rundgren, Gösta Winberg, Erik Sædén, Tord Wallström.

To play a composition just as the composer wrote it and to use the same types of instruments that were available to him may seem a modest goal. Paradoxically, however, there is scarcely anything more radical in our otherwise fairly tolerant music scene than trying to correct the prevailing perception of the classics: you are altering something safe and therefore breaking a taboo.

Nevertheless it is necessary.

In this country, we are fortunate enough to own the best venue in the world for such experiments: The Drottningholm Theatre, with its fascinating medial position somewhere between a cult site and a centre for research. To play Mozart's "Don Giovanni" entirely with the original instruments is to fulfill a mission. It is overwhelming and amazing, because under the surface of generations of well-meaning misconceptions and Rococo ideals is a music that is not at all similar to our picture of the

Olympian Mozart: more grotesque and earthy, but no less human, and no less ingenious.

The violins' pinpoint sharpness, the violas' meaty bass notes, the French horns' flavour of the forest, and the trombones' gentle illumination all contain unimagined possibilities for characterisation, and it certainly allows Arnold Östman to shine when he, for example, rounds out the irony of letting the French horns tease Donna Elvira while Leporello sings his catalogue aria. His control of the young ensemble is gentle but exacting. With Östman, the theatre is entering a new era: for those who did not already recognise it, he must henceforth be considered a world-class conductor.

It is now the task of responsible politicians to protect the orchestra that is being built. The opportunity to achieve an international profile will not come again, but right now we are half a step ahead of Europe.

Great successes have been loudly applauded within the delicate walls of the Drottningholm Theatre, but rarely with such overtones of excitement, gratitude and expectation as last Friday's premiere. This feeling, shared by all participants, was also directed towards the other major player in the production, the director Göran Järvefelt.

A frequently used method of directing is the "anecdotal", i.e., the spicing up of performance diversions from the action. Järvefelt's directorial art rests upon a solid ideal, linking the plot sequences in a logical and inevitable sequence. There is no need to emphasise that Järvefelt's method is highly stimulating and rewarding for performers, provided they are sufficiently responsive.

In that respect, this production of "Don Giovanni" is abundantly blessed. The singers have assumed their roles with a commitment that borders on obsession: Helena Döse's uninhibited and sensual Donna Anna; Birgit Nordin's intellectually distant but nonetheless temperamental Donna Elvira; Anita Sodh's figurative and tonally light-footed Zerlina; Bengt Rundgren's imposing Commander; Gosta Winbergh's perfectly voiced Don Ottavio; Tord Wallgren's furious Masetto. Most fascinating, however, is the combination of Don Juan and Leporello. For Håkan Hagegård's and Erik Saedén's respective portrayals, there is only one word that comes close: brilliant.

Järvefelt's and Hagegård's Don Juan is a study in social disintegration. He displays the classic arrogant posturing of d'Andrade, almost feminine in his self-absorption. Don Juan loves only himself, and does not even look at his victims, narcissistically conscious that he is irresistible. From behind the proud mask – which seems to have borrowed features from Donald Sutherland in Fellini's movie *Casanova* – cowardice emerges. After the murder of The Commendatore, he is desperate, terrified even of Leporello, who here is not a plump glutton but rather a lean, hungry, and dangerous type. It is a fantastic, taut portrayal by Erik Saedén. When The Commendatore or stone guest arrives at Don Juan's castle, the host is completely intoxicated. After all of the first act's suave elegance, here are just tangles and stubble. The wig is the last symbol of dignity Don Juan loses before plunging into the grave.

In Don Juan's destruction, Järvefelt wants to see the collapse of aristocracy. He argues – and this is an interesting discussion point – that he dies because he has sinned against humanity. "The murdered Commander's statue represents the voice of humanism and humanity," he writes in the programme. Through "the theatre's own logic," Mozart brings "a marble statue to life to pass judgment."

Are we to understand that the actual theatre (!) comes to the defence of humanity? Yes, apparently this is what Järvefelt seeks. Theatrical thunder roars and the wind machine howls with artificial wind when the guests at the ball attack Don Juan. The Commendatore's response to the invitation is heard through the curtain (thus the curtain "participates" in the play). Don Juan's demise is not accompanied by the flames of hell; he simply sinks down through a trapdoor. It is the theatre itself which carries out the sentence.

This seems, if I may say so, a little abstract, as if Järvefelt were trying at all costs to avoid the superstructure of religious morality which provides the play's fundamental premise. The opera was called *The Punished Hedonist* (*Den straffade vällustingen*) when staged in Sweden for the first time. Don Juan has sinned against the Most High; when neither the nobility, nor the bourgeoisie, nor the peasants can punish him, the church steps in. That is the intent and there is no getting around this fact.

You can also consider the relationship between Donna Anna and Don Ottavio. Through her, Järvefelt expresses both lust and hatred for the seducer and killer Don Juan, and thus possibilities emerge for a portrayal composed of conflicting forces. However, it is not obvious why she – like all of Don Juan's enemies – so ostentatiously turns her back on Don Ottavio, the man who for Järvefelt represents Don Juan's moral antithesis. It is he, rather than The Commendatore, who ought to advocate humanist ideals.

It should be emphasised that these reservations apply only to the production concept. The theatrical portrayal is superb in its fusion of a contemporary, almost brutal, body language with geometrically arranged scenery, which optimises the baroque setting's aesthetic possibilities. It only becomes a little awkward in terms of musical coordination when the singers stand at the very back of the stage. You could describe and analyse and praise from one moment to the next, but to what avail? Fortunately, TV1 will record the performance and thus widen the circle of its contented viewers and listeners.

Carl-Gunnar Åhlén

NOTES

Chapter 1

1. 'Det låg ett skimmer över Gustavs dagar' is the first line of the Academy Song by Esaias Tegnér, written in 1836, which has become a proverb in Swedish.
2. Nordensvan 1917, Levertin 1889
3. Stockholms Tidning, 20 August 1922.
4. *Slottsteatrarna på Drottningholm och Gripsholm.* An English translation of this book was published, although abbreviated, as late as 1972, *Court Theatres at Drottningholm and Gripsholm*, New York: Benjamin Blom.

Chapter 2

1. The unclear circumstances surrounding this fire are thoroughly investigated in Beijer 1981, pp. 22-242.
2. More details about Monvel's activities on the stage of Drottningholm follow in chapter 4.
3. In 2011 a conference was held in Stockholm on the challenging of illuminating the Drottningholm stage. Experts from a number of European and North American countries participated. But even the collective wisdom of these experts failed to offer a satisfactory solution for recreating the magic of candlelight.
4. Ove Hidemark describes these steps in the book about the Drottningholm Court Theatre published by Byggnadsstyrelsen in 1993. *Drottningholms Slottsteater*, Stockholm 1993
5. Adelcrantz continued to live there after the death of Gustav III in 1792. See his letter of complaint concerning repayment of his expenses in Appendix c. He died in 1796.
6. Anders Zander, *Drottningholms Slottsteater*, p. 124f. mentions Byggnadsstyrelsen, Drottningholms Teatermuseum, ståthållarämbetet, slottsarkitekten och riksantikvarieämbetet.

7. Ove Hidemark, 'Att lyssna till en uråldrig byggnad', in: *Drottningholms slottsteater*, p. 139.

Chapter 3

1. See Zachary Dunbar 'Music Theatre and Musical Theatre' in *The Cambridge Companion to Theatre History*, ed. David Wiles and Christine Dymkowski (Cambridge: Cambridge University Press, 2013) pp.197-207.
2. Cf. David Wiles *A Short History of Western Performance Space* (Cambridge: Cambridge University Press, 2003).
3. The text is widely anthologised. See for example Barrett H. Clark *European Theories of the Drama* (New York: Crown, 1965) pp.322-328.

Chapter 4

1. David Lowenthal used Hartley's phrase as the title of a theoretical book on historiography, *The Past is a Foreign Coutry*, Cambridge: Cambridge University Press 1985.
2. Quoted from Elisabeth Mansén, *Sveriges Historia 1721-1830*, Stockholm: Norstedts 2011, p. 309 (my translation).
3. The distinctions between intimate, private and public are elaborated upon by Jürgen Habermas in *The Structural Transformation of the Public Sphere: An Inquiry into a Category of Bourgeois Society*. Transl. by T. Burger and F. Lawrence, CambridgeMass. 1989 (German original in 1962).
4. Skiöldebrand in Beth Hennings, *Gustav III*, Stockholm: Norstedts 1967, p. 116.
5. His full name was Adolph Ludvig Gustaf Fredrik Couchi (also spelled Coichi), born c. 1747 in St. Croix in the (then) Danish West Indies. At the age of ten he was presented as a gift to Queen Lovisa Ulrika, and later he served Princess Sophia Albertina. He received a number of Swedish honours and decorations and lived until 1822. Two novels have

been written about him, namely Magnus Jakob Crusenstolpe's *Morianen* (1880) and Ylva Eggehorn's *En av dessa timmar* (1996).

6. The actual performance did not take place before 1 September 1786.
7. *Kindlers Literatur Lexikon*, vol. 17, p. 7462 (dtv, München 1974).
8. The story of Victorine was picked up by George Sand, who wrote a sequel in 1851, *Le marriage de Victorine*.
9. Cf. Chapter 2, when his picture was discussed during the guided tour.
10. Her civil name was Anne Francoise Hippolyte Boutet, or after her mother, Salvetat. Born in 1779, she served the Comédie from 1799-1841 and died in 1847.
11. August Strindberg *Memorandum till Intima Teaterns personal från regissören*, Stockholm: Börjeson 1908. English translation (for example) in Barrett H. Clark, European Theories of the Drama (Crown: New York 1965).
12. Published in *Gustaviansk teater, skildrad av Pehr Hilleström*. Inledning av Agne Beijer, bildtexter av Gustaf Hilleström, Stockholm: Wahlström & Widstrand 1947.
13. In Germanic languages, this specialisation of actors is called 'Rollenfach', meaning that each character was neatly put in a box.
14. Cf. Joseph Roach, *The Player's Passion: Studies in the Science of Acting*, Newark: University of Delaware Press 1985.
15. *Dissertatio de actione scenica*, Munich 1727
16. For details see Lisbet Scheutz, *Berömda och glömda stockholmskvinnor*, Stockholm: mbm-förlag 1995, pp. 44-47
17. For a detailed record, including a description of the plot, see Birgitta Schyberg, ''Gustav Vasa' as Theatre Propaganda', in *Gustavian Opera. An Interdisciplinary Reader in Swedish Opera, Dance and Theatre 1771-1809*, Stockholm: The Royal Swedish Academy of Music 1991, nr. 66, pp. 293-322.
18. The circumstances of this play, which can be approximately rendered in English as The Occasion Makes the Thief (a Swedish proverb), and later claims that Armfelt had not written it himself, are minutely

described by Armfelt's latest biographer, Stig Ramel in *Gustaf Mauritz Armfelt 1757-1814*, Stockholm: Bonniers 1997. Others, among them Gunilla Dahlberg in *Den svenska litteraturen*, maintain that Hallström wrote the play. (p.149, 151) A vaudeville usually combines existing and well-known melodies with new texts.

19. This is the same Swedish Academy, to which Alfred Nobel entrusted the election of the Nobel Prize in literature.

20. Kerstin Derkert (ed.), *Den svartsjuke neapolitanar'n, Dram i tre akter av Gustav III*. Stockholm: Stuts 1985. The editor gives very insightful explanations in her introduction and her comments on the play, p.21f.

21. Derkert p. 12.

22. The remarks in italics are the notes from the prompter's copy of the play.

23. P. 87-88.

24. Of course there was no complete darkness on stage. The lighting equipment would not allow for that, but could achieve a relative darkness by turning all lights away from the acting area.

25. Se Kerstin Derkert's comments, p. 104, 107.

26. Swedish translation 1902-42. An excerpt from one of her letters in the diary is reprinted in Appendix b.

27. This divertissement took place in September 1783 and is described in the diary edition from 1903, volume II, p. 34-35.

28. This was the last in a long series of tournaments or carousels that had started in 1777. The first ones were held in or close to the city so that the citizens of Stockholm could watch the proceedings. Between 1778 and 1785, four carousels were held at Drottningholm.

29. Magnus Olausson, in: *Gustavian Opera*, p.223-34.

30. Olausson, p. 231

31. There is no evidence that Vogler actually made such a remark – rather this is my conclusion drawn from the repertoire of Gustavian opera.

32. For details concerning the musical variations see Kathleen Kuzmick Hansell, 'Gluck's "Orpheus och Euridice" in Stockholm – Performance

practices on the way from "Orfeo" to "Orphée" 1773-1786'. In *Gustavian Opera*, p. 253-280.

33. These paintings are exhibited in the rooms of the Drottningholm Theatre, and in the foyer of the Royal Opera, respectively.
34. Referred to by Kathleen Kuzmick Hansell, op.cit. p. 254. She also refers to a second version of this painting with a rougher background, but basically the same dresses.
35. Quoted from *Gustaviansk teater, skildrad av Pehr Hilleström*, p. 38.
36. Quoted in *Gustaviansk teater, skildrad av Pehr Hilleström*, p. 38.
37. Name days rather than birthdays were celebrated in the eighteenth century, despite the fact that the Lutheran Reformation had banned the saints from their churches.

Chapter 5

1. The architectural source appears to be Borromini's Spada Palace in Rome: see Kristopher Neville *Nicodemus Tessin the Elder*, Turnhout: Brepols, 2009, 86. For a theatre historian, the technique evokes Scamozzi's famous vistas in the Palladian Teatro Olympico. Comprehensive documentation of the palace can be found in *Drottningholms slott*. Vol. 1, Från Hedvig Eleonora till Lovisa Ulrika, ed. Göran Alm and Rebecka Millhagen (Stockholm : Byggförlaget Kultur, 2004.).
2. The shelving is authentic, but the books are in fact substitutes.
3. See Merit Laine 'An Eighteenth-century Minerva: Lovisa Ulrika and Her Collections at Drottningholm Palace 1744-1777' *American Society for Eighteenth-Century Studies* 31 (1996) pp. 493-503.
4. Agne Beijer, *Drottningholms slottsteater på Lovisa Ulrikas och Gustaf III's tid*. (Drottningholm: Drottningholms Teatermuseum, 1981) p.15; Catharina Nolin, *Drottningholms slottspark* (Stockholm: Trydells, 2000), p.24.
5. Agne Beijer *Court Theatres of Drottningholm and Gripsholm*, tr. G.Frnölich (New York: Blom, 1972) plates 2 & 3.
6. *Gustavian Opera: an Interdisciplinary Reader in Swedish Opera, Dance*

and Theatre 1771-1809 (Stockholm: Royal Swedish Academy of Music, 1991) p.67; Kjerstin Dellert and Inger Marie Opperud *Confidencen – an Old Theatre Resurrected*, trans. L.Hadorph (Stockholm: Confidencen Rediviva, 1999). On p.47, Opperud follows Beijer in associating the theatre with Laxenburg.

7. On the Italian tradition and its influence on Louis XIV's theatre architecture, see Alice Jarrard *Architecture as Performance in Seventeenth-Century Europe: Court Ritual in Modena, Rome, and Paris* (Cambridge, Cambridge University Press, 2003). Joanna Norman traces the principle of the imperial box back to Vienna in 1704: 'Performance and Performativity,' in *Baroque: Style in the Age of Magnificence 1620-1800*, ed. Michael Snodin and Nigel Llewellyn (London: Victoria and Albert Museum, 2009) 142-165, p.159.

8. Barbara Coeyman 'Theatres for Opera and Ballet during the Reigns of Louis XIV and Louis XV,' *Early Music* 18, (1990): 22-37. For a broader survey see Thomas E.Lawrenson *The French Stage and Playhouse in the XVIIth Century: a Study in the Advent of the Italian Order*, 2nd edn. (New York, AMS Press, 1986). Jarrard Architecture as Performance p. 201 has an illustration of the auditorium of the Salle des Machines.

9. Alfred Marie 'La salle de théâtre du Château de Fontainebleau,' *Revue d'histoire du théâtre* 3 (1951): 237-47.

10. See Joanna Norman 'Performance and Performativity: Baroque Art and Design for the Theatre,' in *Baroque 1620-1800: Style in the Age of Magnificence* (London: V&A, 2009) 142-165, pp.158-9.

11. Alfred Marie 'Les théâtres du Château de Versailles,' *Revue d'histoire du théâtre* 3 (1951): 133-52, p.150; Agne Beijer 'Les théâtres de Drottningholm et de Gripsholm,' *Revue d'histoire du théâtre* 8 (1956): 215-227.

12. *Collection des écrits politiques, littéraires et dramatiques de Gustave III, roi de Suède : suivie de sa correspondance* (Stockholm : C. Delén, 1804-05), v.1, p.176.

13. Epistle 115

14. On Tessin see R. Nisbet Bain *Gustavus III and his contemporaries,*

1746-1792 : an overlooked chapter of eighteenth century history (London: Kegan Paul, Trench, Trübner, 1894) pp.13-20; Carl Fredrik Scheffer *Lettres particulières à Carl Gustaf Tessin, 1744-1752*, ed. Jan Heidner (University of Stockholm, 1982) pp.9-11.

15. *Letters from an Old Man to a Young Prince with the Answers* (London: R.Griffiths, 1759) i.165-6 (Letter 31).

16. Tessin *Letters* i.76 (Letter 17)

17. Stig Fogelmark suggests a location in the park in *Gustavian Opera* p.79.

18. Scheffer *Lettres* p.11.

19. Tessin *Letters* ii.240-51 (Letter 65).

20. Bain *Gustavus* i.25

21. *A Treatise of Human Nature* (Penguin: Harmondsworth, 1969) IV.v , p.301.

22. Ernst Hartwig Kantorowicz *The King's Two Bodies: a Study in Mediaeval Political Theology* (Princeton: Princeton University Press, 1997).

23. The machinery is illustrated in an engraving of 1771: see Simon Tidworth *Theatres: an Illustrated History* (London: Pall Mall Press, 1973), plate 77.

24. Ove Hidemark 'The Advent and Growth of a Theatre Building' in Ove Hidemark, Per Edström, Birgitta Schyberg et al. *Drottningholm Court Theatre* (Stockholm: Byggforlaget, 1993) 29-73, p.42.

25. I am grateful to Robert Franklin for this observation.

26. Birgitta Schyberg 'On Stage at Drottningholm Theatre' in Ove Hidemark, Per Edström, Birgitta Schyberg et al. *Drottningholm Court Theatre* (Stockholm: Byggforlaget, 1993) 13-20, p.13; Anna Johnson 'The Hero and the People: On National Symbols in Gustavian Opera,' in *Gustavian Opera: Swedish Opera, Dance and Theatre 1771-1809* (Stockholm: Royal Swedish Academy of Music, 1991) 173-195, p.176. See p.000 above.

27. Tessin *Letters* ii.121 (letter 54).

28. Neil Kent *The Soul of the North: a Social, Architectural, and Cultural History of the Nordic Countries, 1700-1940* (London: Reaktion Books, 2000) p.258.

29. Epistle 249, in Laurence Senelick (ed.) *National Theatre in Northern and Eastern Europe, 1746-1900* (Cambridge: CUP, 1991) p.22.

30. Ekeblad's journal extracted in Beijer, *Drottningholms slottsteater*, pp.298-9. My translation from the French.

31. On Voltaire's appreciation see: H. Arnold Barton 'Gustav III of Sweden and the Enlightenment' in *American Society for Eighteenth-Century Studies* 6 (1972): 1-34, p.6.

32. Scheffer *Lettres* 20.

33. See Kathleen Kuzmick Hansell 'Gluck's 'Orpheus och Euridice' in Stockholm: performance practices on the way from 'Orfeo' to 'Orphée' 1773-1786' in *Gustavian Opera* pp.253-292.

34. See the discussions by Barbro Stribolt and Per Bjurström in *Gustavian Opera* pp.123-145.

35. Cf. Iain McCalman, 'Philippe de Loutherbourg's Spectacular Simulations,' in *Historical Reenactment: from Realism to the Affective Turn*, eds. Iain McCalman and Paul Pickering (Basingstoke: Palgrave Macmillan, December 2009.

36. 'Letter to a lady of a certain age on the present state of the Opera' in Piero Weiss (ed.) *Opera: A History in Documents* (Oxford: OUP, 2002) p.108.

37. Cited in Roger Savage 'The Staging of Opera' in *The Oxford Illustrated History of Opera*, ed. Roger Parker (Oxford: OUP, 1992) 350-420, p. 370. Rousseau's optimal arrangement of the operatic orchestra, with the Kapellmeiser facing the singers on a central harpsichord, is illustrated on p.60 of this volume.

38. *Mémoires, ou essais sur la musique* (Paris, 1797) pp.40-41.

39. 1786 regulations in *Gustavian Opera* p. 273. An early C19th water colour depicts the Kapellmeister facing the actors and beating time at the Stockholm Opera House, p. 55.

40. 'Dictionnaire de Musique: Opéra' in *Écrits sur la musique, la langue et le théâtre* ed. Bernard Gagnebin and Marcel Raymond (Paris: Gallimard, 1995) p.954-5.

41. See William Weber 'La musique ancienne in the Waning of the Ancien

Régime,' *The Journal of Modern History* 56.1 (Mar., 1984): 58-88.

42. For a historical account of the term, see Helen Hills 'The Baroque: the Grit in the Oyster of Art History' in *Rethinking the Baroque*, ed. H. Hills (Farnham: Ashgate, 2011), pp. 11-36.
43. *The Origin of German Tragic Drama*, tr. J. Osborne (London: Verso, 2003) p.201.
44. For transmission to the Swedish court see Per Bjurström 'Nicodemus Tessin il Giovane: Descriziione delle machine sceniche nei teatri veneziani' in *Giacomo Torelli : l'invenzione scenica nell'Europa barocca*, ed. Francesco Milesi (Fano: Fondazione Cassa di risparmio di Fano, 2000) pp.29-32.
45. Per Bjurström *Giacomo Torelli and Baroque Stage Design* (Stockholm: Almqvist & Wiksel, 1961) p.211.
46. Benjamin Origins 66.
47. Important French-oriented studies include Richard Sennett *The Fall of Public Man* Cambridge: CUP, 1977); Daniel Roche *The Culture of Clothing: Dress and Fashion in the 'ancien regime'* tr. Jean Birrell (Cambridge: CUP, & Paris: Éditions de la Maison des sciences de l'homme (1994). See also Marcia Pointon *Hanging the Head: Portraiture and Social Formation in 18th-Century England* (Cambridge, Mass.: Yale UP, 1993), pp. 107-36, though I do not follow her argument about the inherent masculinity of the wig.
48. See Claude Nordmann *Gustave III, un démocrate couronné* (Lille: Presses universitaires de Lille, 1986) especially pp.194-6.
49. On Blenheim see David Green *Blenheim Palace* (London: Country Life, 1951); Jeri Bapasola *The finest view in England: the landscape and gardens at Blenheim Palace* (Woodstock: Blenheim Palace, 2009); www.blenheimpalace.com; www.british-history.ac.uk/report.aspx?compid=7897.
50. Green *Blenheim Palace*, pp.188-90. On French amateur theatricals at this time see Marie-Emmanuelle Plagnol-Diéval *Le théâtre de société: un autre théâtre?* (Paris: Champion, 2003).
51. See especially Laurajane Smith *Uses of heritage.* (London: Routledge,

2006)

52. Jane Malcolm-Davies 'The TALC and Heritage Sites' in *The Tourism Area Life Cycle* Vol. 1: Applications and Modifications, ed. Richard W. Butler (Clevedon : Channel View Publications, 2005) 162-80, p. 176-7.

53. Raphael Samuel *Theatres of Memory*, Vol.1. Past and present in contemporary culture (London: Verso, 1994). The sociology of cultural memory can be traced back to Maurice Halbwachs' *On Collective Memory* tr. L. Coser (Chicago: University of Chicago Press, 1982) first published in French in 1925.

54. Pierre Nora 'Between Memory and History: Les Lieux de Mémoire,' *Representations* 26, (Spring, 1989): 7-24. His edited 7 volume collection *Les Lieux de mémoire* was published by Gallimard in 1984–1992.

55. *Letters* ii.121 (letter 54).

56. Cited from Josette Féral 'The Art of Acting' in *The Cambridge Companion to Theatre History*, ed. David Wiles and Christine Dymkowski (Cambridge: CUP, 2013) 184-96, pp.186-8.

57. Theodor W.Adorno 'Opera and the long-playing record' in *Essays on Music*, ed. R.Leppert (Berkeley: University of California Press, 2002) 283-7, p.284.

Chapter 6

1. Quote from Gustaf Hilleström, *Drottningholmsteatern förr och nu/The Drottningholm Theatre – Past and Present*, translation by Joseph Stewart, Stockholm: Natur och Kultur, 1980 (new, enlarged edition) p. 106-7.

2. We are grateful to the Friends for financially supporting the costs of illustrating this book.

3. The International Federation for Theatre Research is also known by its French title, Fédération Internationale de Recherche Théâtrale, and abbreviated as IFTR/FIRT.

4. *Drottningholmsteatern förr och nu/ The Drottningholm Theatre – Past and Present, Dramatik på Drottningholm*, Stockholm: Lindqvist, 1975.

5. Quoted from G. Hilleström, *Drottningholmsteatern förr och nu*, p. 24 (revised transl). Hilleström defends the cuts, and informs the reader that only 8 of the 28 arias had to be cut.
6. Hilleström p.29, quoting from Christian Science Monitor
7. Ibid.
8. Cited from Hilleström, p.33 (my transl).
9. Hilleström, p. 34 (my transl.)
10. See Stefan Fogelberg Rota's interpretation in his dissertation *Poesins drottning. Christina av Sverige och de italienska akademierna*, Stockholm University 2008, p. 186-911.
11. Regarding Noverre see chapter 4; John Weaver, *Orchesography or: The Art of Dancing (1706)*, Cirencester: Echo Library, 2005.
12. According to Gustaf Hilleström (1980), p. 21.
13. Hilleström p. 17.
14. Willmar Sauter, *Publiken på Drottningholm*, Teatervetenskapliga småskrifter, Stockholm: Stuts, 1981, p. 30.
15. Göran Järvefelt, *Operaregi – ett sökande efter människan*, Stockholm: Bonniers 1990, p. 97 (my transl.).
16. Järvefelt, p. 93.
17. Järvefelt, p. 97.
18. Interwiew with Jonas Forssell on 7 April 2009.
19. Fredric Jameson, *Brecht and Method*, New York: Verso, 1998
20. Hans-Georg Gadamer, *Wahrheit und Methode. Grundzüge einer philosophischen Hermeneutik*, Tübingen: JCB Mohr 1960 (1975), pp. 284 ff.
21. Karin Helander: 'Tidstypiska gester skapar lätt distans', *Svenska Dagbladet* 31 May 2011
22. Thomas Anderberg: 'Humoristiskt. Bästa uppsättningen på många år', *Dagens Nyheter* 4 August 2012.

Chapter 7

1. Videocassette published by RM Arts in 1993. On Östman, see Chapter 6 p.164ff below.
2. YouTube video, available through www.vadstena-akademien.org.
3. I am grateful to Gilli Bush-Bailey for her comments on this topic, drawing upon her pioneering work with Jacky Bratton using students to 'revive' the work of Jane Scott, a project documented in *Nineteenth-Century Theatre & Film* 29.2 (2002). I was unfortunately not able to see T'Hooft's 2012 production of Haydn's *Orlando Paladino* at Drottningholm, where she used a professional cast. Willmar Sauter tells me there was amongst some but not all the performers a much stronger sense that rococo gesture had been internalised, and a more successful integration of gesture and music.
4. *Practical Illustrations of Rhetorical Gesture and Action* (London: Sherwood, Neely & Jones) 1822, p.2-3.
5. Conference discussion. Stockholm. 26/8/13.
6. Wolfgang Hildesheimer *Mozart*, tr. M. Faber (London: Dent, 1983) p.288.
7. *Encyclopédie, ou dictionnaire raisonné des sciences, des arts et des metiers* Vol.4 (1757) p.652. My translation.
8. *Art of Gesture: The Practices and Principles of 18th Century Acting* (Heidelberg: C. Winter, 1987). An important UK exponent of Barnett's method in the field of opera is Ian Caddy: see www.BaroqueGestures.com. For a critique of Barnett, see Virginia Scott *Women on the Stage in Early Modern France: 1540-1750* (Cambridge: CUP, 2010) pp.202-3. Knowledge of the past is never objective: Kindermann is usually mentioned nowadays in connection with his harnessing of a scientific theatre history to the ideology of fascism in the 1930s and 40s: see Sandra Richter *A History of Poetics: German Scholarly Aesthetics and Poetics in International Context, 1770-1960* (Berlin & New York: Walter de Gruyter, 2010) pp.255-60.
9. Barnett *Art of Gesture* p.14.
10. *De Oratore* 193-4, *Noctes Atticae* 6.5, *Life of Cicero* 5.5, *Institutio Oratoria* vi.2.25-36.

11. 'The Passions Dissected, or, On the Dangers of Boiling down Alexander the Great', in *Early Music*, 37. 1 (2009): 101-112; 'Gaps, Pauses and Expressive Arms: Reconstructing the Link between Stage Gesture and Musical Timing at the Académie Royale de Musique', in *Journal for Eighteenth-Century Studies* 32. 4 (2009): 607-623. The text of Austin's Chironomia appears in Barnett *Art of Gesture* pp.467-71.
12. On Brutus and the French revolution, see David Wiles *Theatre and Citizenship: The History of a Practice* (Cambridge: CUP, 2011), pp.148-154.
13. Shearer West *The Image of the Actor: Verbal and Visual Representation in the Age of Garrick and Kemble* (London: Pinter, 1991) p.87.
14. See, for example, Emery's introduction to Carlo Gozzi *Five Tales for the Theatre*, ed. Albert Bermel and Ted Emery (Chicago: University of Chicago Press, 1989).
15. *Encyclopédie* iv.684. Scott *Women* pp. 236-8 offers some examples of how Baron pushed at the rules.
16. Alan S. Downer 'Nature to Advantage Dressed: Eighteenth-Century Acting' *PMLA* 58.4 (1943):1002-1037, p.1005.
17. *The Player's Passion: Studies in the Science of Acting* (Newark: University of Delaware Press, 1985) p.55 – cited in Wentz 'Gaps' p.621.
18. For the director function in the baroque period, see Roger Savage and Matteo Sansone 'Il Corago and the staging of early opera: four chapters from an anonymous treatise circa 1630,' *Early Music* 17 (1989): 495-511.
19. Richard Wagner 'Speech on the laying of the foundation stone of the Bayreuth Festspielhaus on 22 May 1872' - www.bayreuther-festspiele.de/documents/_the_bayreuth_festival_theatre_341.html
20. 'The Pastness of the Present and the Presence of the Past' in *Authenticity and Early Music*, ed. Nicholas Kenyon (Oxford: OUP, 1988) 137-207, esp. p. 152.
21. Cf. Peter Kivy *Authenticities: Philosophical Reflections on Musical Performance.* (Ithaca: Cornell University Press, 1995) esp. pp.140-1. James O. Young offers an overview in 'Authenticity in Performance'

in *The Routledge Companion to Aesthetics* ed. Berys Gaut and Dominic McIver Lopes (London: Routledge, 2005) pp. 501-512. On authenticity in popular music, see Allan Moore 'Authenticity as authentication' *Popular Music* 21 (2002): 209-223.

22. Bertil H. van Boer, Jr (ed.) *Gustav III and the Swedish stage : opera, theatre, and other foibles : essays in honor of Hans Åstrand* (Lewiston, N.Y & Lampeter: Mellen, 1993) p.10.

23. *The Confessions of Jean-Jacques Rousseau* tr. J.M Cohen (London: Penguin, 1953) pp.294-5. Layout modified.

24. *Eighteenth Century* Music 8.2 (2011) 349-50. Paul Menzer addresses the same problem in his 'Afterword' in *Inside Shakespeare: Essays on the Blackfriars Stage*, ed. Paul Menzer (Cranbury: AUP, 2006), pp.225-9.

25. Walter Benjamin 'The Work of Art in the Age of Mechanical Reproduction' (1936) – most recently republished in *The Work of Art in the Age of Mechanical Reproduction*, tr. J.A.Underwood (London: Penguin, 2008).

26. Laurajane Smith. *Uses of Heritage.* (London: Routledge, 2006) pp. 34, 69. Her argument echoes Raphael Samuel's *Theatres of Memory: Past and Present in Contemporary Culture.* Vol.1 (London: Verso, 1994).

27. Rebecca Schneider *Performing Remains: Art and War in Times of Theatrical Reenactment* (London: Routledge, 2011) p. 60. On re-enactment see also Gilli Bush-Bailey 'Re: enactment' in *The Cambridge Companion to Theatre History*, ed. David Wiles and Christine Dymkowski (Cambridge: Cambridge University Press, 2012) pp. 281-98.

28. See also *Historical Reenactment: from Realism to the Affective Turn*, eds. Iain McCalman and Paul Pickering (Basingstoke: Palgrave Macmillan, December 2009.

29. For the term, see Jeremy Lopez 'A Partial Theory of Original Practice' *Shakespeare Survey* 61 (2008): 302-317.

30. See Penelope Woods *Globe Audiences: A Comparison of Early Modern and Current Spectatorship* (Ph.D. thesis, King's College London, 2011) pp. 91, 144.

31. A representative attack was Dennis Kennedy 'Shakespeare and Cultural Tourism' *Theatre Journal* 50 (1998): 175-188. Cf. the balanced discussion of W.B.Worthen in *Shakespeare and the Force of Modern Performance* (Cambridge: CUP, 2003) pp. 93-5. On the US context, cf. John Butt *Playing with History: The Historical Approach to Musical Performance* (Cambridge: CUP, 2002), pp. 164, 173-82.

32. Raphael Samuel *Theatres of Memory* Vol.1: Past and Present in Contemporary Culture (London: Verso, 1994) – reissued in paperback in 2012; Barbara Kirshenblatt-Gimblett 'Theorizing Heritage' *Ethnomusicology* 39.3 (1995): 367-80. Italic added.

33. cited in Lopez 'Original Practice' note 6.

34. Blurb to the expanded 1997 edition (New York: Applause).

35. Tiffany Stern *Rehearsal from Shakespeare to Sheridan* (Oxford: OUP, 2000) was inspired by and continues to foster such work.

36. Production by The Factory at Blackwell's bookshop, Oxford, March 2012.

37. Jenny Tiramani analyses the problem in *Shakespeare's Globe: A Theatrical Experiment*, ed. Christie Carson and Farah Karim-Cooper (Cambridge: CUP, 2008), pp.58-9.

38. Cited by Martin White in Carson and Karim-Cooper *Shakespeare's Globe* p.170.

39. Woods *Globe Audiences* pp.71, 83. Cf. Catherine Silverstone 'Shakespeare live: reproducing Shakespeare at the 'new' Globe theatre.' *Textual Practice* 19.1 (2005) 31-50, pp.42-3.

40. Carson and Karim-Cooper *Shakespeare's Globe* pp.113, 43.

41. Carson and Karim-Cooper *Shakespeare's Globe* p.109. The term 'sacred geometry' was doubtless borrowed from Iain Macintosh.

42. See my discussion in 'Seeing is believing: the historian's use of images' in *Representing the Past: Essays in the Historiography of Performance*, ed. Charlotte Canning and Tom Postlewait (Iowa: Iowa University Press, 2010) pp. 215-239. I am grateful to Franklin Hildy for further information.

43. W.B.Worthen *Shakespeare and the Authority of Performance* (Cam-

bridge: CUP, 1997) p.104 – citing Michael Schulman and Eva Mekler.

44. Carson and Karim-Cooper *Shakespeare's Globe* p. 170. Cf. John H. Astington *Actors and Acting in Shakespeare's Time* (Cambridge: Cambridge University Press, 2010), a book which skirts around questions of style in order to concentrate on the material context. Bernard Beckerman's chapter on acting in *Shakespeare at the Globe: 1599-1609* (New York: Macmillan, 1967) pp. 109-156 marks a cusp in the shift of fashion from historicism to organicism.

45. Carson and Karim-Cooper *Shakespeare's Globe* p.108.

46. Woods *Globe Audiences* pp. 147-8, 180-1. Her study relates to the period from 2005 when Dominic Dromgoole was artistic director.

47. Helen Hills *Rethinking the Baroque* (Aldershot: Ashgate, 2011) p. 30.

48. See most famously the opening scene of *L'Impromptu de Versailles*.

49. On Andrew Gurr's account of the theatre as 'original instrument', see Butt *Playing with History* pp. 53-4.

50. Worthen *Authority* p.102.

51. Woods *Globe Audiences* p.267. At the time of writing in 2012, the forestage has been extended forwards to reach the centre.

52. *Hatred of Democracy* (London: Verso, 2006).

53. Richard A. Lanham *The Motives of Eloquence: Literary Rhetoric in the Renaissance* (New Haven: Yale University Press, 1976) p.4. I have preferred homo democraticus to Lanham's homo seriosus.

54. *English Professional Theatre 1530-1660*, ed. Glynne Wickham (Cambridge: Cambridge University Press, 2000) p.181.

55. Hamlet III.ii.1-36.

56. Quintilian xi.3.112-3.

57. Shakespeare's relation to rhetoric is the subject of current research by Quentin Skinner, reported in his 2011 Clarendon lectures in Oxford and 2012 Clark lectures in Cambridge. It is the focus of my own ongoing research.

58. See Lopez 'Theory of Original Practice'.

59. Savage and Sansone 'Il Corago' p.501.

60. See for example Stephen Orgel 'The authentic Shakespeare' *Representations* 21 (1988): 1-25
61. See Claudio Vicentini *La teoria della recitazione: dall'antichità al Settecento* (Venice: Marsilio, 2012).
Translation in http://www.actingarchives.unior.it/Essays.
62. Pierre Nora 'Between Memory and History: Les Lieux de Mémoire,' *Representations* 26, (Spring, 1989): 7-24, p.10.
63. www.albaemoting.cl/english-2/. A pioneering work on theatrical gesture was Eugenio Barba and Nicola Savarese *A Dictionary of Theatre Anthropology: The Secret Art of the Performer* (London: Routledge, 1991).

Chapter 8

1. Conference discussion. Stockholm. 26/8/13.
2. Bo Löfvendahl in *Svenska Dagbladet* 28/5/13.
3. Conference discussion. Stockholm. 26/8/13.
4. Willmar Sauter, *Pubilken på Drottningholm. Rapport från publikundersökningen sommaren 1980* (Stockholm: Stuts – Teatervetenskapliga småskrifter nr. 13, 1981); Magnus Kirchhoff, *Publiken på Drottningholm. Rapport från publikundersökningen sommaren 1996, jämförd med publikundersökningen från sommaren 1980.* (Stockholm: Stuts – Teatervetenskapliga småskrifter nr. 19, 1998); Mikael Strömberg, *Rapport om publiken på Drottningholm sommaren 2008*, unpublished document (Stockholm University 2009).
5. http://whc.unesco.org/en/list/559/documents/
6. http://whc.unesco.org/en/list/559/
7. http://whc.unesco.org/en/conventiontext
8. http://www.unesco.org/culture/ich/index.php?lg=en&pg=00002

Appendices

1. Von Düben were a family of musicians from Leipzig, Germany who

became counts in 1719. Henrik Fredrik von Dûben was the secreterary of the Music Academy in Stockholm.

2. Wife of Gustav III:s brother Karl

3. Gustav III:s sister

4. Carl Gottfried Seuerling, German actor who came to Sweden in 1760, established his own troup in 1768 later and became famous for introducing Shakespeare in Sweden (Romeo and Juliet, 1776).

5. Most probably, Saint-Croix refers to Badin (see chapter 4, note 5), whose birthpalce served as a code name.

6. The Swedish monetary unit of the time. As a word, daler is closely related to the German T(h)aler.

BIBLIOGRAPHY

This bibliography intends to give an overview of some of the literature that has been published about the Drottningholm Court Theatre, its building and historical activities as well as more general studies of the Gustavian era. Therefore, the sections contain 'literatures focusing on the Drottningholm Court Teatre', 'anthologies', 'varia', 'articles' and finally 'publications in other languages than Swedish and English'. A short list of CD:s, DVD:s and VHR:s concludes the bibliography.

Literature focusing on the Drottningholm Court Theatre

Att underhålla och konservera Drottningholms slottsteater, Statens fastighetsverk, Stockholm, 2005

Beijer, Agne, *Slottsteatrarna på Drottningholm och Gripsholm*, Lindfors, Stockholm, 1937

Beijer, Agne, *Court Theatres of Drottningholm and Gripsholm.*, Benjamin Blom, New York, 1972

Beijer, Agne, *Drottningholms slottsteater på Lovisa Ulrikas och Gustaf III:s tid*, Birgitta Schyberg (ed.), LiberFörlag, Stockholm, 1981

Bæckström, Arvid, *Drottningholmsteaterns brand år 1762*, Stockholm, 1948

Bilder från Slottsteatern på Drottningholm, Agne Beijer (ed.), Stockholm, 1950

Cameron, Cathleen, *'China' as Theatrical Locus: Performances at the Swedish Court, 1753-1770*, ProQuest, Diss. (PhD). Indiana University, Department of Comparative Literature, 2005, Ann Arbor, MI, 1963[1931]

Drottningholms slottsteater: dess tillkomst, öden och bevarande, Hidemark, Ove, Per Edström & Birgitta Schyberg (eds), Byggförlaget, Stockholm, 1993. In English translation: *Drottningholm court theatre: its advent, fate and preservation*, Byggförlaget, Stockholm, 1993

Drottningholms slottsteater: teknisk antikvarisk undersökning, Hidemark, Ove (ed.), Byggnadsstyrelsen, Stockholm, 1987

Gustav III, *Gustav III:s dramatiska skrifter*, Stockholm 1857

Gustav III, *Den svartsjuke Neapolitanar'n: drame i tre akter*, Med inledning och kommentar av Kerstin Derkert, Stiftelsen för utgivning av teatervetenskapliga skrifter, Stockholm 1985

Hedvig Elisabeth Charlottas dagbok, ofversatt och utgifven av Carl Carlson Bonde, del 1 (1775-1782), 2nd ed. 1908, del 2 (1783-88), 2nd ed. 1911

Hilleström, Pehr, *Gustaviansk teater*, Inledning av Ague Beijer, bildtexter av Gustaf Hillström. Föreningen Drottningsholmsteaterns vänner, Malmö, 1947

Hilleström, Gustaf, *Drottningholmsteatern förr och nu: The Drottningholm Theatre - Past and Present*, Natur o. kultur, Stockholm, 1956 (enlarged ed. 1980)

Hilleström, Gustaf, *Drottningholms föreställningar 1922-1966: Performances given at the Drottningholm Theatre from 1922*, Stockholm, 1966

Hilleström, Gustaf, *Dramatik på Drottningholm*, Lindqvist, Stockholm, 1975

Hilleström, Gustaf, *Levande 1700-tal: Drottningholms slottsteater*, Natur o. kultur, Stockholm, 1981

Kull, Gustaf, *Drottningholms slottsteater: scenmaskineriet = Drottningholm Court Theatre : the Stage Machinery*, Bjärtrå Teatertekniska, Härnösand, 1987

Larsson, Barbro, *Drottningholms slottsteater: repertoar 1954-1978*, Borås, 1978

Levertin, Oskar, *Teater och drama under Gustav III*, Norstedts, Stockholm, 1889

Lindqvist, Herman, *Drottningholms slottsteater: världens enda orörda 1700-talsteater som fortfarande är i bruk : the only intact 18th-century theatre still in use : das einzige noch heute benutzte Theater der Welt aus dem 18. Jahrhundert : le seul théâtre au monde du xviiième siècle encore utilisé aujourd'hui*, Stiftelsen Drottningholms teatermuseum, Stockholm, 1998

Lorraine, Philip L., *Drottningholm Court Theatre*, Föreningen Drottningholms vänner, Stockholm, 1956

Rangström, Ture, *Drottningholms slottsteater och dess belysning*, Drottningholms teatermuseum, Stockholm, 1985

Reimers, Gerd & Karlsson, Stig T., *En operakväll i Drottningholm: An Opera Evening at Drottningholm : Ein Opernabend in Drottningholm : Une soirée d'opéra à Drottningholm*, Nordiska musikförlaget, Stockholm, 1964

Stribolt, Barbro, *Scenery from Swedish Court Theatres: Drottningholm, Gripsholm*, Stockholmia, Stockholm, 2002

Teatermuseet på Drottningholm, Stribolt, Barbro (ed.), Drottningholms teatermuseum, Stockholm, 1984

Wichman, Holger, *Drottningholmsteaterns brand år 1762*, Stockholm, 1971

Anthologies

Drottningholms slott. Bd 1, Från Hedvig Eleonora till Lovisa Ulrika, Alm, Göran & Rebecka Millhagen, (eds), Byggförl./Kultur, Stockholm, 2004, samt

Drottningholms slott. Bd 2, Från Gustav III till Carl XVI Gustaf, Alm, Göran & Rebecka Millhagen (eds), Votum i samarbete med Kungl. hovstaterna och Statens fastighetsverk, Karlstad, 2010

Gustavian Opera: an Interdisciplinary Reader in Swedish Opera, Dance and Theatre 1771-1809, Mattsson, Inger (ed.), Royal Swedish Academy of Music [Kungl. Musikaliska akad.], Stockholm, 1991

Hilleström, Gustaf, 'En levande slottsteater', *Drottningholm : en konstbok från Nationalmuseum.*, S. 189-112, 1966

Varia

Aronsson, Kjell-Åke, Emma Karlsson & Terese Magnusson, *Forskning om hur turister värderar ett svenskt världsarv*, ETOUR, Östersund, 2001

Artéus, Gunnar, *Gustav III:s hov*. Stockholm: Medströms Bokförlag 2013

Berlova, Maria, *Performing Power. The Political Masks of Gustav III (1771-1792)*, Stockholm, Department of Musicology and Performance Studies, 2013

Hennings, Beth, *Gustav III*, Norstedts, Stockholm 1957

Holmström, Kirsten Gram, *Monodrama, Attitudes, Tableaux Vivants. Studies on some trends of theatrical fashion 1770-1815*. Acta, Stockholms universitet, 1967

Klenoder i tiden: en utredning om samlingar kring scen och musik: betänkande, Fritze, Stockholm, 2006
http://www.regeringen.se/sb/d/108/a/67300

Lönnroth, Erik, *Den Stora Rollen. Kung Gustav III spelat av honom själv*, Norstedts, Stockholm 1986

Magnusson, Terese, *Världsarv och turism: de svenska världsarven ur ett turistiskt perspektiv*, European Tourism Research Institute (ETOUR), Östersund, 2002

Mansén, Elisabeth, *Sveriges historia: 1721-1830*, Norstedt, Stockholm, 2011

Marker, Frederick J. & Marker, Lise-Lone, *The Scandinavian theatre: a short history*, Blackwell, Oxford, 1975

Marker, Frederick J. & Marker, Lise-Lone, *A history of Scandinavian Theatre*, Cambridge Univ. Press, Cambridge, 1996

Mullin, Donald C., *The Development of the Playhouse: a Survey of Theatre Architecture from the Renaissance to the Present*, Univ. of California Press, Berkeley, Calif., 1970

Nell, Jennie, *Vivat vår monark! Carl Michael Bellmans panegyrik över Gustav III 1771-1793*, Ellerströms, Lund 2011

Nordensvan, Georg, *Svensk teater och svenska skådespelare från Gustav III till våra dagar*: Förra delen: 1772-1842. Stockholm: Bonniers 1917

Rangström, Lena, *Kläder för tid och evighet. Gustav III sedd genom sina dräkter*, Livrustkammaren, Stockholm 1997

Skunke, Marie-Christine, *Gustav III – det offentliga barnet. En prins retoriska och politiska fostran*, Atlantis, Stockholm 1993

Tandefelt, Henrika, *Konsten att härska. Gustav III inför sina undersåtar*, Söderbergs, Helsingfors 2008

Utredningen rörande verksamheten vid Stiftelsen Drottningholms teatermuseum m. m., *Drottningholms teatermuseum: betänkande*, LiberFörlag/Allmänna förl., Stockholm, 1982

Articles

Atterfors, Göran, 'Perspektiv på Mozart: Drottningholmsteatern', *Musikrevy.*, 1993 (48:5), s. [12]-17, 1993

Computer Modeling as a Tool for the Reconstruction of Historic Theatrical Production Techniques, *Theatre Journal* - Volume 51, Number 4, December 1999, pp. 417-431

Driscoll, F. Paul, 'Drottningholm : a visit to Sweden's eighteenth-century jewel', *Opera news.*, 2009 (73:11), s. 18-21, 2009

Falk, Johan, 'Drottningholm court theatre: a Stradivarius among theatres', *Nordic sounds.*, 1999:3, s. [15]-20, 1999

Forsström, Per & Per-Erik Öhrn, 'Drottningholmsteatern i ny törnrosasömn: debatt', *Tidskriften Opera.*, 2002:5, s. 6-7, 2002

Hanes Harvey, Anne-Charlotte, 'Vacker som faux' – The Drottningholm Theatre Aesthetic, *TijdSchrift voor Skandinavistiek* vol. 27 (2006), nr. 2

Husmark, Elisabeth, 'Hur ska det gå för Drottningholms Slottsteater?', *Tidskriften Opera.*, 2006:4, s. [4]-8, 2006

Marklund, Hedvig, 'Tankar om ljusdesign.', *Tidig musik.*, 2010:2, s. 26-27, 2010

'The Swedes and their theatre king: The Stockholm symposium on "Opera and Dance in the Gustavian Era, 1771–1809"', *Dance Chronicle*, Volume 10, Issue 2, 1986

Tranberg, Sören, 'Sverige: ett u-land på tidig musik', *MD : Musikdramatik.*, 2000:4, s. 9-11, 2000

'Theaters in the Courts of Denmark and Sweden from Frederik II to Gustav III', *Journal of the Society of Architectural Historians*, Vol. 43, No. 4, Dec., 1984

Volpe, Erika, 'Tillbaka till 1700-talet', *Kulturvärden.*, 2010:4, s. [28]-[35], 2010

Publications in other languages than Swedish and English

Beck-Friis, Regina, 'Tanz und Choreographie auf der Bühne des Schlosstheaters Drottningholm.', *Tanz und Bewegung in der barocken Oper* / herausgegeben von Sybille Dahms und Stephanie Schroedter., S. 19-29, 1996

Beijer, Agne & Duchartre, Pierre Louis, *Le recueil Fossard*, Éd. augm. et précédée de Vive et revive la Commedia dell'arte, Librairie théâtrale, Paris, 1981

Hilleström, Gustaf, *Das Schlosstheater von Drottningholm*, Drottningholmsteaterns vänner, Stockholm, 1958

Hilleström, Gustaf, *Le théâtre de Drottningholm.*, Drottningholmteaterns vänner, Stockholm, 1960

Hidemark, Ove, Per Edström & Birgitta Schyberg (eds), *Le théâtre du château de Drottningholm: sa naissance, son destin et sa conservation*, Byggförlaget, Stockholm, 1994

Kuhnmunch, Jacques (red.), *"Théâtres de cour - théâtres privés": actes du colloque international organisé les 18 et 19 octobre 1996 au musée national du château de Compiègne, sous la direction scientifique*, Éd. du Mécène, Paris, 1998

Reus, Klaus-Dieter (red.), *Faszination der Bühne: barockes Welttheater in Bayreuth ; barocke Bühnentechnik in Europa*, (2., unveränd. Aufl.)., Rabenstein, Bayreuth, 2001

CD/DVD/VHS

Mozart, Wolfgang Amadeus & Petrosellini, Giuseppe, *La finta giardiniera from the Drottningholm Court Theatre*, Polygram, London, 1998

Mozart, Wolfgang Amadeus, Da Ponte, Lorenzo & Biel, Ann-Christine, *The Drottningholm Theater production of Così fan tutte*, Arthaus Musik, München, 1989

Mozart, Wolfgang Amadeus & Dahlberg, Stefan, *Die Zauberflöte*, Arthaus Musik, München, 1989

Mozart, Wolfgang Amadeus & Schäffer, Emmerich, *Die Entführung aus dem Serail*, Arthaus Musik, München, 1989

Mozart, Wolfgang Amadeus & Biel, Ann-Christine, *Idomeneo*, Arthaus Musik, München, 1990

Mozart, Wolfgang Amadeus, *La clemenza di Tito*, Arthaus Musik, München, 1991

Rameau, Jean-Philippe, *Zoroastre opéra*, Opus Arte, Waldron, Heathfield, East Sussex, 2007

Åhlén, Carl-Gunnar, *Från museum till musikinstitution: Drottningholms slottsteater 1922-1992 = From museum to music institution : Drottningholm Court Theatre 1922-1992*, Caprice Records, Stockholm, 1993

LIST OF ILLUSTRATIONS

Abbreviations:

MTB – Musik- och teaterbiblioteket (Library of Music and Theatre), Musikverket
SSM – Stockholms stadsmuseum (City Museum of Stockholm)
NM – National Museum, Stockholm

Illustrations

Frontispiece: Gustav III. Sketches by Johan Tobias Sergel. NM

1. View of Drottningholm from the English Park. Photo: Max Plunger
2. The interior of the theatre in 1921. MTB
3. *Zemire and Azor* by A. E. M. Grétry, performed in 1778 with a vision of Zemire's family seen through a mirror. Painting by Pehr Hilleström, Royal Theatre
4. *The Magic Flute* by W. A. Mozart in a performance from 1989. On the backdrop the palace of Drottningholm seen from the lake side. Photo: Bengt Wanselius, MTB
5. Entrance of the Drottningholm Court Theatre. Private photo
6. Groundplan of the Drottningholm Court Theatre. The numbers indicate the order of the rooms visited during the guided tours. MTB
7. Queen Lovisa Ulrika (1720-1782). Painting by Lorens Pasch d.y. NM
8. View of the auditorium and stage upon entering the inner sphere of the theatre. Photo: Max Plunger
9. The auditorium photographed in the 1930s. The Royal chairs were, as in the Gustavian period, not yet surrounded by the benches (cf. ill. 57); the shutters of the rear windows were painted in green (cf. ill. 18). Clearly visible is also the false proscenium for the curtain to cut off the lower class visitors in the back rows. MTB
10. Painting of the carousel *The Conquest of Galtare Rock* by Pehr Hilleström from 1779. MTB

11. The actor Jaques-Marie Boutet de Monvel. Painting by Carl Fredric von Breda. MTB
12. Gustav Kull's drawing of the stage machinery 1973-86. MTB
13. A painted rock on stage as used in the production of Joseph Haydn's *Orlando Paladino* in 2012. On stage Magnus Staveland and Kirsten Blaise. Photo: Mats Bäcker
14. Lighting pole at the Drottningholm Court Theatre in the position of renewing the 'candles'. Photo: E. Schaaf, MTB
15. The machinery of the theatre as used since 1766 and again since 1922: ropes and capstans moved by stage hands ever since. Photographers unknown. MTB
16. As above.
17. The cloud machinery as it appeared in a rehearsal of the solo performance of the Russian soprano Julia Lezhneva in August 2013. The musicians are not dressed in period costumes. Photo: Elias Gammelgård
18. View of stage and auditorium from the reversed perspective – from the wave machine to the auditorium. The backdrop depicting a town square is still hanging upside-down. The false proscenium cutting off the last rows is fully visible as well as the shutters which have been painted white in the 1950s. Photo: Lennart af Petersens. SSM
19. Dressing room with original wall papers as it appears today. Agne Beijer's prints illustrating theatre history have been removed (Cf. ill. 53). Photo: Max Plunger
20. The wear and tear of history: deteriorations and damages of the wallpapers that have to be preserved and restored. Photos: Max Plunger
21. Monteverdi's *Return of Ulysses* on the Drottningholm stage 2008. Photo: Bo Ljungblom
22. The gods in Monteverdi's *Return of Ulysses* 2008. On stage Susanne Rydén, Niklas Björling Rygert, Lukas Jakobski. Photo: Bo Ljungblom
23. The scholars discussing Monteverdi in the Drottningholm park. From left Rikard Hoogland, Willmar Sauter, Inga Lewenhaupt and Eske Tsugami. Private photo

24. The courtiers entertaining themselves at Drottningholm 1779. Painting by Pehr Hilleström. NM
25. Gustav III overlooking Stockholm. Bronze statue by Johan Tobias Sergel in the Old Town. Private photo
26. The cards that indicated fine or bad weather, according to Gustav III:s opinion. Private photo.
27. The eminent actor Monvel. Drawing by Carl August Ehrensvärd 1782. Private
28. A group of actors as painted by Johan Pasch on a wall of Confidensen at Ulriksdal. Private photo
29. A group of actors as painted by Johan Pasch on a wall of Confidensen at Ulriksdal. Private photo
30. Louis Gallodier, the ballet master in a sketch by Johan Tobias Sergel. MTB
31. Actors of the Comédie Française in the 1760s. Feulie and Monvel in the comedy *Les Rendez-vous*. Coloured engraving to a drawing by Louis Foech, reprinted in *Les Souvenirs et les regrets d'un vieil amateur dramatique* by A. V. Arnault. MTB
32. Gustav Mauritz Armfelt in a scene of Gustav III:s play *Gustaf Adolf's Magnanimity*. Painting by Pehr Hilleström. NM
33. Kjerstin Dellert as Elisabeth Olin in front of a portrait of opera singer Elisabeth Olin. Still from Vilgot Sjöman's movie *Syskonbädd*. Photo: Rangvi Gylder
34. *Gustav Vasa* by J. G. Naumann and Gustav III. Act I, scene 8: King Christian threatens the young Svante Sture, son of Christina Gyllenstierna. Painting by Pehr Hilleström. MTB
35. Gustaf Mauritz Armfelt. Portrait by Adolf Ulrik Wertmüller, pained in Paris 1784. NM
36. View of stage and auditorium of the Confidensen theatre in Ulriksdal. Private photo
37. *The Jealous Neapolitan*, act III, scene 3, Gustav III:s last play. Aquatint by M. R. Heland to a drawing by C. W. Swedman. *Gustaf III:s skrifter i politiska och vittra ämnen*, Stockholm 1807. MTB

38. The Drottningholm domain. Water colour by Cecilia Uhrstedt 1993
39. A contemporary ballet scene *Pierrot in the Park*, 1982, in the Leaf Theatre in the Drottningholm park. The dancers are John Massey and Solveig Åkerberg. Photographer unknown. MTB
40. Painting of the carousel *The Conquest of Galtare Rock* by Pehr Hilleström from 1779. The towers of the temporary castle, built in the park for this occasion, resemble the structure of the Freemason's Temple in Paris. Spectators were placed on a particular scaffold (see detail). MTB
41. C. W. Gluck's *Orfeus and Euridice*, pained by Pehr Hilleström in 1773. DTM
42. C. W. Gluck's *Orfeus and Euridice*, pained by Pehr Hilleström in 1786. DTM
43. The Royal brothers: Gustav, Carl and Fredrik Adolf. Painting by Alexander Roslin 1771. NM
44. The staircase of the Drottningholm palace. Engraving by Erik Dahlberg in *Svecia antiqua et hodierna* 1697
45. Queen Lovisa Ulrika depicted as goddess Minerva on the theatre curtain. In front of the curtain Staffan Liljas and Frida Jansson in Mozart's *Così fan tutte* 2011. Photo: Mats Bäcker
46. Hedvig Eleonora's bedchamber in the palace, where Gustav III:s levee was held during his stay at Drottningholm. The Royal Castle
47. The Baroque design of the French park emphasised by snow. Photo: Alexis Daflos. The Royal Castle
48. Section and groundplan of the 1754 Drottningholm Theatre, demonstrating the prominence of the Royal box and heated withdrawing room behind. NM
49. The auditorium of Confidensen, in which the Royal box has been re moved. Private photo.
50. The auditorium of the theatre at Gripsholm. MTB
51. The stage of the theatre at Gripsholm. The cassette roof of the auditorium is repeated in the set on stage. MTB

52. Charles de Valois and his family watching a play in 1640. Wall-painting attributed to Abraham Bosse

53. Prince Gustav as a child. Painting by Ulrika Pasch. NM

54. Elisabeth Söderström in the dressing room of the primadonna. Agne Beijer's print exhibition illustrating theatre history were still on the wall. (Cf. ill. 19). Photo: Lennart af Petersens, SSM

55. Stucco and paint create the illusion of a column. Detail from the auditorium. Photo: Max Plunger

56. Groundplan of the theatre before the Déjeuner-Salon was added in 1791. Uppsala University Library

57. The Royal chairs as they are placed today, with the front benches next to it. Photo: Max Plunger

58. The west facade with Louis-Jean Desprez' original design of the Déjeuner-Salon. To the right Gustav III:s signature. MTB

59. *Orpheus and Euridice* at the Confidensen theatre 2009. From left: Mikael Mengarelli, Love Enström, Karolina Blixt, Sofia Niklasson, Joakim Schuster, Sandra Bundy, Tiia Kokkonen, Bétina Marcolin. Photo: Rikard Westman

60. The orangery of the Blenheim palace. Private photo

61. *Orlando Paladino* by Joseph Haydn, Drottningholm 2012. From left: Daniel Ralphson, Ditte Andersen, Pietro Spagnoli, Rikard Söderberg, Tova Svenningsen, Magnus Staveland, Kirsten Blaise. Photo: Mats Bäcker

62. In this photograph, taken around 1930, Agne Beijer has hand-painted some of the soufittes that cover the cloud machinery. MTB

63. *The Birthday Celebrated in a Fisherman's Hut* by C. M. Bellman, 1936, was one of the first plays performed at the Drottningholm theatre in the modern era. On stage: Sarah Quarnström, Set Svanholm, Gunvor Olsson, Folke Sällström. Photo: Hugo Edlund, MTB

64. The Drottningholm Court Theatre was, until Beijer died in 1975, a museum in the first place. Pictures, furniture and costumes were among the dominating items that were exhibited in the rooms of the theatre. Photo C. G. Rosenberg. MTB

65. *Orlando furioso* by G. F. Händel, 1950. On stage Sven Nilsson, Leon Björker, Carl-Axel Hallgren, Lilly Furlin, Eva Prytz. Photographer unknown. MTB

66. *Orpheus and Euridice* by C.W. Gluck, 1957. Kerstin Meyer as Orpheus, conductor Albert Wolff. The musicians are wearing wigs. Photo: Lennart af Petersens, SSM

67. *Orpheus and Euridice* by C.W. Gluck, 1957. The costumes of Kerstin Meyer and Elisabeth Söderström represent classical Greek images. Photo: Enar Merkel Rydberg. MTB

68. *Die Entführung aus dem Serail* by W. A. Mozart, Drottningholm 1965. Curtain call with Lennart Lindberg, Tord Slättegård, Mattiwilda Dobbs, Gunilla Slättegård, Gunnar Drago and Bengt Rundgren. Photo: Beata Bergström, MTB

69. Dancer stretching in one of the corridors of the theatre. Photo: Lennart af Petersens. MTB

70. *Cupido out of His Humor*, ballet by Mary Skeaping with music by H. Purcell, 1966. Among the dancers Catharina Ericson, Viveka Ljung and Aulis Peltonen. Photo: Enar Merkel Rydberg. MTB

71. *Cupido out of His Humor*, ballet by Mary Skeaping with music by H. Purcell, 1966. Photo: Enar Merkel Rydberg. MTB

72. *Don Giovanni* by W. A. Mozart, 1979. Håkan Hagegård, Birgit Nordin and Erik Saedén. Photo: Beata Bergström. MTB

73. *The Garden* by Jonas Forssell, 1999. Loa Falkman and Ulf Montan. Photo: Bo Ljungblom. MTB

74. Two singers sitting on the floor – a popular position for modern directors and completely impossible in the eighteenth century. Vivianne Holmberg and Peter Mattei in concert 2013. Photo: Markus Gårder

75. *Il matrimonio segreto* by D. Cimarosa, 2013. Solid doors were placed on the floor and the flat wings turned backwards – a dubious entertainment for visitors to a historical theatre. On stage Frida Josefine Östberg, Anna Hybiner, Jens Persson. Photo: Mats Bäcker

76. *Il Giasone* by F. Cavalli, 2012. Maria Sanner's Jason attacks the 'bull', performed by Joseph MacRae Ballantyne on stilts. Photo: Mats Bäcker

77. *La clemenza di Tito* by W. A. Mozart, 2013. The Roman theme of the opera inspired a mixture of costume styles. On stage: Annemarie Kremer, Markus Schwartz, Luciana Mancini. Photo: Mats Bäcker
78. *Orlando paladino* by J. Haydn, 2012. Magnus Staveland and Kirsten Blaise. Photo: Mats Bäcker
79. *Così fan tutte* by W. A. Mozart, 2011. From left: Frida Jansson, Katja Zhylevich, Sara Widén. Photo: Mats Bäcker
80. *Così fan tutte* by W. A. Mozart, 2011. On stage: Joel Anmo, Sara Widén, Staffan Liljas, Katja Zhylevich, Luthando Qave. Photo: Mats Bäcker
81. The Dutch flutist and performer Jed Wentz in a demonstration of a historically informed speech. Private photo
82. Scene from Gustav III:s historical drama *Helmfelt*, performed at Gripsholm theatre in 1783. Painting by Pehr Hilleström. NM
83. From this bench the musicians could see and be seen by the actors on the forestage. Gripsholm theatre. Private photo
84. The auditorium of Richard Wagner's Festspielhaus in Baureuth. Drawing of a performance of Rheingold in 1786.
85. Suzanne Rydén in the guest performance of *Orlando* by G. F. Händel from the Händelfestspiele Göttingen at Drottningholm 2009. Photo: Bo Ljungblom
86. An audience dressed in Rococo costumes during a television recording in 1955. Photo: Beata Bergström. MTB
87. Mark Rylance as *Richard III* by W. Shakespeare at the Globe Theatre in London. Photo: Simon Annand. Shakespeare's Globe Picture Library
88. The walls of the banqueting hall in the castle of Český Krumlov are decorated with figures from the Commedia dell'Arte. In front of the painted Pantalone a performer imitates the gesture depicted on the wall. Photo: Michal Tuma
89. View of Drottningholm Palace in 1697. Engraving by Erik Dahlberg from *Svecia antiqua et hodierna* 1697.
90. *La clemenza di Tito* by W. A. Mozart, 2013. From left Elena Galitzkaya, Annemarie Kremer and Katja Dragojevic. Photo: Mats Bäcker

91. *Il matrimonio segreto* by D. Cimarosa, 2013. From left Sofie Asplund, Richard Hamrin and Anna Hybiner. Photo: Mats Bäcker
92. The domain of Drottningholm according to a tourist brochure from the 1920s. The Royal Castle.
93. *The Magic Flute* by W. A. Mozart, performed at Confidensen at Ulriksdal in 2013 with live candle light. On stage Randi Rössaak Photo: Linn Sandholm
94. Arlecchino and Columbine in the ballet *Arlecchino – the Sorcerer of Love*, performed by Madeleine Onne and Mikael Mengarelli, 1996. Photo: Mats Bäcker

LIST OF REPERTOIRE DURING GUSTAVIAN PERIOD

The French titles indicate that the plays were performed by French acting companies. Titles in *italics* mark opera performances given by the national Swedish opera (from 1773). Performances on 22 July were given in honour of the Queen's name day; the date 19 August refers to celebrations of Gustav III's coup d'etat in 1772.

1766
Rhadamiste et Zénobie by Crébillon; tragedy (9 July)
Psyché by J-B Lully & F A Uttini; tragi-comédie-ballet (28 Oct)
Le Philosophe sans le savoir by M-J Sedaine; comedy (12 Nov)
Tom Jones by A Poinsinet; comedy (13 Nov)
Les Chinois by C S Favart; opera-comique (14 Nov)

1768
L'Aveugle de Palmyre, opera-comique by F A Uttini

1770
Gaston et Bayard by De Belloy; tragedy (14 May)
Athalie by J Racine; tragedy with music by F A Uttini
Semiramis by Voltaire; tragedy (27 Aug)

1778
Zémire och Azor by A E M Grétry; opera-comique (22 July)

1779
Arsène by P A Monsigny; opera-comique (22 July)
Iphigenia uti Auliden by C W Gluck; opera

1781
Orlando by N Piccini; opera (22 July)

Alceste by C W Gluck; opera

1785
Andromaque by A E M Grétry; opera (22 July)

1786
La Folle Journée ou le Mariage de Figaro by Beaumarchais; comedy (29 March)
La Comtesse D'Escarbagnas by Molière; comedy ballet (5 April)
Les Trois Sultanes ou Soliman II by Favart; opera comique (7 April)
Blaise et Babet (ou la Suite des Trois Fermiers) by Monvel; opera comique (7 (April)
Olympie by Voltaire; tragedy (26 April)
Le Veuf by Carmontelle; comedy (26 April)
L'Etourdi, ou Les Contre-temps by Molière; comedy (3 May)
La Gageure by M J Sedaine; comedy (3 May)
Pierre Le Cruel by De Belloy; tragedy (5 May)
La Bavard by Carmontelle; proverb (5 May)
Beverley by Saurin; bourgeois tragedy (10 May)
Le Procureur arbiter by Ph Poisson; comedy (10 May)
Eugénie by Beaumarchais; drame (12 May)
Le Somnambule by Pont-de-Veyle (12 May)
Dupuis et Desronais by Collé; comedy (17 May)
Les Deux Nieces by Boissy; comedy (17 May)
L'Esprit de condradiction by Dufresny; comedy (2 June)
Le Siege de Calais by Beeloy; tragedy (2 June)
Hypermnestre by Le Mierre; tragedy (9 June)
Le Depot by Destouches; comedy (9 June)

Democrite Amoureux by Regnard; comdy (14 June)

La Coupe Enchantée by Champmeslé and La Fontaine; comdy (14 June)

Les Menechmes ou les Jumeaux by Regnard; comedy (21 June)

L'Enfant Prodigue by Voltaire; comedy (28 June)

Les Plaideurs by J Racine; comedy (5 July)

La Surprise de l'amour by Maricaux; comedy (12 July)

Le Medecin malgré lui by Molière; comedy (12 July)

Le Malade imaginaire by Molière and M A Charpentier; comedy ballet (22 July)

Le Méchant by J B L Gresset; comedy (26 July)

Les deux Oncles by N J Forgeot; comedy (26 July)

Zaïre by Voltaire; tragedy (28 July)

Le Retour imprévu by Regard; comedy (28 July)

Giannina e Barnadone by D Cimarosa; opera buffa (30 July)

L'Amour conjugal, ou L'heureuse crédulite by NJ Forgeot; comedy (2 Aug)

Oedipe chez Admete by J F Ducis; tragedy (4 Aug)

Iphigenia uti Auliden by C W Gluck; opera (6 Aug)

Le Siège de Calais by De Belloy; tragedy (9 Aug)

Le Dépôt by Destouches/Monvel; comedy (9 Aug)

L'Ecole des amis by La Chaussée; comedy (11 Aug)

Iphigenia uti Tauriden by G W Gluck; opera (14 Aug)

Le Cocher suppose by Hauteroche; comedy (16 Aug)

Le Mariage fait et rompu by Dufresny; comedy (25 Aug)

Crispin Médecin by Hauteroche; comedy (25 Aug)

Athalie by J Racine; tragedy (28 Aug)

Tom Jones à Londre by Deforges; comedy (30 Aug)

L'Ile déserte by Collet; comedy (1 Sept)

Le Philisophe sans le savoir by M J Sedaine; comedy (1 Sept)

Alceste by G W Gluck; opera (3 Sept)

Le Sage étourdi by L de Boissy; comedy (6 Sept)

Le Mort Marié by M J Sedaine (6 Sept)

Monsieur de Pourceaugnac by Molière & J B Lully; comedy ballet (8 Sept)

Amour pour amour by La Chaussée; comedy (12 Sept)

La Metromanie ou Le Poète by A Piron; comedy (20 Sept)

Le Distrait by J F Regnard; comedy (27 Sept)

L'Avare by Molière; comedy (29 Sept)

L'Oracle by Saint-Fox; comedy (29 Sept)

Le Grondeur by Brueys and Palaprat; comedy (4 Oct)

Le Barbier de Seville ou la Précaution inutile by Beaumarchais; comedy (6 Oct)

Le Mari retrouvé by Dancourt; comedy (6 Oct)

L'Hypocondre ou la Femme qui ne parle point by J-B Rousseau; comedy (18 Oct)

Le Jeu de l'amour et du hazard by Marivaux; comedy (20 Oct)

Le Mort marié by M J Sedaine; opera comique (20 Oct)

Turcaret by Le Sage; comedy (25 Oct)

Les Deuz oncles by Forgeot; comedy (25 Oct)

Le Glorieux by Destouches; comedy (27 Oct)

L'Anglais ou le fou raisonable by Patras; comedy (27 Oct)

Eugenie by Beaumarchais; drame (1 Nov)

Le Chocher suppose by Hauteroche; comedy (1 Nov)

La Mere jalousie by Barthe; comedy (3 Nov)

Le Mercure gallant ou la comédie sans titre by Boursault; comedy (3 Nov)

Le Festin de Pierre by Th Corneille; comedy (8 Nov)

La Fille capitaine by Montfleury; comedy (15 Nov)

Blanche et Guiscard by Saurin; tragedy (24 Nov)

Le Temps passé by Le Grand; comedy (24 Nov)

Tartuffe by Molière; comedy (29 Nov)

Les Deuz billets by Florian; comedy (29 Nov)

Le Joueur by Regnard; comedy (1 Dec)

Les Fourberies de Scapin by Molière; comedy (8 Dec)

L'Ecole des bourgeois by Allainval; comedy (15 Dec)

Les Vendangeurs ou les deux baillis by Barré and Piis; opera comique (20 Dec)

L'Officieux by La Salle d'Offremont; comedy (29 Dec)

La Fête d'amour ou Lucas et Colinette by Favart, Mme Favart and Chevalier; opera comique (29 Dec)

1787

Amphitrion by Molière with music by J M Kraus; comedy

Electra by J C F Haeffner; opera (22 July – world premiere)

Queen Christina by J H Kellgren; Swedish drama with music by C F Müller (19 Aug)

1791

Iphigenia uti Tauriden by G W Gluck; opera (14 Aug)

Les Graces by Saint Foix; comedy (16 Aug)

L'Obstacle imprévu ou l'obstacle sans obstacle by Destouches; comedy (17 Aug)

LIST OF REPERTOIRE SINCE 1922

1922

Inauguration of the Drottningholm Court Theatre

Divertissement: changement à vue, music by Mozart, Bellman, Gluck and Händel (19 Aug)

1924

Concert in the Déjeuner-Salon (27 July)

1930

Divertissement on the occasion of an international museum congress with changement à vue and music by Händel, Uttini and Bellman (6 June)

Den bedragna Bachan (Bacchus Deceived), comedy with songs by Gustav III, in the Leaf Theatre (27-29 June, 3 performances)

1931

Divertissement for the visiting actors of the Comédie Française (11 Oct)

1933

Pax, Labor et C's: Nya skapelsen eller överklaga månde Elektra (Peace, Work and C's New creation or Electra's appeal), free interpretation of Johan Henric Kellgren's play about the court of Gustav III. Conference of Nordic architects (8 June)

Divertissement for the XIIIme Congrès International d'Histoire de l'Art (9 Sept)

1934

Matinee for Swedish Vegetable Oil Producers (7 June)

Soiree and dance for Aging Artists (Höstsol) and the establishment of the association of the Friends of the Drottningholm Theatre (7 Sept)

1935

Divertissement by a Latvian ballet troupe (29 Sept)

1936

Divertissement for the Royal Theatre in Copenhagen (30 April)

Divertissement for the Danish Royal family (30 Aug)

Divertissement for the Friends of the Drottningholm Theatre, including a short play by Bellman, as well as *Födelsedagen firad i fiskarstugan* (A Birthday Celebrated in a Fisherman's Hut), a comedy ballet by Bellman with music by Kraus (16 Sept)

1937

Divertissement for the Scandinavian Theatre Congress, including a comedy by Olof Kexel, *Captain Puff eller Storprataren*, after de Boisy's *Le Babilard* (22 May)

Subscribed divertissement (4 June)

Subscribed divertissement (5 Oct)

1938

Subscribed divertissement (27 June)

Memorial performance in honour of the actors of the Royal Dramatic Theatre at the time of Gustav III, including Bellman's *A Birthday Celebrated in a Fisherman's Hut* (16 Oct)

1939

Concert in the Déjeuner-Salon by the Swedish Association for Soloists (9 Aug)

Concert in the Déjeuner-Salon by the Swedish Association for Soloists (16 Aug)

Concert in the Déjeuner-Salon by the Swedish Association for Soloists (23 Aug)

Concert in the Déjeuner-Salon by the Swedish Association for Soloists (30 Aug) with different programmes on each occasion.

1940

Rococo play with dance by the St. Olof School (7 June)

Concert by the Swedish Association for Soloists for the Friends of the Drottningholm Theatre, the Bellman Society and Par Bricole (20 Oct)

1941

Divertissement during the 'Danish Week' (20 March)

Herculi Wägewahl (Hercules choice at the crossroads), play by Stiernhielm and Columbus from the 17th century in the framework of a divertissement by the Friends of the Drottningholm Theatre

Public tours of the museum including a divertissement (21 Sept, five times until 19 Oct)

Public tours of the museum including a divertissement for the youth organisation of the Social Democratic Party (26 Oct)

1942

Public tours of the museum including a divertissement (on Sundays from April to Oct)

Orchestra recitals (May to Aug)

Celebration of 20 years of performance at the Drottningholm Court Theatre, including Kexel's *Michel Wingler eller Bättre Brödlös än Rådlös* (Michel Wingler or better without bread than without wit) (4 Oct)

Celebration of 20 years of performance at the Drottningholm Court Theatre, including Lesage's play *Crispin Maître de son rival*, in French (11 Oct)

1943

Public performance recorded by Lux Film with scenes from Molière's *L'École des femmes* (3 June)

Divertissement for the Friends of the Drottningholm Theatre, including de Beauchamp's comedy *Le Portrait* (19 Sept)

1944

De löjliga precisiöserna (Les Précieuses ridicules), comedy by Molière, presented by two theatre schools from Stockholm. (premiere 5 June, 14 performances, i.e. the first en suite performances in this theatre!)

Divertissement with and for Nordic theatre artists (1 July)

Memorial recital in honour of Roman (17 Sept)

Memorial recital in honour of Almquist and Stagnelius (24 Sept)

1945

Celebration of 10th anniversary of the association of the Friends of the Drottningholm Theatre (9 May, repeated 10 May)

Den sköna okända (The Unknown Beauty) by Holberg presented by Students of the Humanities in honour of their Professor Martin Lamm (4 June, repeated 2 more times)

1946

Divertissement for the Estonian Association (26 May)

Divertissement for Scandinavian Museum Employees (31 May)

Martin och Gripon eller De bägge giriga (Les Deux avares), opéra-comique by A E M Grétry and C G Fenouilat de Falbaire (4 June and 7 more performances)

Divertissement for the XVIIth International Pen Congress (5 June)

1947

Äktenskapsskolan (*L'École des femmes*) by Molière in a production by the Royal Dramatic Theatre (18 May)

Bastien och Bastienne, singspiel by Mozart for the audience organisation Skådebanan; first appearance of Elisabeth Söderström at Drottningholm; conductor Sixten Ehrling (31 May and 13 more performances in 1947 and repeated in the following years)

Celebration of the 25th anniversary of the Drottningholm Theatre Museum (5 Oct)

1948

– **Gustaf Hilleström artistic director (until 1968)**

Den talande tavlan (*Le Tableau parlant*) opéra-comique by A E M Grétry (9 May with 12 more performances)

Il matrimonio segreto, opera buffa by D Cimarosa. First guest performance by the Royal Theatre (the Royal Opera) at Drottningholm (5 Aug and 7 more performances)

1949

Bastien och Bastienne, singspiel by Mozart (13 May)

Maskerade by L Holberg, performed by the Danish Acting Academy (14 May)

L'Europe galante, opéra-ballet by Campra together with *Birger Jarl*, Swedish national dances to music by Uttini (22 May)

Il matrimonio segreto, opera buffa by Cimarosa, produced by the Royal Opera (27 Aug)

Le Mariage forcé by Molière with music by Campra, performed by Théâtre Athenée from Paris (3 Sept)

1950

Divertissement for an agricultural congress (7 June)

Den rasande Roland (*Orlando*) opera by Händel, produced by the Royal Opera. (1 Sept and 5 more performances this year)

Den farliga vänskapen (*Les fausses confidences*), comedy by Marivaux, produced by the Royal Dramatic Theatre (10 Sept and 2 more times that year)

Divertissement for Swedish Bankers (12 Sept)

Divertissement for children in English (4 Oct)

1951

Den rasande Roland (*Orlando*) opera by Händel, produced by the Royal Opera. (22 May and 7 more performances)

Divertissement for the Art Association of Stockholm's Merchants (9 June)

Il matrimonio segreto, opera buffa by Cimarosa, produced by the Royal Opera (9-10 June)

Divertissement for a Congress of Cristallographs (28 June)

Divertissement for a Lighting Congress (29 June)

Divertissement for C.I.E. (3 July)

Den farliga vänskapen (*Les fausses confidences*), comedy by Marivaux, produced by the Royal Dramatic Theatre (2 Sept)

1952

Divertissement for school children: "From Baroque to Romanticism" (15 May)

Divertissement by students of Bromma Highschool (25 May)

Divertissement for Stockholm's Arts Associations (5 June)

Den rasande Roland (*Orlando*) opera by Händel, produced by the Royal Opera (14 June and 3 more times)

Il matrimonio segreto, opera buffa by Cimarosa, produced by the Royal Opera (7 July and 3 more times)

1953

Bastien och Bastienne, singspiel by Mozart, together with *Bågspännaren*, ballet pantomime by Rousseau (20 May, official premiere 4 July)

Herde-spel (Pastoral Play) by Olof von Dalin. Guest performance by the Royal Dramatic Theatre (29 May)

Livietta og Tracollo (*La contadina astuta*), opera by Pergolesi. Guest performance by the Royal Theatre of Copenhagen (26 June)

Kärlekens och slumpens lek (*Le Jey de l'amour et du hazard*), comedy by Marivaux (transl. by A. Beijer). Guest performances by Parkteater Stockholm

Concert for the Japanese Prince Akihito (17 Aug)

Divertissement for the committee 'Stockholm 700 years' (6 Sept)

1954

Anette och Lubin, comical opera by A. B. Blaise. Performed as divertissement with Rousseau's ballet pantomime (20 May)

Iphigénie en Aulide, opera by Gluck, presented by Bromma Highschool (29 May)

Baroque concert by the Royal Opera (4 June)

Festival performance of *Anette och Lubin* by Blaise and *Pantalones misslyckade kärleksäventyr*, ballet pantomime by Domenico Scarlatti (6 June)

Divertissements (7 June to 29 Sept)

1955

Bastien och Bastienne, singspiel by Mozart – first program from Drottningholm on Swedish Television (5 May)

Divertissement for the Press Institute (15 May)

Fêtes galantes, opera by Campra, produced by the Royal Opera, together with *A Birthday Celebrated in a Fisherman's Hut*, by Kraus with text by Bellman (5 June)

Un curioso accidente, comedy by Goldoni, produced by I Classici Italiani (7 June)

Il maestro di musica, opera buffa by Pergolesi (4 Aug). Recording on gramophone LT 33117, LP SCD 1029 (25 Sept). Performed every year in a number of performances until 1961

1956

Divertissement for the High Soviet Delegation (8 May)

Monsieur de Pourceaugnac, comédie-ballet by Molière. Produced by the Highschool Association Brage (27 May)

La finta semplice, opera buffa by Mozart (3 June)

Gl'innamorati, comedy by Goldoni, produced by I Classici Italiani (5 June)

Il maestro di musica, opera buffa by Pergolesi (4 June)

Cupid out of His Humor (*Den fångna Cupido*), ballet by Mary Skeaping with music by Purcell (14 June, in Honour of Queen Elizabeth of England)

Così fan tutte (*Så gör alla*), opera by Mozart (18 Aug)

Il servitore di due patroni, comedy by Goldoni, presented by Piccolo Teatro di Milano with Marcello Moretti (9 Sept)

1957

Cupid out of His Humor, ballet by Mary Skeaping with music by Purcell (2 June)

Chamber concert (2 June)

Kärlek och dårskap (Les Folies amoureuses), comedy by Regnard (6 June)

Orfeus och Euridice, opera by Gluck, production by the Royal Opera (8 June)

En tjener og to herrer (Il servitore di due padroni), comedy by Goldoni, presented by the Danish Theatre Academy (12 June)

Rodelinda, opera by Händel (27 July)

Divertissement for the Congressus Internationales Dermatologorum (2 Aug.)

1958

Il Ventaglio (The Fan) comedy by Goldoni, presented by I Classici Italiani (21 May)

Orfeus och Euridice, opera by Gluck, production by the Royal Opera (1 June)

Lucretia, opera by Britten (7 June)

Il trionfo dell'onore, opera by Scarlatti, production by the Stockholm Festival (14 June)

Divertissements (until September)

Chamber concerts (with recording, until 25 Sept)

1959

Pimpinone (Det omaka äktenskapet), opera intermezzo by Telemann (22 May)

Orfeus och Euridice, opera by Gluck (31 May)

Il trionfo dell'onore, opera by Scarlatti, production by the Stockholm Festival (2 June)

Il filosofo di campagna, comedy by Goldoni, presented by the Virtuosi di Roma (9 June)

Divertissements by the Virtuosi di Roma (until 12 June)

Rodelinda, opera by Händel (15 July)

Divertissement by Pro Arte Antiqua, Prague (18-19 July)

Concerts

1960

Ifigenia på Tauris, opera by Gluck, produced by the Royal Opera (29 May)

Kinesiskorna (Le cinesi) opera by Gluck (together with Cupido) the Radio Orchestra (31 May)

Orfeus och Euridice, opera by Gluck, production by the Royal Opera (4 June)

Il trionfo dell'onore, opera by Scarlatti, production by the Stockholm Festival (11 June)

Concert of romances by Haydn, Schubert, Mahler and Wolf (15 July)

Concert of romances by Mozart, Strauss and Schubert (17 July)

Il barbiere di Siviglia, opera by Paisiello (19 July – 21 performances this summer)

Pimpinone (Det omaka äktenskapet), opera intermezzo by Telemann. Special performance for the patients of a hospital for mental diseases (17 Aug)

Divertissement for the XIth International Astronautical Congress (17 Aug)

Divertissement for King Bhumidol Adulyadej and Queen Sirikit of Thailand (22 Sept)

1961

La vedova scaltra, comedy by Goldoni, presented by I Classici Italiani (24 May)

Ifigenia på Tauris, opera by Gluck, produced by the Royal Opera (4 June)

Orfeus och Euridice, opera by Gluck, production by the Royal Opera (9 June)

Il barbiere di Siviglia, opera by Paisiello (9 June – 21 more performances this summer)

Chamber concert with music by Purcell, Haydn, Mozart, Åhlström and Monteverdi (10 Aug)

Divertissement in celebration of Gustaf Hilleström's 50th birthday (14 Aug)

Bach concert (27 Aug)

1962

Dido and Aeneas, opera by Purcell, presented by The English Opera Group in Britten's edition (16 May – 5 performances)

Orfeus och Euridice, opera by Gluck, production by the Royal Opera (2 June)

Alkestis, opera by Gluck, produced by the Royal Theatre (8 June)

L'infedeltà delusa (Tröstlöshet och list), opera by Haydn (13 June)

Così fan tutte, opera by Mozart (1 July – to be performed until 1978) with Elisabeth Söderström, conducted by Hans Schmidt-Isserstedt

Il barbiere di Siviglia, opera by Paisiello (5 Aug – another 6 performances this summer)

Chamber music – 4 concerts (2 – 23 Sept)

Divertissement in the context of an exhibition on Venetian Art at the National Museum (21 Oct)

1963

Spring soiree by the Esselte choir and orchestra (9 May)

L'infedeltà delusa (Tröstlöshet och list), opera by Haydn (13 June on the occasion of the opening of the East-Indian Museum)

Choir concert conducted by Eric Ericson (29 May)

Orfeus och Euridice, opera by Gluck, production by the Royal Opera (29 May)

Theater-Directeuren (L'impresario in angustie) opera buffa by Cimarosa in a translation by Nordforss from 1799 (17 June)

L'infedeltà delusa (Tröstlöshet och list), opera by Haydn (29 June – on the occasion of the General Assembly of the European Broadcasting Union)

Così fan tutte, opera by Mozart (2 July)

Concert with the soprano Mattiwilda Dobbs (19 July)

Il barbiere di Siviglia, opera by Paisiello (9 June – 5 more performances this summer)

Divertissement with music by Wolf and Schuman (17 Aug)

Bach concerts (21, 27 Aug)

Pimpinone (Det omaka äktenskapet), opera intermezzo by Telemann. Swedish Radio concert (28 Sept)

1964

Divertissement for the Swedish Association of Break Regulators (6 May)

Divertissement for the Belgian King and Queen (13 May)

Divertissement for 103rd Session of the Council of the International Chamber of Commerce (25 May)

Il maestro di musica, opera buffa by Pergolesi (25 May)

Iphigénie en Aulide, opera by Gluck, produced by the Royal Opera (28 May)

Signor Bruschino, opera buffa by Rossini, and *Atis*

and Camilla, ballet by Mary Skeaping with music by Roman (6 June and 8 more performances)

Così fan tutte, opera by Mozart (12 June)

Il barbiere di Siviglia, opera by Paisiello (25 June)

Il pittore parigino, opera buffa by Cimarosa, presented by the Teatro dell'Opera della Città di Genova (28 July – 3 performances)

L'amante di tutte, opera buffa by Galuppi, presented by the Teatro dell'Opera della Città di Genova (7 Aug – 5 performances)

Musical Salons with the Swedish Radio Corporation (15 Aug etc.)

Ariodante, opera by Händel (18 Aug – 5 performances this summer)

Così fan tutte, opera by Mozart (28 Aug)

Guest performances by the Jyske Opera with various arias (15-17 Sept)

1965

Così fan tutte, opera by Mozart (18 May and 5 more performances)

Il maestro di musica, opera buffa by Pergolesi (19 May- 3 more performances)

Iphigénie en Aulide, opera by Gluck, produced by the Royal Opera (30 May and 3 June)

Il barbiere di Siviglia, opera by Paisiello (16 June)

Die Entführung aus dem Serail, singspiel by Mozart (23 June and 10 more performances)

Madrigal concert with Dorow Bell Consort (9 July)

Concert with Hamburger Barockensemble (16 July)

La clemenza di Tito, opera by Mozart, presented by the Landestheater Salzburg (20 July, 6 performances)

Concert with Nicolai Gedda (23 Aug)

Chamber concert with music by Haydn (25 Aug)

Guest performance by Camerata Nova from Prague (2 Sept)

1966

Acis and Galatea, opera by Händel, presented by the English Opera Group, Covent Garden, London (2 May, 4 performances)

Così fan tutte, opera by Mozart, presented by the Wiener Staatsoper (10 May, 2 performances)

Così fan tutte, opera by Mozart, The Royal Theatre (21 May)

Orfeus och Euridice, opera by Gluck, production of the Royal Opera (24 May)

Die Entführung aus dem Serail, singspiel by Mozart (26 May)

Iphigénie en Aulide, opera by Gluck, produced by the Royal Opera (30 May)

Divertissement in celebration of the 200th anniversary of the Drottningholm Court Theatre (2 June, repeated 4 June)

L'honestà negli amori, opera by Scarlatti, produced by the Association of the Friends of the Drottningholm Theatre DTV (29 June)

Il barbiere di Siviglia, opera by Paisiello (21 July)

Ifigenia paa Tauris, opera by Gluck, presented by the Royal Theatre of Copenhagen (5 Aug)

Orfeo, opera by Monteverdi, guest performance by the Sommerspiele Herrenhausen (13-16 Aug)

Concerts and Liederabend (20-24 Aug)

Three ballets choreographed by Mary Skeaping, including *Cupido*, *Vårens återkomst* (The Return of Spring) and *Giselle*, act 2 (31 Aug)

Atis and Camilla, ballet by Mary Skeaping (with *Vårens återkomst* and *Giselle*) (11 Sept)

Le Triomphe de l'amour, comedy by Marivaux, presented by the Centre Dramatique National du

Nord (Lille) (16 Sept, 2 performances)

Concert with music by the Viennese classical composers (20 Sept)

1967

Matinee for the ITI symposium (29 April)

Orfeus och Euridice, opera by Gluck, production of the Royal Opera (25 May)

Giselle, ballet by Mary Skeaping (2 June)

Die Entführung aus dem Serail, singspiel by Mozart (16 June)

Le nozze di Figaro, opera by Mozart, guest performances by the Deutsche Staatsoper, Berlin, GDR (29-30 June)

Così fan tutte, opera by Mozart, guest performances by the Deutsche Staatsoper, Berlin, GDR (2-3 July)

Il barbiere di Siviglia, opera by Paisiello (11 July)

Don Giovanni, opera by Mozart, guest performance by the Glyndebourne Festival Opera (6-7 Sept)

Il matrimonio segreto, opera by Cimarosa, guest performance by the Glyndebourne Festival Opera (8-9 Sept)

Divertissement with Svenska Riksteatern (19 Sept)

Orfeus och Euridice, opera by Gluck, production by the Royal Opera (29 May)

1968

Bertil Bokstedt takes over as Artistic Director (until 1980)

Divertissement for the 300th anniversary of the founding of the Bank of Sweden (14 May)

Den rasande Roland (Orlando), opera by Händel, new production by the Royal Opera (21 May)

Die Entführung aus dem Serail, opera by Mozart (11 June)

Il barbiere di Siviglia, opera by Paisiello (28 June)

Così fan tutte, opera by Mozart, revival of the 1962 production (26 July)

Zémire och Azor, opera by Grétry, transl. by Lenngren 1778 (9 Aug)

L'honestà negli amori, opera by Scarlatti (23 Aug)

1969

Ballet programme with two choreographies by Mary Skeaping and two choreographies by Elsa Marianne von Rosen (21 May)

Die Entführung aus dem Serail, opera by Mozart (24 May)

Concert by soloists from the Royal Opera (27 May)

Oidipus i Aten, opera by Sacchini, production by Royal Opera (3 June)

Il barbiere di Siviglia, opera by Paisiello (27 June)

Così fan tutte, opera by Mozart, revival of the 1962 production (25 July)

Zémire och Azor, opera by Grétry, transl. by Lenngren (15 Aug)

Livet på månen (Il mondo della luna), opera by Haydn (22 Aug)

Il pastor fido, opera by Händel in the 1734 version by Farncombe (4 Sept)

Pinpinone, opera by Telemann (Sept – six subscribed performances)

1970

Concert by soloists from the Royal Opera (20 May)

Ballet programme with three choreographies by Mary Skeaping (26 May)

Il pastor fido, opera by Händel in the 1734 version by Farncombe (31 May)

Die Entführung aus dem Serail, opera by Mozart (5 June)

Scipio, opera by Händel, guest performances by The Handel Opera Society, London (30 June)

Charlatanen (Livietta e Tracollo), opera by Pergolesi (7 July)

Kärlek på prov (La pietra del paragone), opera by Rossini (15 July)

Concert with The All-Philadelphia Boys Choir (19 July)

Livet på månen (Il mondo della luna), opera by Haydn (7 Aug)

1971

Concert by soloists from the Royal Opera (18 May)

Il maesto di musica, opera by Pergolesi, in honour of the Fédération Internationale en Propriété Industrielle (19 May)

Ballet programme with two choreographies by Mary Skeaping (23 May)

Il pastor fido, opera by Händel in the 1734 version by Farncombe (31 May)

King Arthur, opera by Purcell, guest performances by the Royal Opera House, Covent Garden, London, The English Opera Group (4 July)

Av ont kommer got (Dal male il bene), opera by Marazzoli, guest performances by the Vadstena Akademi (3 Aug)

Livet på månen (Il mondo della luna), opera by Haydn (13 Aug)

Orfeus och Euridice, opera by Gluck, 1762 Vienna version, production by the Royal Opera (3 Sept)

Divertissement in honour of the 200th anniversary of the Royal Academy of Music (7 Sept)

1972

Concert by soloists from the Royal Opera (24 May)

Ballet programme with two choreographies by Mary Skeaping (26 May)

Orfeus och Euridice, opera by Gluck, 1762 Vienna version, production by the Royal Opera (2 June)

Programme for the United Nations Conference on the Human Environment, including *Il pastor fido* and *Cupido* (9 June)

Scipio Africanus, opera by Cavalli, production by the Royal Opera (14 June)

Kärlek på prov (La pietra del paragone), opera by Rossini (18 June)

Divertissement for passengers from the M T S Argonaut (19 June)

Così fan tutte, opera by Mozart, revival of the 1962 production (22 Aug)

Joseph Martin Kraus concert (7 Sept)

1973

Concert by soloists from the Royal Opera (17 May)

Scipio Africanus, opera by Cavalli, production by the Royal Opera (23 May)

Gustaf Adolf och Ebba Brahe, opera by Vogler, libretto by Gustav III and Kellgren, production by the Royal Opera (7 June)

Ballet programme with two choreographies by Mary Skeaping (13 June)

Kärlek på prov (La pietra del paragone), opera by Rossini (29 June)

Così fan tutte, opera by Mozart, revival of the 1962 production (9 Aug)

Orfeus och Euridice, opera by Gluck, 1762 Vienna version, production by the Royal Opera (24 Aug)

Den dubbla trolösheten (La Double inconstance), comedy by Marivaux, guest performance of the Royal Dramatic Theatre (6 Sept and four more performances)

1974

Concert by soloists from the Royal Opera (16 May)

Il pastor fido, opera by Händel in the 1734 version by Farncombe (23 May)

Kärlek på prov (La pietra del paragone), opera by Rossini (29 June)

Ottone (Otto), opera by Händel, guest performances by The Handel Opera Society, London (1-6 Aug)

Orfeus och Euridice, opera by Gluck, 1762 Vienna version, production by the Royal Opera (18 Sept)

Gustaf Adolf och Ebba Brahe, opera by Vogler, libretto by Gustav III and Kellgren, production by the Royal Opera (27 Aug)

1975

Concert by soloists from the Royal Opera (22 May)

Gustaf Adolf och Ebba Brahe, opera by Vogler, libretto by Gustav III and Kellgren, production by the Royal Opera (26 May)

Mozart concert by the orchestra of the Royal Opera (6 June)

Lully concert with artists from the Royal Opera (14 June)

Kärleksdrycken (L'Elisir d'amore), opera by Donizetti (25 June)

Così fan tutte, opera by Mozart, revival of the 1962 production (14 Aug)

Concert with the chamber orchestra of the National Museum (17 Aug)

Ballet programme with two choreographies by Mary Skeaping (9 Sept)

1976

Poppeas kröning (L'incoronazione di Poppea), opera by Monteverdi, production by the Royal Opera (20 May)

Concert with Catarina Ligendza (6 June)

Dans-vurmen (La Dansomanie), ballet with music by Méhul, choreography by Skeaping and Ivo Cramér (12 June)

Kärleksdrycken (L'Elisir d'amore), opera by Donizetti (30 June and eleven more performances this summer)

Concert with Nicolai Gedda (8 August)

Così fan tutte, opera by Mozart, revival of the 1962 production (13 Aug)

1977

Concert by soloists from the Royal Opera (24 May)

Poppeas kröning (L'incoronazione di Poppea), opera by Monteverdi, production by the Royal Opera (27 May)

Dans-vurmen (La Dansomanie), ballet with music by Méhul, choreography by Skeaping and Ivo Cramér (10 June)

Kärleksdrycken (L'Elisir d'amore), opera by Donizetti (30 June and nine more performances this summer)

Oskuld på landet (La buona figliuola), opera by Piccinni, production by the Royal Opera (18 Aug)

Orfeus och Euridice, opera by Gluck, 1762 Vienna version, production by the Royal Opera (10 Sept)

1978

Concert by soloists from the Royal Opera (26 May)

Platée, opera by Rameau, produced by the Royal Theatre (3 June)

Kärleksdrycken (L'Elisir d'amore), opera by Donizetti (4 July and six more performances this summer)

Oskuld på landet (La buona figliuola), opera by Piccinni, production by the Royal Opera (18 July)

Così fan tutte, opera by Mozart, revival of the 1962 production (10 Aug)

Ballet programme with two choreographies by Mary Skeaping and Ivo Cramér (9 Sept – seven performances until 23 Sept)

1979

Annual divertissement for the Friends of the Drottningholm Theatre (28 May)

Gustaf Adolf och Ebba Brahe, opera by Vogler, libretto by Gustav III and Kellgren, production by the Royal Opera (2 June plus five performances)

Xerxes, opera by Händel (29 June and 7 more performances)

Don Giovanni, opera by Mozart, first cooperation of the team Järvefelt/Östman at Drottningholm (3 Aug and 9 more performances)

Dans-vurmen (La Dansomanie), ballet with music by Méhul, choreography by Skeaping and Ivo Cramér (1 Sept)

1980

Arnold Östman becomes artistic director (to 1993)

Proserpin, opera by Kraus, produced by the Royal Opera (31 May)

Il matrimonio segreto, opera by Cimarosa (5 July)

Fiskarena eller skärgårdsflickan (The Fishermen or the Girl from the Archipelago), ballet by Mary Skeaping and Ivo Cramér, music by Kraus (30 Aug)

Divertissement for the Agne Beijer Memorial Foundation (2 Sept)

1981

Dido and Aeneas, opera by Purcell, concert performance (3 June)

Proserpin, opera by Kraus, produced by the Royal Opera (6 June)

La nozze di Figaro, opera by Mozart, directed by Järvefelt (15 July)

Don Giovanni, opera by Mozart (20 Aug)

Två Arlequiner (Two Harlekins), ballet pantomime in Commedia dell'Arte style by Ivo Cramér (12 Sept)

1982

Två Arlequiner, ballet pantomime in Commedia dell'Arte style by Ivo Cramér (29 May)

Trollflöjten (Die Zauberflöte), opera by Mozart, directed by Järvefelt (10 July)

Haydn concert (23 July)

Montezuma, opera by Graun, guest performances by the Deutsche Oper, Berlin (18 Aug)

La Cenerentola (Cinderella), opera by Rossini, production by the Royal Opera (4 Sept)

1983

Ballet programme with choreographies by Skeaping and Gardel (21 May)

Ballet programme with two choreographies by Skeaping (*Cupido, Fiskarena*) staged by Regina Beck-Friis (27 May)

Divertissement for the Agne Beijer Memorial Fund (30 May)

Ballet programme with two choreographies by Skeaping (*Vårens återkomst, Två Arlequiner*) staged by Regina Beck-Friis (3 June)

Il fanatico burlato (The Fanatic Deceived), opera by Cimarosa (18 June)

Don Juan, comedy by Molière, directed by Järvefelt (20 July)

La Cenerentola (Cinderella), opera by Rossini, production by the Royal Opera (22 Aug)

1984

The School for Scandal, comedy by Sheridan, performed by the Duke of York's Theatre, London (19 May)

La Cenerentola (Cinderella), opera by Rossini, production by the Royal Opera (22 May)

Henrik og Pernille, comedy by Holberg, performed by Grønnegårds Teatret, Copenhagen (1 June)

Così fan tutte, opera by Mozart, directed by Järvefelt (4 July)

Il maestro di capella by Cimarosa and *Medea* by Benda (1 Aug)

Dianas träd (L'arbore di Diana), opera by Martín y Soler, production by the Royal Theatre (31 Aug)

1985

Divertissement "Oh Amadeus" for the Agne Beijer Memorial Foundation (19 May)

Ballet programme with three choreographies by Beck-Friis, including *Don Juan* with music by Gluck (24 May)

Divertissement for the Friends of the Drottningholm Theatre (28 May)

Agrippina, opera by Händel, presented by the Oper der Stadt Köln (27 June)

Die Entführung aus dem Serail, opera by Mozart (13 July)

Così fan tutte, opera by Mozart, directed by Järvefelt (4 July)

Divertissement for Queen Margrethe and Prince Henrik of Denmark (4 Sept)

Il maestro di musica, opera by Pergolesi, production by the Royal Opera (13 Sept)

Divertissement in honour of the 50th anniversary of the Friends of the Drottningholm Theatre (23, 25, 26 and 28 Sept)

1986

Ballet programme with three choreographies by Beck-Friis, including *Don Juan* with music by Gluck (30 May)

Dans-vurmen (La Dansomanie), ballet with music by Méhul, choreography by Skeaping and Ivo Cramér (4 June)

Två Arlequiner, (Two Harlequins) ballet pantomime in Commedia dell'Arte style by Ivo Cramér (10 June)

Don Giovanni, opera by Mozart (19 June)

Idomeneo, opera by Mozart (12 July)

De löjliga preciöserna (Les Précieuses ridicules), and *Läkare mot sin vilja (Le Médicin malgré lui)*, comedies by Molière, performed by the Royal Dramatic Theatre (19 Aug)

1987

Divertissement in celebration of Elisabeth Söderström's 40th anniversary at the Drottningholm Theatre (4 June)

Paris och Helena (Paride ed Elena), opera by Gluck, produced by the Royal Opera (8 June)

La clemenza di Tito, opera by Mozart, directed by Järvefelt (18 June)

La nozze di Figaro, opera by Mozart, Järvefelt/Östman (15 July)

1988

Ballet programme with three choreographies by Beck-Friis (4 June)

La finta giardiniera, opera by Mozart, directed by Järvefelt (23 June)

La clemenza di Tito, opera by Mozart, directed by Järvefelt (9 July)

Die Schöpfung (The Creation) by Haydn: orchestra oratory (17 July)

Symphony concert with works by Mendelssohn (7 Aug)

Paris och Helena (Paride ed Elena), opera by Gluck, produced by the Royal Opera (30 Aug)

1989

Soliman II, opera by Kraus, produced by the Royal Opera (27 May)

Trollflöjten (Die Zauberflöte), opera by Mozart, directed by Järvefelt (15 June)

Iphigénie en Aulide, opera by Gluck, directed by Järvefelt (5 Aug)

Concert – Classics from Vienna (17 Aug)

1990

Gustaf Adolf och Ebba Brahe, opera by Vogler, libretto by Gustav III and Kellgren, production by the Royal Opera (31 May)

Die Entführung aus dem Serail, opera by Mozart (13 July)

Concert: songs and cantatas (10 July)

Iphigénie en Aulide, opera by Gluck, (28 July)

La finta giardiniera, opera by Mozart, (10 Aug)

Gustavian concert and ballets (27 Aug)

1991

Electra, opera by Haeffner, transl. by Ristell 1787, production by the Royal Opera (27 May)

Idomeneo, opera by Mozart (20 June)

Concert (10 July)

1992

Figaro eller Almaviva och kärleken (Figaro or Almaviva and Love), ballet pantomime by Ivo Cramér after Beaumarchais (22 May)

Der Handwerker als Edelmann (L'artigiano gentiluomo), opera by Hasse, presented by the Bayerische Kammeroper, Veitshöchheim (3 June)

Falstaff ossia Le tre burle, opera by Salieri, presented by the Opera Academy/ Operahögskolan (11 June)

Haydn Concert (4 July)

Orfeus och Euridice, opera by Gluck: 1769 Parma version (18 July)

Armida, opera by Haydn; concert presentation in honour of Arnold Östmans period as artistic director (20 Sept)

1993
Elisabeth Söderström as artistic director

La fedeltà premiata, drama pastorale by Haydn, produced by the Royal Theatre and the Opera Academy (20 May)

Figaro eller Almaviva och kärleken (Figaro or Almaviva and Love), ballet-pantomime by Ivo Cramér (19 May)

Zemire och Azor, opera by Grétry (12 June)

Chamber concert: 'Around the Revolution' (15 June)

Una cosa rara ossia Bellezza ed onesta (A Rare Thing or Beauty and Honesty), opera by Marín y Soler (10 July)

Concert: *The Drottningholm Music* by Roman and *Les Indes galantes* by Rameau (28 July)

Concert with Edita Gruberova (3 Sept)

1994

Ungdom och dårskap (Youth and Folly), singspiel by Du Puy (26 May)

Orlando paladino, opera by Hayden (2 July)

'Himmelske Händel' (Heavenly Handel), music composed by Händel (22 July)

'Strindberg i kulisserna' (Strindberg in the Wings), produced by Svenskt Festspel (5 Sept)

1995

Dido and Aeneas, opera by Purcell, produced by the Royal Opera (25 May)

'Ack, säll är denna tiden' (Lovely is this time); Spring concert in the Déjeuner-Salon (13 June)

Divertissement with music by Bellman (14 June)

'Från Monteverdi till Monte Hekla' (Songs of Love and Death), Déjeuner-Salon (17 June)

Una cosa rara ossia Bellezza ed onesta (A rare thing or Beauty and honesty), opera by Marín y Soler (2 July)

Tom Jones, opera by Philidor (29 July)

Concert with Doris Soffel (4 Aug)

1996

Divertissement on the occasion of the World Scout Foundation Royal Birthday Celebration (10 May)

Mäster Pergolesis spektakler (La serva padrona, Il maestro di musica), produced by the Royal Opera (1 June)

Tom Jones, opera by Philidor (7 July

Orfeus och Euridike, opera by Gluck (27 July)

Concert with Anne Sofie von Otter (6 Aug)

Arias from the repertoire of Jenny Lind, sung by Lena Nordin (1 Sept)

Harlekiner och rövare (Harlequins and Robbers), Swedish ballets from the 1790s interpreted by Ivo Cramér (2 Sept)

1997

Per-Erik Öhrn artistic director (until 2007)

Harlekiner och rövare (Harlequins and Robbers), Swedish ballets from the 1790s interpreted by Ivo Cramér (4 June)

Euridice, opera by Jacobo Peri (5 July)

L'Orfeo, opera by Luigi Rossi (2 Aug)

1998

Baroque concert in the Déjeuner-Salon (27 May)

Concert with Anders Paulsson, soprano saxophone (5 June)

Harlekiner och rövare (Harlequins and Robbers), Swedish ballets from the 1790s interpreted by Ivo Cramér (8 June)

Divertissement on the occasion of The International Society for the Performing Arts Foundation International Congress XII (10 June)

Orfeus and Euridike, opera by Gluck in the 1762 Vienna version (26 June)

Alceste, opera by Gluck in the 1967 Vienna version (18 July)

Paris och Helena, opera by Gluck in a semi-staged version (27 July)

Don Juan, ballet choreographed by Regina Beck Friis with music by Gluck (27 Aug)

1999

'Salle des machines' with Susanne Rydén and Mikael Bellini (26 May)

Divertissement for the European Business Press Annual Meeting (17 June)

Trädgården (The Garden), opera by Jonas Forssell (10 July)

I re pastore, opera by Mozart (7 Aug)

Don Juan, ballet choreographed by Regina Beck-Friis with music by Gluck (28, Aug)

2000

Semiramis, ballet by Regina Beck-Friis and music by Gluck, and *Medea*, pantomime by Noverre and Ivo Cramér, music by J-J Rodolphe, produced by the Royal Opera (31 May)

Così fan tutte, opera by Mozart (30 June)

Tamerlano, opera by Händel (29 July)

2001

Semiramis, ballet by Regina Beck-Friis and music by Gluck, and *Medea*, pantomime by Noverre and Ivo Cramér, music by J-J Rodolphe, produced by the Royal Opera (1 June)

Divertissement on the occasion of the Silver Wedding of King Carl XVI Gustav and Queen Silvia (19 June)

Julius Caesar, opera by Händel (21 June)

Così fan tutte, opera by Mozart (22 July)

2002

Ungdom och dårskap (Youth and Folly), singspiel by Du Puy, produced by the Royal Opera (30 May)

Trollflöjten (Die Zauberflöte), opera by Mozart (4 July)

Tamerlano, opera by Händel (3 Aug)

2003

Dans-Vurmen (La Dansomanie), pantomime-ballet by P-G Gardel with music by E N Méhul, staged by Cramér/Skeaping. Production of the Royal Opera (29 May)

Alcina, opera by Händel (26 July)

2004

Kastrater (Castratos), opera by Miklós Maros on the basis of Sven Delblanc's novel, produced by the Royal Opera (3 June – world premiere)

Cecilia och Apkungen (Cecilia and the Monkey King), opera by Reine Jönsson, (10 July – world premiere)

2005

La capricciosa corretta, opera by Martín y Soler, production by the Opera Academy (27 May)

Kärlekens triumf, (Le Triomphe de l'amour), comedy by Marivaux, guest performances by the Royal Dramatic Theatre (11 June)

Zoroastre, opera by Rameau (2 Aug)

2006

Figaros bröllop, opera by Mozart, production by the Opera Academy (27 May)

Zoroastre, opera by Rameau (13 July)

Den fångne Cupido and Fiskarena, ballets by Skeaping, with music by Kraus (31 Aug)

Divertissement for Stena Line (22 Sept)

2007

Mark Tatlow **appointed as artistic director (to 2013)**

Xerxes, opera by Händel, production by the Opera Academy (26 May)

Divertissement for Kauping Bank (31 May)

Divertissement for the Europa Nostra Annual Congress with 'open changement' (8 June)

L'Orfeo, opera by Monteverdi (28 July)

2008

Livet på månen, (Il mondo della luna), opera by Haydn, production by the Opera Academy (24 May)

Il ritorno d'Ulisse in patria, opera by Monteverdi (26 July)

L'opera seria, opera buffo by Gassmann, guest performances by Fäviken Opera Society (2 Aug)

2009

Ariodante, opera by Händel, production by the Opera Academy (30 May)

L'incoronazione di Poppea, opera by Monteverdi (25 July)

Orlando, opera by Händel, guest performances by the Händelfestspiele Göttingen (21 Aug)

2010

La finta giardiniera, opera by Mozart, production by the Opera Academy (30 May)

Don Giovanni, opera by Mozart (31 July)

2011

Così fan tutte, opera by Mozart, production by the Opera Academy (29 May)

Don Giovanni, opera by Mozart (31 July)

Les Petits Riens & Don Juan, ballets by Marie-Geneviève Massé, guest performances by La Companie de danse l'Éventail, Paris (12 Aug)

2012

Il Giasone (Jason och Medea), opera by Cavalli, production by the Opera Academy (27 May)

Orlando paladino, opera by Haydn 29 July)

Concert with Peter Mattei (4 and 8 Aug)

'Gustav III' – an evening with Christopher O'Regan (8 and 15 Sept)

'Marie Antoinette', solo performance by Anna Järvinen (21 Sept)

2013

Il matrimonio segreto, opera by Cimarosa, production by the Opera Academy (26 May)

Concert with Anne Sofie von Otter and Elin Rombo (26-27 July)

La clemenza di Tito, opera by Mozart (11 Aug)

Concert with Julia Lezhneva (23 Aug)

Trollflöjten (Die Zauberflöte), opera by Mozart, trivialized concert version (26-27 Aug)

'Gustav III' – an evening with Christopher O'Regan (31 Aug)

'Marie Antoinette', solo performance by Anna Järvinen (7 Sept)

INDEX

Aare, L. 233

Abenius, F. 141

Adelcrantz, C.F. 5, 16, 19, 40, 109, 111, 120, 123, 126, 132, 133, 231, 232

Adolf Fredrik 6, 15

Adorno, T.W. 138

Aleotti, G.B. 39

Anderberg, T. 247

Andersen, D. 141, 266

Anmo, J. 187, 268

Antoine, A. 122

Armfelt, G.M. 76–85, 92, 95, 239, 240, 264

Arnaud, B. d' 86

Asplund, K. 146

Asplund, S. 220, 269

Astington, J.H. 252

Austin, G. 192

Badin (Couschi, A.L.G.F.) 63, 64, 67, 68, 71, 72, 90, 92, 254

Baeckström, A. 255

Bain, R.N. 242

Baker, G.P. 204

Bapasola, J. 245

Barnett, D. 191–195, 248, 249

Baron, M. 78, 193, 249

Barton, H.A. 244

Bassi, G. 230

Beaumarchais, P.-A. de 7, 67, 129, 270, 271, 285

Beckerman, B. 252

Beck-Friis, R. 164, 165, 260, 283, 284, 287

Beijer, A. 2–9, 31, 41–44, 117, 125, 139, 141–149, 158, 160, 176, 224, 237, 239, 241–244, 255, 256, 260, 263, 266, 276, 283, 284

Bellman, C.M. 9, 94, 145–147, 258, 266, 273–276, 286

Benjamin, W. 66, 132, 134, 200, 201, 250

Bergman, I. 149, 166, 167

Berlova, M. 258

Bermel, A. 249

Berry, W. 159

Bertati, G. 216, 232

Bjurström, P. 244, 245

Björling Rygert, N. 52, 263

Blaise, K. 29, 141, 180, 263, 266, 268

Blixt, K. 133, 266

Blomkvist, T. 165

Boer, B.H. von 250

Bokstedt, B. 155, 280

Boland, H. 233

Borg, K. 154

Bourdieu, P. 137

Bratton, J. 248

Brecht, B. 217, 247

Broberg, B. 163

Brook, P. 177

Brown, J.R. 203, 204, 217

Brown, L.C. 127, 137

Bundy, S. 133, 266

Bush-Bailey, G. 248

Butt, J. 251

Cahusac, L. de 190–193

Calzabigi, R. de' 53, 134

Cameron, C. 255

Campra, A. 150, 275, 276

Carlsten, R. 158

Carroll, T. 204, 205

Catherine II 113

Cavalli, F. 177, 178, 181, 216, 217, 267, 281, 288

Christina 104, 161, 162, 272

Churchill, W. 136

Cicero, 192, 248

Cicognini, G.A. 216

Cimarosa, D. 149, 150, 158, 174, 216, 220, 232, 233, 267, 269, 271, 275–280, 283, 284, 288

Clark, B.H. 238

Coeyman, B. 242

Cohen, R. 204

Colonna, D.C. 180, 181, 216–221

Corneille, P. 119

Couchi: see Badin

Cramér, I. 164, 282–287

Crébillon, P.J. 6, 270

Crusenstolpe, M.J. 239

Cullberg, B. 163

Dahlberg, G. 240

Dalin, O. von 80, 276

Dellert, K. 79, 242

Derkert, K. 240

Descartes, R. 194

Desprez, L.J. 9, 22, 40, 84, 88, 99, 126–129, 266

Diderot, D. 51, 63, 72, 76, 190, 193

Dobbs, M. 154, 267

Downer, A. 194, 249

Dragojevic, K. 216, 268

Dunbar, Z. 238

Düben, H.F. von 229, 253

Dymkowski, C. 238

Dönch, K. 159

Edh, B. 163

Edwards, S. 229

Eggehorn, Y. 239

Ehrenstrahl, D. K. 106, 115

Ehrensvärd, C.A. 63, 264

Elizabeth II 160, 163

Engländer, R. 232, 233

Enström, L. 133, 266

Ericson, C. 161, 267

Eschenbach, C. 169

Falkman, L. 170, 177, 267

Farncombe, C. 155

Favart, C.-S. 141, 270, 272

Féral, J. 246

Fersen, A. von 89, 90

Florin, M. 171

Fogelberg Rota, S. 247

Fogelmark, S. 243

Forman, M. 166

Forssell, J. 170–172, 267

Forsström, P. 165

Franklin, R. 243

Frederick II 15, 118

Fredrik Adolf 89, 92, 100, 101, 265

Friedrich, G. 154

Furlin, L. 150, 267

Gadamer, H.-G. 179, 180, 247

Galitzkaya, E. 216, 268

Gallodier, L. 63, 68–72, 97, 99, 264

Gardelli, L. 155, 232

Garrick, D. 76, 195, 249

Gassmann, F. 53, 134, 288

Gellius, A. 192

Gjörwell, C.C. 98

Gluck, C.W. 7, 9, 39, 67, 85, 95–99, 128, 150–155, 159, 165, 167, 209, 233, 234, 240, 244, 265, 267, 271, 273, 276–287

Goethe, J.W. von 88

Goldoni, C. 158, 193, 276–278

Gozzi, C. 193, 249

Gram Holmström, K. 258

Green, D. 245

Grétry, A.E.M. 6, 37, 97, 130, 149, 150, 262, 270, 275, 280, 285,

Gros de Gasquet, J. 195

Gurr, A. 252

Gustav III passim

Gustav VI Adolf 163

Habermas, J. 238

Hagegård, H. 167, 169, 267

Halbwachs, M. 246

Hallgren, C.-A. 150, 267

Hamrin, R. 220, 269

Händel, G. F. 9, 39, 96, 140, 145, 150, 152, 158, 175, 178, 221, 267, 268, 273–288

Harbage, A. 206

Hartley, L.P. 59, 238

Haydn, J. 29, 96, 141, 180, 248, 263, 266, 268, 277–285, 288

Hedvig Eleonora 103–107, 114, 241, 257, 265

Hedvig Elisabeth Charlotta 84, 90, 95, 256

Helander, K. 181, 247

Hennings, B. 238, 258

Hidemark, O. 43, 237, 238, 243, 255, 256, 260

Hildesheimer, W. 248

Hill, H. 245

Hilleström, G. 149, 154, 155, 164, 246, 247, 256, 257, 260, 275, 278

Hilleström, P. 23, 73, 76, 77, 95–98, 156, 239, 241, 256, 262–265, 268

Hills, H. 207, 252

Hjortsberg, L. 65, 71, 72

Holbach, Baron d' 130

Holberg, L. 122, 274, 275, 284

Holmberg, V. 173, 267

Hoogland, R. 57

Hume, D. 118

Hybiner, A. 174, 220, 267, 269

Jakobski, L. 52, 263

Jameson, F. 178, 247

Jansson, F. 105, 185, 265, 268

Jarrad, A. 242

Johnson, A. 243

Johnsson, Busk M. 153

Joseph, S. 206

Jouvet, L. 158

Järvefelt, G. 165–170, 234–236, 247, 283–285

Jönsson, R. 171, 287

Kantorowicz, E. 243

Karl (XIII) 16, 90, 91, 95, 98, 100, 101, 265

Karl X 104

Karl XI 104

Karlsson, S.T. 257

Kellgren, J. H. 80, 86, 88, 272, 273, 281–285

Kemble, J.P. 193, 249

Kennedy, D. 251

Kent, N. 243

Kexel, O. 146, 273, 274

Kindermann, H. 191

Kirchhoff, M. 253

Kirshenblatt-Gimblett, B. 203

Kivy, P. 249

Kmentt, W. 159

Kokkonen, T. 133, 266

Koltay, F. 154

Kraus, J.M. 141, 272, 273, 276, 281, 283, 285, 287

Kremer, A. 179, 216, 268

Kuhnmunch, J. 260

Kull, G. 27, 263

Kullnäs, Å. 157

Kuzmick Hansell, K. 240, 241, 244

Laine, M. 241

Lalin, J.S. 98

Lang, F. 76

Lanham, A. 252

Lanham, R. 209, 252

Larsson, B. 256

Lawrenson, T.E. 242

Lekain, H.L. 65, 76

Lenngren, A.M. 98

Lewenhaupt, I. 56, 57

Levertin, O. 237, 258

Lezhneva, J. 35, 263

Liljas, S. 105, 187, 265, 268

Lindqvist, H. 256

Linné, C. von 171, 172

Ljung, V. 161, 267

Loney, G.M. 153

Lopez, J. 210, 250–252

Lorraine, P.L. 257

Louis XIV 48, 60, 103–106, 109, 112, 113, 118, 125, 130–136, 242

Lowenthal, D. 238

Lovisa Ulrika 5, 6, 15, 16, 47, 48, 63, 104–119, 122, 126, 134, 212, 238, 241, 255, 257, 262, 265

Ludwig, C. 125, 159

Lully, J.-B. 6, 7, 130, 132, 212, 270, 271, 282,

Lydén, A. 157

Löfvendahl, B. 253

Lönnroth, E. 258

MacRae Ballantyne, J. 179, 267

Malcolm-Davis, J. 246

Malmborg, L. af 151

Mancini, L. 179, 268

Mansén, E. 238, 258

Marcolin, B. 133, 266

Marie Antoinette 90, 288

Marie, A. 242

Marivaux, P. de 7, 271, 275, 276, 280, 282, 287

Marker, F.J. 258

Marker, L.-L. 258

Mars, Mlle 66

Martin, E. 1

Massey, J. 93, 265

Mattei, P. 173, 267

McCalman, I. 244

McCaw, D. 199

Meldahl, Å. 171

Mengarelli, M. 133, 227, 266, 269

Menzer, P. 250

Meyer, K. 152–156, 267

Molière, J.-B. 7, 75, 115, 119, 122, 129, 132, 142, 146, 148, 157, 158, 167, 193, 194, 206, 207, 212, 270–276, 284

Montan, U. 170

Montelius, L. 9

Monteverdi, C. 48–53, 56, 57, 96, 159, 177, 189, 209, 221, 263, 286–288,

Monvel, J.-M. de 24, 25, 65–76, 82, 103, 237, 263, 264, 270, 271

Moore, A. 250

Moretti, M. 158

Mozart, W.A. passim

Mullin, D. 258

Naumann, J.G. 80, 81, 264

Nell, J. 258

Neville, K. 241

Niklasson, S. 133, 266

Nilsson, S. 150, 267

Nora, P. 137, 212, 246, 253

Nordenfelt, E. 158

Nordensvan, G. 237, 258

Nordin, B. 169, 267

Nordmann, C. 245

Norman, J. 242

Noverre, J.-G. 70, 163, 247, 287

Oberle, C.F. 165

Olausson, M. 240

Olin, B. 80

Olin, E. 79, 80, 264

Olofsson, T. 166, 170

Olsson, G. 146, 266

Onne, M. 227, 269

Oreglia, G. 157

Orgel. S. 253

Oxenstierna, J.G. 141

Palmstedt, E. 7

Pasch, J. 66, 69, 264

Peltonen, A. 161, 267

Pergolesi, G.B. 145, 149, 157, 160, 276–279, 281, 284, 286

Persson, J. 174, 267

Picinni, N. 97

Pirandello, L. 200

Pixérecourt, R.C.G. 88

Plagnol-Diéval, M.-E. 245

Plutarch 192

Pointon, M. 245

Poisson, J. 192

Pope, A. 134

Provenzale, F. 165

Prytz, E. 150, 233, 267

Purcell, H. 161, 267, 277, 278, 281, 283, 285

Qave, L. 187, 268

Quarnström, S. 146, 266

Quintilian 192

Racine, J. 133, 134, 193, 194, 270, 271

Ralphson, D. 141, 266

Rameau, J.P. 130, 261, 282, 285, 287

Ramel, S. 240

Rangström L. 258

Rangström T. 257

Rasch, E. 163

Regnard, J.-F. 158, 270–272, 277

Reimers, G. 257

Reus, K.-D. 260

Richelieu, A.-J. 112

Richter, S. 248

Ristell, A.F. 82

Roach, J. 194, 195, 239,

Roche, D. 245

Roman, J.H. 145, 179, 274, 279, 285

Rosen, E.M. von 163, 280

Roslin, A. 101, 265

Rothman, G. 98

Rousseau, J.J. 130, 131, 135, 154, 188, 192, 193, 199, 200, 244, 250, 276

Rydén, S. 52, 176, 200, 201, 263, 268

Rylance, M. 202–207, 268

Rössaak, R. 225, 269

Saedén, E. 169, 267

Sages, R. 154

Salieri, A. 96, 285

Samuel, R. 137, 203, 246, 250, 251

Samuelson, M. 169

Sand, G. 239

Sandberg, H. 148

Sauner, M. 177, 267

Sansone, M. 249, 252

Sartori, A. 158

Savage, R. 244, 252

Scarlatti, D. 146, 149, 158, 276, 277, 279, 280

Schaffer, P. 166

Scheffer, C.F. 116, 127, 243, 244

Scheutz, L. 239

Schiller, F. von 38

Schmidt-Isserstedt, H. 153

Schneider, R. 202

Schuster, J. 133, 266

Schwartz, M. 179, 268

Schwarzkopf, E. 159

Schyberg, B. 239

Sciutti, G. 159

Scott, V. 248

Sedaine, M.-J. 63, 64, 270, 271

Senelick, L. 244

Sennett, R. 245

Serlio, S. 39

Seuerling, C.G. 230, 254

Shakespeare, W. 116, 202–211

Sheridan, R.B. 193

Siddons, H. 186

Silverstone, C. 251

Sjöberg, A. 167

Skeaping, M. 142, 160–166, 267, 277, 279–284, 287

Skiöldebrand, A.F. 62, 238

Skunke, M.-C. 258

Smith, L. 137, 201, 245, 250,

Sofia Magdalena 7, 92, 101

Spagnoli, P. 141, 266

Stadig, S.F. 98

Stanilawski, K.S. 77

Staveland, M. 29, 141, 180, 263, 266, 268

Stenborg, C. 80, 96, 98, 230

Stern, T. 251

Stiernhjelm, G. 161

Stopani, D. 5

Stormare, P. 167

Stradella, A. 165

Strehler, G. 158

Stribolt, B. 244, 257

Strindberg, A. 51, 54, 72, 73, 163, 239, 286,

Strömberg, M. 253

Svanholm, S. 146, 266

Svenningsen, T. 141, 266

Sällström, F. 146, 266

Söderberg, R. 141, 266

Söderström, E. 117, 149, 153, 155, 160, 171, 234, 266, 267, 275, 278, 284, 285

T'Hooft, S. 180, 181, 185–191, 196, 211, 216, 220, 221, 248

Talma, F.J. 66

Tandefelt, H. 258

Tatlow, M. 49, 177–182, 196, 200, 215–221, 287

Tegnér, A. 9

Tegnér, E. 237

Tessin, C.G. 114–116, 121, 127, 138, 242, 243

Tidworth, S. 243

Tiramani, J. 251

Toll, J.C. 85

Torelli, G. 33, 39, 133, 245

Treichl, M. 52, 263

Tsugami, E. 57

Tsugami, M. 56, 57

Tucker, P. 204

Turcoy, V. 175, 180

Twycross, M. 199

Uhrstedt, C. 91, 265

Ulrika Eleonora 104, 107, 115

Uttini, F.A. 5, 6, 96, 145, 146, 270, 273, 275

Valois, C. de 113, 114, 266

Vicentini, C. 253

Vogler, G.J. 67, 71, 96, 240, 281–285

Voltaire, F.-M. A. 7, 16, 61, 99, 108, 114, 122–126, 134, 154, 188, 195, 244, 270, 271

Wagner, R. 122, 125, 154, 196–198, 200, 249, 268

Wanamaker, S. 203

Weaver, J. 163

Weber, W. 244

Wentz, J. 192–194, 208, 249, 268

Wenzinger, A. 159

Wertmüller, A.U. 83, 264

West, S. 249

White, M. 251

Wichman, H. 257

Widén, S. 185, 187, 268

Wolff, A. 152, 153, 267

Woods, P. 204, 206, 208, 250–252

Worthen, W.B. 206, 251

Young, J.O. 249

Zander, A. 237

Zhylevich, K. 185, 187, 268

Åhlén, C.G. 234, 236

Åkerberg, S. 93, 265

Öhrn, P.E. 171, 173, 177, 259, 286,

Östberg, J. 174, 267

Östman, A. 164–171, 177, 185, 234, 235, 248, 283–285

ACTA UNIVERSITATIS STOCKHOLMIENSIS (AUS)

Corpus Troporum
Romanica Stockholmiensia
Stockholm Cinema Studies
Stockholm Fashion Studies
Stockholm Oriental Studies
Stockholm Slavic Studies
Stockholm Studies in Baltic Languages
Stockholm Studies in Classical Archaeology
Stockholm Studies in Comparative Religion
Stockholm Studies in Economic History
Stockholm Studies in English
Stockholm Studies in Ethnology
Stockholm Studies in Film History
Stockholm Studies in History
Stockholm Studies in History of Ideas
Stockholm Studies in History of Literature
Stockholm Studies in Human Geography
Stockholm Studies in Modern Philology. N.S.
Stockholm Studies in Musicology
Stockholm Studies in Philosophy
Stockholm Studies in Russian Literature
Stockholm Studies in Scandinavian Philology. N.S.
Stockholm Studies in Social Anthropology, N.S.
Stockholm Studies in Sociology. N.S.
Stockholm Theatre Studies
Stockholm University Demography Unit - Dissertation Series
Stockholmer Germanistische Forschungen
Studia Fennica Stockholmiensia
Studia Graeca Stockholmiensia. Series Neohellenica
Studia Juridica Stockholmiensia
Studia Latina Stockholmiensia

STOCKHOLM THEATRE STUDIES

1. Kirsten Gram Holmström, *Monodrama, Attitudes, Tableaux Vivants. Studies on some trends of theatrical fashion 1770-1815.* Stockholm 1967, 278 pp. Ill.

2. Gösta M. Bergman, *Lighting in the Theatre.* Stockholm and Totowa, N.J., 1977. 426 pp. Ill.

3. Jacqueline Martin & Willmar Sauter, *Understanding Theatre. Performance Analysis in Theory and Practice.* Stockholm 1995, 272 pp. Ill.

4. Willmar Sauter & David Wiles, *The Theatre of Drottningholm – Then and Now Performance between the 18th and 21st centuries.* Stockholm 2014, 296 pp. Ill.